Susan Prescott is Winthrop Professor at The University of Western Australia and a practising paediatrician at the Children's Hospital in Perth, where she specialises in treating children with asthma and allergic diseases. Her research in this field is internationally recognised, and she is author of *The Allergy Epidemic: A Mystery of Modern Life*. Her inspiration to study medicine came from her grandmother, one of the few women to study medicine in the 1930s, and her love of research and academia was inspired by her grandfather Sir Stanley Prescott, former Vice-Chancellor of The University of Western Australia. She travels widely, but always loves coming home to her family in Western Australia.

The Calling

A TRUE STORY OF
FAITH, HOPE & LOVE

SUSAN L PRESCOTT

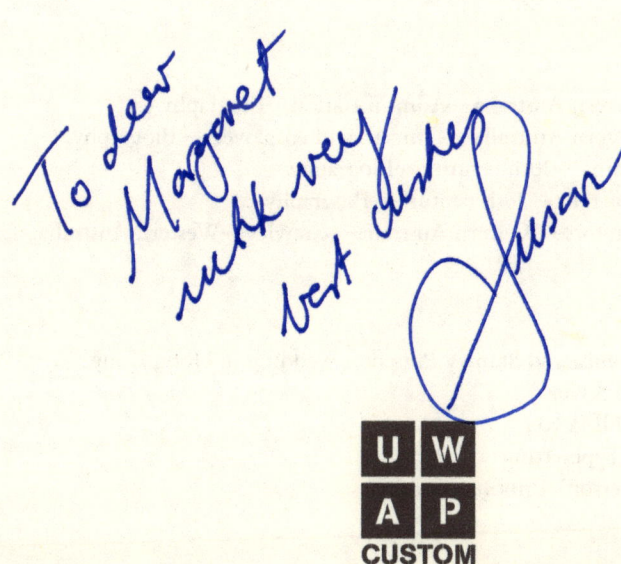

To dear Margaret
with very
best wishes
Susan

U W
A P
CUSTOM

First published in 2013 by
UWA Publishing
Crawley, Western Australia 6009
www.uwap.uwa.edu.au

UWAP Custom is an imprint of UWA Publishing
a division of The University of Western Australia

THE UNIVERSITY OF
WESTERN AUSTRALIA
Achieve International Excellence

National Library of Australia
Cataloguing-in-Publication data:
Prescott, Susan L.
The calling : a true story of faith, hope and love / Susan L. Prescott.
9781742584898 (pbk.)
Includes index.

Prescott, Monica.
Prescott, Stanley.
University of Western Australia—Administration—Biography.
University of Western Australia—Officials and employees—Biography.
Missionaries—China—20th century—Biography.
Missionaries—Australia—20th century—Biography.
College administrators—Western Australia—Crawley—Western Australia.

266.0092

Cover image: Monica and Stanley Prescott's wedding in Hong Kong,
courtesy of Helen Silver
Cover design by Jill Porter
Typeset by J&M Typesetting
Printed by McPherson's Printing Group

For Eleanor, James and Elliott

*In celebration of the lives and hearts
of Stanley and Monica Prescott*

Contents

Prologue
A life to remember

Monica Mary Prescott
4 February 1913 – 9 June 2007

St George's Cathedral, Perth

It is a beautiful day to say farewell to an astonishing woman. We gather today to celebrate the life and achievements of Monica Mary Prescott, to thank God for the privilege of knowing her and for having had the opportunity to be influenced by her.

It is far too hard, in a short service, to do justice to a long, rich and varied life. Even were we able to hear all the memories gathered here, together with those who would like to be here, and those who are welcoming Monica into her new life, we would still not have the full measure of Monica, of who she was to each of us.

You all have your own private memories, those which bring joy in the midst of sadness, perhaps those less resolved remembrances. All these together convey something of the truth of how Monica touched our lives in many ways.

I had the privilege of seeing Monica regularly. With indomitable will, she would make the journey in all weathers for our time together. I heard something of her story, of where she came from, of her life as a student in Manchester, of her adult life, her coming to this cathedral and knowing she belonged here.

I knew of her great love and understanding of her family, her huge appreciation of them and of all they were to her; of her wide ranging interests, her activities and her passion for people. But above all, I met a woman who knew God and knew she was known and loved by God.

Monica was one of those rare people who lived, breathed and epitomised the two great commandments. She loved God with all her heart and soul and mind and strength, and she loved her neighbour. She could, however, be a bit tough on herself, particularly towards the end of her life when she was so longing to die. I can hear her now: 'I have no fear of death, no fear at all'. And she would ask, 'Is it wrong to want to die?' to which I could only reassure her and respond to her next question, 'Why doesn't God want me?' with the suggestion that perhaps she still had things to teach us.

The closing down of life is so difficult and painful for the one concerned and, often, for those most closely connected. It was hard to watch Monica's struggles in recent weeks and months. Living became much more costly than slipping into the gentle dark of death. Yet Monica's spirit and tenacious hold on life made it hard for her.

When someone is travelling through death's dark vale, it is not only the one who is dying, but all those near and dear who are being drawn along that same road. Christians, Monica absolutely, believe that we travel this road accompanied by Jesus, who knows it well, who travelled it himself and who, having risen from the dead, shows us the way to the new life that we believe follows this.

Jesus has also gone before us, as John's gospel so comfortingly assures us, to prepare our final home. I can imagine Monica, being as astonished with the beauty of it all as she was when she first saw this, her beloved cathedral. She had a favourite spot to sit in here, where she could take in all the wonder of the place and be drawn into worshipping the God who had brought her here, who had had her in the palm of his hand all her life.

Quite by chance on Sunday evening I met two ladies of Monica's age, who had met her on Monica's last recent holiday in Scotland. They are both sprightly and it was a tour for the elderly, but they told me of their amazement at Monica's energy and curiosity, leaping from the coach at every opportunity, bounding up hills to see the view, to see what was around the corner, to see whatever there was to see.

This was the Monica I knew and loved. Skipping, swinging, dancing, jumping. There was no stopping her. Her loss is immense and we will miss her more than she could ever imagine.

But she lives on, in our minds, our memories. She will bring warmth, a smile to your heart and the love and the memories shared by each of you, and Monica will ensure she will not be forgotten. The love we share with and for Monica is part, I believe, of the infinitely greater and unimaginably deeper love that is God's – for Monica and for each of us. And while we do grieve as the finality of death hits us, even though we know it is how it is, even though we are conscious of the gulf now separating us, this bigger love can hold and sustain us across the divide.

I imagine Monica, even now, dancing joyously towards the gates of heaven, confident in her reception, as God, whom she knew and loved, waits to welcome her with delight and to enfold her in his eternal grace.

We commend her soul to the Everlasting Arms. May she rest in peace, Amen.

Canon Theresa Harvey
Wednesday 13 June 2007

Opposite: Portrait of Monica, aged 20, in 1932
Courtesy of Helen Silver

Preface
A reluctant heroine

It might seem strange to begin a story at the end, but that is how this started. She was so small and fragile, but her eyes were still as bright as they had been at her birth almost a century before, I doubt the nurses could have suspected Monica's adventures as they puffed her pillows and folded her into her sheets. As she got closer to the edge I could feel her stories circling closer to gently enfold her. When her eyes closed that final time, all I wanted was to give her story a life of its own. Perhaps it is my way of keeping her memory alive: I want to celebrate her and this is the best way I know.

Much of the story comes directly from Monica. I am so glad I had the foresight to record her words and memories in the months before she died, so I have been able to include these reflections, together with the many letters she wrote as a young doctor and medical missionary escaping from Japanese-occupied China with her tiny son David, my father.

The seeds for this book were sown in 2007 when I was invited to give the keynote address at the Centenary Trust for Women's annual luncheon at The University of Western Australia (UWA). It was the fiftieth anniversary of the UWA medical school, and the Governor-General of Australia and many other dignitaries were present for this important celebration. At the time I was a new 'young' medical professor at the university, and I was invited to tell the story of my grandfather Sir Stanley Prescott and his role as the founding Vice-Chancellor of the medical school. But as it was an occasion to celebrate the academic development of women, I decided instead to tell the story from my grandmother Monica's perspective.

I have had other opportunities to celebrate small parts of this story and on each occasion I have been urged to tell more. Of course, Monica's story is also very much the story of Stanley, another truly remarkable person and the hero of many of the memories that Monica kept alive for us over the decades. Their life together was the stuff of fairy tales, and his great devotion to her was beyond compare. Stanley's deep commitment and purpose were equally evident in his passion and spiritual connection with his community. He was a great leader and an engineer of positive change, but he always did this gently, with the greatest of diplomacy and with a humorous twinkle in his eyes. And Monica was the heroine of his life.

Just as Monica did, I want to keep our tradition of storytelling alive, and I hope to achieve my task as narrator and bit player using what I have been told, read and lived. I do not presume to know her mind, but I feel her spirit in me, and her story is also a part of me. I say this because although many of these words are mine, they somehow come from her.

I am not sure that Monica would be at all comfortable with being the focus of so much attention, but I am sure she would suggest a cup of tea before beginning.

I admired Monica most for her way of being, her truth, her heart and her utter and selfless devotion to her family and her community. She was a person of apparent contradictions. On the one hand, she was a reserved and private person. I suspect that this was partly a product of her era. Her family was quite poor but very proud of who they were. Although she was born in the colonies, she always had the air of being very 'British' and of being quite proper. This was natural and not at all affected. It was just who she was. She was immaculately dressed and spoke with a delightful Anglo-Australian accent.

On the other hand, she had an amazing childlike quality. Even when she was in her nineties she would still embarrass her children – but most certainly not her grandchildren – by skipping through the park and playing on the swings. She even admitted to jumping up and down on her bed in the retirement home when no one was looking, making it very clear to me that she was in full possession of her faculties at the time. 'And why not?!' she always said.

Through both her words and her actions Monica emphasised that you should never stop having fun, because otherwise what is the point of life? Her bright blue eyes always shone with the excitement of just being alive. She had a humble confidence that was never arrogant.

I did not meet Monica until she was in her fifties, and I adored her as a doting and loving grandmother who patiently took me for walks down Thomas Street in the well-to-do suburb of Nedlands. This was in the 1960s when the family was living close to in the university. By the time I was an adult, she was in her late sixties. Even then, she seemed fitter and more active than ever. When I was sixteen I could hardly keep up with her as we climbed the steps of St Paul's Cathedral in London. Her mind was quick and she had so many stories. Monica's memory for detail was incredible.

Monica made the most of every minute of her ninety-four years. In telling her story, I hope to let Monica shine for who she was more than for what she did. She never stopped appreciating her life and she never stopped having fun. We always marvelled at her love and excitement, and her positive attitude and enthusiasm touched so many. We are all heroes of our own kind, but it is good to be reminded of the possibility and adventure in our own lives, and that we can do anything if we set our minds to it.

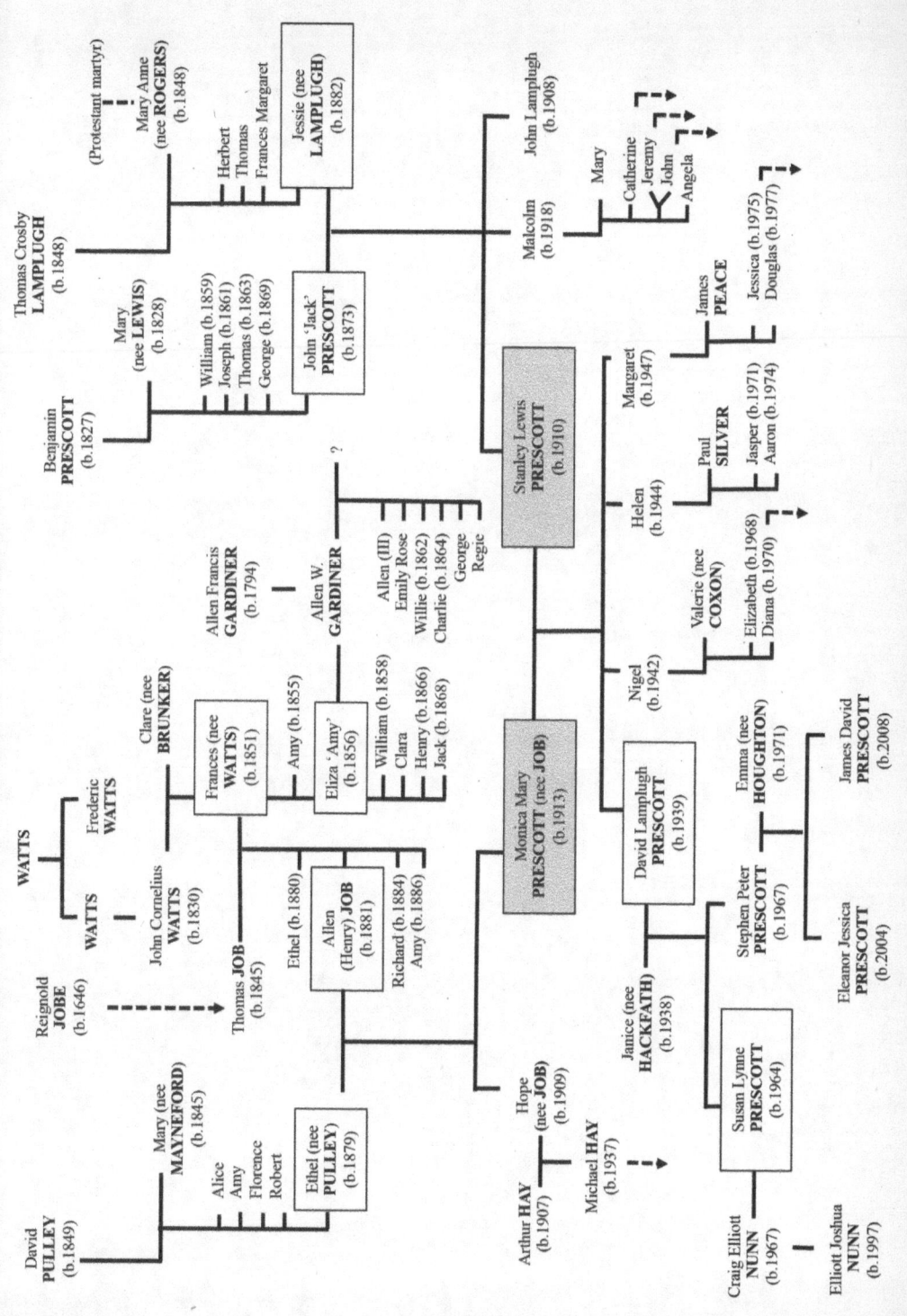

From distant lands

Shaped by the stories of our past

From a long line of adventurers

In the heavy half-darkness of her last hours, the air felt dense with the stories that had filled Monica's past, like happy phantoms calling her home. Monica was the keeper of stories and the custodian of our past. She faithfully told the humble but courageous tales of our family identity, to her children and to her grandchildren, keeping the spirit of our forefathers alive in an age when storytelling is dying. As we all gathered quietly at her bedside, so too did the spectres of our family legends, so well known to us from her telling they could remain unspoken. As a child, these stories told me of 'my people' and who I was. From generations of nomadic wanderers, Monica's place was of the heart and soul, and her stories are still the connection between us all.

In the final weeks before her death, Monica relaxed her struggling grip on the present and happily let her mind fall into the past. I treasured her remembering, as she conjured the spirits of our ancestors once again. As her eyes closed forever and her breath grew thin, I could feel all those who had gone before gathering unseen around her. And I knew that she could not wait to be with them all again.

Monica was born into a family of travellers, explorers and missionaries. At a time when storytelling was central to family life, the stories of her predecessors laid the foundations of her own identity and played a profound role in shaping her ideas, philosophies and life plans.

I cannot hope to tell all of Monica's family stories here, because my main purpose is to tell her own story and that of her life with Stanley. But to understand something more of Monica, of her deep sense of purpose and her quiet commitment to helping others, we need to know of the history that shaped her convictions and her values. As her family story was so important to her, I will introduce some of its main characters here. In particular, the stories of her father Allen in Peru, her grandmother Frances in outback Australia, and her great-aunt Eliza in Africa, were foundations for her deep spirituality.

FRANCES AND ELIZA

Frances (b. 1851), Monica's grandmother, and her sister Eliza (b. 1856) were born in the Australian outback. Later in life, Frances was 'known throughout the district for her practical religion, [she] was always missionary-minded, and instilled into her children a love of missions'.[1] Eliza also married into a strong missionary family, and Monica grew up enthralled by stories of Eliza's travels to Africa and beyond.

Frances, Eliza and their five younger siblings spent their childhood on the Australian goldfields. It was their father John Cornelius Watts (Monica's great-grandfather), who originally brought the family to Australia. Search as I might, I have no convict heritage: John C. Watts came from a respectable family and his 'transportation' to Australia in 1849 was entirely

10

voluntary. The brief description by Eliza of John C. Watts' cheerful personality and his appearance – fair with blue eyes, always gay, happy and loveable[2] – is reminiscent of both Monica and her father Allen. According to the London papers many years later, Allen was known for 'his happy nature and ready smile', which gained him the soubriquet 'Sunshine Allen'.[3]

Frances and Eliza grew up knowing scarcity and hardship, but were always full of appreciation for the little they had. Their father tried to find fortune by prospecting for gold and doing odd jobs as a carpenter, but their mother still had to take in sewing to make ends meet. Frances recalled:

> Among my earliest recollections was watching men sinking a deep shaft and getting up the dirt with buckets on the windlass and taking it to the puddling machines and cradles to get the gold. It was always a great fascination to watch them washing a great deal of dust and dirt, and thinking at every moment that the dirt would wash out and take the gold with it. But within a few minutes you could see all the beautiful specks of gold lying in the bottom of the dust.
>
> After the heavy rains all of the old people and children would go 'specking' which was picking up specks of gold. I often remember picking up a penny-weight of gold. Sometimes it was fine, sometimes coarse, but always valuable.
>
> Once to my great joy, I found a little nugget of gold, valued at 10 shillings. It was very beautiful. Gold at that time was getting very hard to find. The little nugget came just at the time when we were badly in need of money.[4]

They would travel in a covered wagon with four horses. Every night the horses were hobbled and bells put on them to warn off rustlers. Then they would sit by the campfire huddling close to their mother while their father played the flute. When the children were put to bed under the big hood of the wagon, they would happily fall asleep to the sound of his music. They had few possessions and the only toys the girls had were dolls made from wax, which they were careful never to leave in the sun.

When she was still quite small, Frances almost lost her life falling into a deep shaft that had filled with mud. She was saved by her pet dingo Paddy, who barked until her mother came.

> Mother followed him and found me floating in the waterhole, nearly drowned. Father was on the hill cutting down a tree when he heard my mother scream. As he threw down the axe the tree fell down and caught the back of his trousers and tore a piece right out. He got down in time before I sank and jumped in to pull me out.

As she got a little older, she was allowed to travel alone on her father's mule to run errands and collect the post twice a week, always with her dingo Paddy as trusty companion. Even though she was a girl, Frances learned to use a cross-cut saw and would help the men with tree-cutting, fencing, and building.

> Mother was never afraid to let me go among all the rough miners and Chinamen as dog Paddy would allow no man or woman to touch me.

Living on the gold diggings in the 1850s, Frances and her brothers and sisters had very few opportunities to go to church. But it was still something that they all took very seriously.

The minister came once every three months and gave us children so much catechism to learn by the time he came back.

Frances was diligent in her religious studies and was soon putting this into practice. Still a child, she would take her younger sisters Amy and Eliza to visit the road workers with prayer books and hymn books. The men were building a new highway, though the only traffic was the daily coach-and-four and most people travelled on foot or by horse. The workers did not seem to mind these young missionaries-in-training according to Eliza's recollections:

We got there just after their daily meal and Frances had a little service with them and they were awfully nice to her. They did not know the hymns but she and I sang. She had a good voice and they soon joined in. She preached to them and then asked if we might come again, and they said that they would like to see her as often as she could come.[5]

Their lives were darkened for a time when one of the younger ones, Clara, died of pleurisy in their mother's arms. She was only two.

It was a very great grief to my mother, who was a very happy woman, always singing at her work. I never remember her singing again.[6]

The remaining sisters were very close, but Amy was also a sickly child with a weak heart. When she died prematurely some years later, Eliza took her name, and became known to all as 'Amy'.

John C. Watts finally had enough money to buy a small farm at Borenore, near Orange in New South Wales, but could still scarcely support their many children. When the girls were barely old enough, they were each sent to live and work with families that could better look after them. Eliza notes, 'Oh, the dreadful wordless parting and the awful fear of going alone to unknown people'.[7]

In 1864, when she was just thirteen, Frances was sent to work on a cattle station. She earned enough to buy a horse and a saddle of her own, so she could ride to church in Orange every Sunday. Soon after that Eliza was sent to the English missionary family of Mr Allen W. Gardiner, who had arrived from South America following his ministries in Chile. The stories of Gardiner's mission work had a great influence on Frances. He was greatly admired for his preaching and his labours with the Patagonian Indians. Gardiner was the only son of famous British naval officer Commander Allen Francis Gardiner (1794–1851),[8] the first missionary to bring Christianity to the Zulu tribes of Africa (1834–1838). His father also went on to establish Protestant missions in Patagonia (1838–1843) but was foiled by Roman Catholic opposition. Gardiner (junior) faced similar opposition in 1856 when he sailed to Patagonia to continue his father's work. Now he had come to preach in the Australian outback and everyone was excited to have such a knowledgeable traveller in their midst.

The Gardiners had six children, and Eliza was taken on to assist with their new baby, Reggie. She was adept at this, having helped her own mother with her many younger siblings, and she quickly became indispensable. Eliza was only seventeen when Mrs Gardiner died, and Mr Gardiner decided to take her as his wife. He wanted her as a companion and to tend to his children:

She will be a wholesome sister to them and will be able to ride about with me and keep the house for us. I want our marriage to be kept quiet for some time, even from the boys. She and I will be in separate rooms, in fact she is my companion. I will be very good to her as long as I live and I am sure my children will always love her and be kind to her. I am a very lonely and broken man, and must have someone full of life and joy and hope in her to find the broken ends and bind them up, and go on serving my Master, Christ with her young life to help me along to my journey's end.[9]

Meanwhile, Frances fell in love with teamster Tom Job (pronounced *Jobe*), who ran a cartage business.[10] Even as an old woman, she still recalled the white dress with the little blue flowers and a blue ribbon about her waist that Tom admired the day they met.[11] She was just eighteen years old. Their courtship was protracted because Tom frequently travelled away for many months with his bullocks and wagon. They were eventually married in 1878, and Frances was not too impressed that much of their honeymoon was spent riding on a three-horse dray with all their goods and chattels. But they were very happy. While Frances settled in their modest cottage to raise her own four children, she always watched in admiration as her sister Eliza raised another woman's children. Frances named two of her children after Allen and Eliza 'Amy' Gardiner, and made sure their story was well known to all her children and grandchildren.

Within a year or two, Frances was saddened when Gardiner decided to return to England and took Eliza with him. Although Eliza was careful never to say so directly, it is clearly inferred that Gardiner had gone into debt and was pursued by creditors. The situation was bad enough to force Gardiner to part with several family heirlooms in order to settle what was owed and to afford their passage home:

> Before he left for England my husband gave away many lovely bits of plate, and his gold watch he gave to a man who had been very unkind and hard, and whom we marked down as a black shadow when we left.[12]

This is the only reference made to his situation. In those times this had the power to undermine his reputation and his credibility as church parson. With the possible shame of ruin upon him, it is likely that Gardiner had little choice but to lead his young family and new wife away from humiliation.

Although Eliza was more of a daughter than a wife to him, Frances was glad that her sister did come to love Gardiner. And he was happy to leave his problems behind and return to his homeland.

> My husband was so light-hearted and happy with everyone. We all clustered around him in some snug place and he would read to us. How big and strong he was, and how nice to feel his loving heart beating against our young bodies, Charlie always with an arm around his neck. I was very much a child and felt him a beautiful father. My love was very much the love of a child to a father. I loved him devotedly.
>
> Every night we knelt together by my bed. He took my hand, and folding it into his two hands, said the Lord's Prayer and the evening hymn, and there was a very holy feeling that came like a cloud of comfort overshadowing us.

During the voyage, Gardiner taught Eliza to read and write and to appreciate poetry. But this did not prevent her trepidation at arriving to meet his esteemed and cultured family:

> The landing in England and all the wonder of England was overshadowed by the thought of people and what they would think of me, so young and ignorant, and what we should do, and where we should live, and all that awful shyness pressed down upon me.

She was judged harshly and was very glad when, in the late 1870s, Mr Gardiner decided to retrace his father's footsteps to the Zulu country near Port Natal in Africa. They arrived to the sight of 300 Zulus clothed in sacks, each with holes cut for their head and limbs.

> Such beautiful creatures, some of them over six feet high. Their shining copper coloured limbs and easy grace of movement was fascinating.

Gardiner's father was well remembered and they received a warm welcome. He began his preaching and they settled into a lovely home. All went well until Gardiner developed a fever. Eliza tended him night and day, but at his urging she went with the children to a social gathering, agreeing it was important that they make a good impression. She returned later that day to find her husband dead in his bed.

> I can't write much about all this for the horror of it all comes back now. I was crushed into an old woman, all feeling seemed turned to stone.

He was buried in African soil, next to the grave of his much older sister Julia, who had died many years before when their father first came to begin mission work with the Zulus. Alone in a wild country, responsible for Gardiner's orphaned children, and mourning her husband and father figure, Eliza decided to take the children back to England. Although she was still a young woman, her husband's family bought her the black 'widow's weeds' of an old lady, which added to her misery: full, plain black skirts and a white cap with tails to her waist. But over the years she became glad of this outward indication of her painful past.

This dress was a great comfort to me as it explained me to the outside world and I was not hurt by questions.

In the face of strong opposition from Gardiner's family, who planned to divide his children between orphan schools and various relatives, Eliza miraculously won her bid to keep her stepchildren together and look after them herself. To begin with, they lived in the slums and depended on handouts from more kindly relatives, but they were happy to be together.

The boys were delighted at first, but the first night I found we were next to an Incurables' Home and looked into a low gin shop on the other side, and the boys discovered that we were in the slums and were ashamed to let their school fellows know where they lived and pretended they lived in quite the opposite direction.

Her fortunes changed when she eventually inherited £3,000 from one of the English relatives, and this helped her return to visit her Australian family. Eliza could hardly contain her joy at the 'bright sunshine, the song birds and the glory of the flowers', even the sound of the 'locusts' (cicadas) as the ship pulled into Sydney Harbour. She took the train from Sydney to the tiny outback side-station and walked, just as she had as a child, all the way to her old home, to surprise her mother.

> I stood at the door and said 'Mother'. She turned with a cry of joy, and I was in her arms. Oh, those mother-arms and that mother-heart.

She stayed a month and 'grew fat with happiness' (although this still only amounted to seven stone) being with her old family again. The farm was doing well and by then her father, John C. Watts, had been able to take on more land. Frances was married by that time and all the family was filled with the wonder of Eliza's stories, which became fireside legends for generations to come. Eliza's many stepchildren had become her life, and so she travelled on with them to live in New Zealand as they too pursued their family's calling to continue mission work. Incredibly, she later remarried another widower with a missionary background, Allen Williams, and became stepmother to his children as well. Although Eliza never had any children of her own, her sister Frances (my great-great-grandmother) made sure her stories were passed on, and a century later I also came to enjoy them.

Frances remained a devout Christian all her life. Her life was a happy one, although frugal. The old 1890s sepia photos of their home reveal little more than a small wooden shack. One of the greatest joys before she died was to see her granddaughter when Monica arrived in 1941 as a refugee from China.

19

ALLEN AND ETHEL (MONICA'S PARENTS)

Monica's father, H. Allen Job, was born in 1881 while his father was away carting copper. A drought had set in and Tom Job had to divert his bullock team to the hills where there was enough scrub for them to feed. He was away for seven months and three days, and arrived back to find a new son, whom Frances had named after 'that good man Allen Gardiner'. Looking back proudly at her son's life, Frances said:

> I always think that the missionary spirit and mantle fell upon him with the name.[13]

With his aunt Eliza's many stories to colour his imagination, it is easy to imagine why Allen was also set on becoming a missionary.

Allen's pioneering adventures provided a strong theme throughout Monica's childhood. His family stories instilled a sense that anything was possible if you put your mind to it. He probably had the greatest effect on the woman Monica was to become and on the way she approached life. He was one of the first Protestant missionaries to work with the descendants of the Incas in South America in the early 1900s. He believed that travel was the best education. Although he had little formal education himself, he went on to become an honoured member of the Royal Geographical Society in London with quite an incredible story of his own. Monica was clearly very proud of him:

> My father was a protestant missionary in Peru, but his story began in Australia, in New South Wales. He grew up near Parkes at Goobang

Creek, but he never went to a proper school. His mother taught him to read and write, and I think he started work by selling newspapers. Then one day a colporteur came through the town. A colporteur was a man who sold Bibles. He told Dad all about his work and his travels. This must have deeply fascinated Dad. He asked the man how and where he was trained to do this, and the man told him all about Harley College [a missionary training institute] in London. Meeting this man must have had a profound influence, because after that he decided that he wanted to go to England, even though he had no idea how to get there. He had no money, none at all. Well, Dad's motto always was 'Where there is a will, there is a way'. He didn't tell anybody, but he saved enough by killing kangaroos and selling their skins. That got him enough for a steerage passage to London. He arrived at the doors of Harley College and said 'I've come'. They had no idea who he was but they hadn't the heart to turn the poor boy away. They took him in and he became known as the 'boy with the baggy trousers', because of his strange attire. He hadn't even got a change of suit. So he stayed at Harley College, London, and they trained him, although he never got a degree or anything like that.[14]

Although Monica has attributed Allen's spiritual revelations to a visiting Bible seller, it is also on record, in the London newspapers that published his obituary in 1947, that his mother, Frances, played a major role.

When he was only fourteen, Allen was sent off to the local town of Parkes, to work on the *Western Champion* newspaper. But he was already dreaming of more distant travels. He had virtually no money or training, and it still seems quite remarkable that a teenage boy living in outback Australia would set off by himself on an expedition as a missionary, without any correspondence or clear idea of what might await him at the other end. He was driven by a deep spiritual conviction as much by his youthful desire to see the world.

So, full of hope, faith and adventure he embarked on a selfless career as a missionary. He began his journey on 15 August 1902, and kept a daily account of his two-month voyage in a diary that he called 'From the land of my birth to the land of my Fathers'. He had very little direct knowledge of the world beyond outback New South Wales, and he was enthralled by everything he saw. In his journal he carefully recorded descriptions of the places, the people and even the daily conditions of the sea. He wanted to capture every moment. With his religious disposition he naturally gravitated towards the many other Christians on board and was clearly dismayed by a small group of passengers who indulged in 'a great deal of drinking and smoking' throughout the voyage. Although he set off alone, he made many dear friends and was sad to be parted from them at their journey's end. Allen was keen not to arrive at Harley College without some preparation, so he took lessons in Latin every day of his travels. Allen's mantra of 'where there is a will, there is a way' was clearly demonstrated in his own actions. This became fundamental to Monica's belief systems; something that she in turn passed onto her own children and grandchildren.

Once he finished missionary school at Harley College in 1904, Allen travelled the country to religious meetings with his new peers. His existence was still very much hand-to-mouth when he met Monica's mother, Ethel Pulley, 'a school teacher with a love of learning and fine character'.[15] Monica also liked to recount her father's story from that time:

He toured England with the religious congresses. But he had no money and could hardly afford to tour. He would always disappear at mealtimes because he did not have enough money to eat with the others. He used to sit on the street and eat peanuts and other scraps. Mother [Ethel Pulley] met him when he was touring. Her people were from Birmingham. Her father was an iron founder or something like that. Eventually, when they were engaged to be married, she took him home to meet her family. They lived in a three-storey house, and had a maid. It was then that they were shocked to discover that he had never worn a pair of pyjamas. He had always slept in the nuddy, but that would not do in Birmingham. Her mother was horrified. So my mother's first gift to Allen was a pair of pyjamas. Rather, it was a nightshirt. A nightshirt! Can you imagine? So then he was on his way to becoming respectable![16]

In one of the few letters kept from this time (1904), Allen writes to his mother about his new love. He was clearly captivated and in love, but as a man with such strong religious convictions, he seemed most drawn by her missionary philosophies.

I believe it was God who brought Miss Pulley and I together. When I said goodbye to her I little thought of ever visiting her in her own home, but here I am and here I have found a home in England.

Ethel is the youngest of four daughters and is 25 years of age. Like all of her sisters, she is a very earnest Christian worker, but she is also a real missionary enthusiast. I had seen her several times during the last day of the convention and had a good talk with her about mission work. But that night when I said goodbye I hardly dreamed of meeting her again. But strange to say, that day she lost her notes and asked me to let her have a copy of the notes that I had taken. We have had many good

23

talks and have decided that should God continue to lead us and open up the way we will someday labour together. I hardly imagined meeting someone so good and true and so well-fitted for missionary work. She is very healthy and prepared to make any sacrifice for Christ.[17]

It is hard to gauge the Pulley family's exact position in society. Although they seemed lofty from Allen's perspective, they certainly weren't gentry. But they weren't labouring classes either. They owned their own home and they had a maid. Ethel's father, David Pulley, was either a tradesman or a 'middleman' in what was an emerging middle class. Whichever way we look at this, Ethel and Allen made a very unlikely couple.

Mr Pulley was born in the country and left school when only eight years old and worked on a farm until he was fifteen. Then he came to Birmingham to work. After spending several years in various occupations he got a position at a very large factory of iron workers and engine makers, where he now occupies the position of manager. He has been there for almost thirty years and recently received a silver medal in recognition of his punctuality and good service. He is quite a noted politician in Birmingham, and is a strong liberal. Mrs Pulley was also brought up in the country, a model housekeeper, and splendid mother. Each of the four girls won a scholarship and passed through Birmingham University and became school teachers.

From any perspective, Allen must have appeared unusual and excitingly exotic to Ethel. However, in those days these qualities are more likely to have been alarming rather than desirable to Ethel's parents. This said, Mr Pulley was clearly a man of liberal ideas, who believed in an education for his daughters – at university no less. Allen was clearly not of the 'establishment' and so there may have been the foundations of mutual respect.

Although Monica's portrayal paints a picture of almost comical amusement at Allen's colonial ways, we can be fairly sure that there would have been grave consideration of his limited means to support their daughter. Although it is difficult to gauge what their reaction would have been when Allen announced his calling as a pioneer missionary to Peru, it is easy to imagine that they would have had some concerns for their daughter. Perhaps they hoped that Allen's departure would fatefully end his engagement to Ethel. It is hard to believe they were not worried when Ethel persisted in her plans to leave England indefinitely and join him in Peru. As it was, Ethel did not return to her motherland for over ten years.

On a mission to Peru

With little formal education and no family influence, Allen's prospects in England were limited. But his first-hand knowledge of other lands at least gave him an advantage. It is quite easy to imagine the appeal of Peru. Ethel remained behind for more than a year while he went ahead to settle there. He needed to establish his mission and make preparations for her arrival.

At three o'clock on the afternoon of 6 December 1906, Allen began his journey:

> this afternoon I boarded a tender boat at Princess Stage Liverpool which was to take passengers to the SS *Mexican* then lying in the harbour. I was the passenger and Miss Pulley and Mrs A Hall were my friends. At last, the tender boat moved out and we were soon alongside the SS *Mexican* which was to carry me to Colon. My friends accompanied me aboard, and looked over the boat before they were called to return to the tender.
>
> Needless to say this goodbye was the hardest I have ever said, but it seemed to be called for by God so it had to be said. I stood on the boat and waved to my friends until they were out of sight. As I turned to go I saw another young man standing by my side with tears in his eyes. We were soon in conversation and took a stroll along the deck. He was off to a cotton mill to take charge of the spinning department

and had just said goodbye to his young wife. A few minutes of exercise before writing a few lines to friends from whom we just parted. After a wash and brush up, the bell called dinner at 6 o'clock. Dinner over, I had a short read and then went to bed.[18]

It is perhaps curious to us that he refers to his fiancee only as 'Miss Pulley' and there are very few words of sentimentality. There is also little mention of her in the diary entries that follow during the voyage. These are more focused on the daily happenings and the people on board than any personal reflections, but that seems to be the nature of his journal and a likely reflection of the times. For us it may seem oddly stiff and formal, with so much left unsaid and little sense of the person underneath it. When I first read it, I was very much reminded of Monica and how she was for most of the time I knew her. It is perhaps easier to see how she was a product of this way of life. My own father David (her son) has this way about him too. I don't think it has come as far as me though, but others might not agree.

Having said this, I really did see a change in Monica as she got older. When we were younger (in the 1960s and 1970s) there was never any hugging in the family but this slowly changed, though a stiffness and an awkwardness remained. Although Monica was always singing our praises and celebrating the smallest achievements of her grandchildren with others, she would rarely bestow this praise directly, at least not in the early days. It seemed to be part of some conditioning against personal demonstrations of affection or displays of emotion. This was made ever so much more meaningful when, in the years before she died, we started to see a more affectionate side of Monica. Her attempts at becoming more modern were often amusing

27

but frequently disconcerting. I recall my surprise when, in her nineties, she tried to demonstrate this in a brief discourse on contraception and premarital sex. She was hasty to point out that she herself had never indulged in such things, because in those days a chaperone was required and it was not acceptable for an unmarried woman to even be alone with a man. I know that several of my other female cousins were also subjected to similar unexpected information. As far as I know, the boys escaped. To know Monica was to know what a radical departure this was from any of her usual behaviour. Her early conditioning was so strong that for most of her life she held her world together with an often artificial sense of propriety. For example, it was decades before she acknowledged that her eldest daughter, Helen, had been divorced before she met my uncle Paul or that they had a child before they were actually married. This was of little concern to the rest of the family, but it did not fit with Monica's preferred view of the world in the 1970s. It was much harder for her to ignore that Paul Silver had a ponytail. But she came to adore him and thought he was 'the best thing that ever happened' to Helen. Paul came from a demonstrative family and would always hug Monica whenever they met. This must have been very unsettling for her at first, but probably led the way to her being more physically affectionate.

I reflect on these things now, because it is really quite striking how this early twentieth-century 'Britishness' seemed to pervade the family over so many years. It is even more curious as Allen was born in the colonies, and Monica's mother was from what we can assume to be a liberal tradesman's family.

According to Allen's commentary, the SS *Mexican* was a cargo steamer built in 1891, and was said to be a 'good behaved boat at sea but rather slow'. They were well fed (with things like soup, boiled fish, duck, green peas, carrots and potatoes, apparently), and although tea and coffee were brought to their cabins before breakfast, Allen was teetotal and would not indulge. These beverages were considered as evil as alcohol. The weather was cold and it seems that Allen spent much of his time 'wrapped in my rug and working away at my Spanish', aiming to get through twenty-four pages of grammar each day. His other reading materials appeared to include Alexander Robertson's *The Roman Catholic Church in Italy*, with a sense that he was checking up on his competition. Perhaps the closest we get to Allen's feelings come from a brief comment he made about a chapter he had read in another book, which I think he called *Black Rock*. He wrote:

> The chapter entitled 'Love is not all' touched me particularly, for if love was all, I would never have come on this voyage alone.[19]

In addition to the crew, it seems that there were only twelve passengers aboard his boat. This included two women (each with two children) and five other men. One of the women was going to Panama to join her husband on the canal works. Allen's closest companions appeared to be the man he had met on deck, despite initial reservations that he was 'from Bolton and a member of the Anglican church' and a man called Dr East, who had a commission with the British Government in the Virgin Islands. The latter was described as 'a fine fellow in many ways, very manly, well read'. Allen seemed to admire him greatly, despite that fact that he was also 'a catholic spirit – and fond of whisky'.

While on board, Allen had opportunities to discuss his mission work, which gives us some insight into his calling:

I was just going to bed when I heard a knock at the door. It was the purser. He had been told in Liverpool that I was a missionary and came to pay me a visit. I went around to his cabin and we had a long talk. He told me of both his joys and his sadnesses. He is a very earnest soul endeavouring to follow the Saviour from day to day. It was a real joy to me to know that there is another follower of Jesus of Nazareth on board the SS *Mexican*. We had a prayer together before parting for the night.

There were also discussions on politics, which confirm, unsurprisingly, that Allen was very much against the conservative parties:

After dinner the six male members of the company and the captain discussed politics. The Dr and I were one on the subject, all the others were conservative, but we held our own.[20]

At a time of wide social divide, the religious division was not only between Catholics and Protestants, but also between the different Protestant faiths. This was clearly a major issue for a young Protestant missionary going to evangelise in a Catholic country, as Monica later explained:

Peru was a Catholic country, and in those days Dad could not go out as a Protestant missionary. Officially, he had to be a farmer so they would let him in. With funding from the Mission Society he bought a whole farm area in Peru, somewhere in the mountains near Arequipa. Although he worked as a farmer, he also started preaching the gospel. He went on many trips through the mountains. He used to travel the treacherous terrain on a mule, along the edges of precipices to talk to the villagers and the miners working up there. He told them all about God.[21]

We might suppose that his early life in rural Australia may have prepared Allen in some way for life as a farmer in the mountains of Peru, but it is unlikely that there were many similarities. Presumably in the five or so years he was there, he must have done some farming in addition to his true calling. My impression is that his community and local activities intensified after Ethel arrived and they were married. Before that he focused on his travels to mountain communities, fluent in Spanish by then.

Allen became well liked and greatly respected, and Monica told me that there is still an area in the mountains, a natural reserve of some kind, that was named after him. At that time, the rest of the world knew relatively little about Peru, and Allen took the opportunity to learn a great deal about the Incas. He was later made a Fellow of the Royal Geographical Society for the detailed records and information that he provided and, when he eventually returned to England, he was frequently invited to give lectures in London on this subject. He was also granted the distinction of Fellow of the Royal Zoological Society for his work in lecturing on the fauna of Australia. In later years, Allen became well known for his radio broadcasts for schools and other societies. He seemed to marvel most at the simple things such as the supply of fish! The Incas 'had gained such a high degree of civilisation in their day that there were records of fresh fish being transported over 200 miles from the regions over the Andes Mountains where it never rains, arriving fresh the same day'.[22]

Allen wrote many accounts of his journeys and adventures in Peru. His exotic tales and sometimes hair-raising adventures went on to become favourite bedtime stories for Monica and her sister throughout their childhood. They revelled in his adventures and I am sure that this inspired them to believe anything was possible if they set their mind to it. I remember my own father David continuing this tradition and reading the same stories to me when I was a child.

Travelling by mule, Allen navigated the treacherous mountain paths to the mines and settlements to meet and work with the local people. His journeys took him to the many small mountain villages, some at more than 14,000 feet (4,000 metres), with mud houses and thatched roofs. There he would enjoy the distant views of Incan huts and llamas grazing across snowy mountains. From there he would take 'the highest wagon road in the world' although at 16,800 feet (5,100 metres) along a cliff edge it could hardly be described as a road. Allen found mountain life invigorating and did not seem to suffer from altitude sickness, unlike a Spanish travelling companion to whom he referred only as 'the Captain'. The following vivid descriptions of one such mountain journey from Agualani to Quitún, later became part of one of Monica's favourite bedtime tales.

The road over which we passed today is by far the most wonderful that I have ever seen. Our hearts were beating nearly twice their usual pace, and now and then they would stop altogether and our hair would stand erect while our mules crawled along a narrow groove cut out of solid rock of an almost perpendicular hill. To describe this road is for me utterly impossible. No one can have any conception of it unless they have passed along it. But try and conceive of a mighty chasm hundreds of feet deep with sides almost wholly perpendicular. It is leagues long and miles of it is solid rock mostly covered with tropical vegetation – trees, vines and flowers all matted together. A roaring torrent runs down the centre and here and there a crystal stream is running or pouring down the sides. The road, varying between two to five feet, is cut into the side, and sometimes this is only a ledge along the slanting wall. At other places it is but a groove blasted out of an upright cliff.

Then put yourself in imagination, on the back of a lively mule. Your left foot is within an inch of the rugged rock and you press it close to the animal's side. You bow your head to save it from bumping on the rocks above, and as you bow your head you see that your right foot is dangling over an awful precipice a hundred feet or more above the foaming waters. A strange feeling creeps over you which is impossible to explain. As you turn the corner and the path widens a little, you give a deep sigh of relief and your hair lies down and your heart starts beating. But it is only for a second, for the groove comes to a sudden stop on this side of the chasm and on the other side it commences. From one point to the other several wire ropes are stretched and planks are laid across them. You cannot turn back so you go ahead. The bridge swings from side to side and moves up and down as you approach the centre. The mule staggers and you glance below at the water dashing itself on the mighty rocks below. You hold your breath until you have reached the groove on the other side. Today we have passed along miles and miles of such roads and crossed six such bridges.[23]

Sometimes the precipice would be more than 1,000 feet above the rushing waters. At some of the worst points there were small wooden crosses to mark the places where others had fallen.

But a few months ago, a poor fellow fell over the cliff and was dashed to pieces on the rocks below.

Several of the small villages had acquired telephones, and there was one little cottage called Aroya where Allen would stay. These were important communication points to coordinate travel. The phone line ran all the way along the road side.

After my description of the road you will realise how necessary the telephone is. For when mules are travelling in opposite directions along this track, the passing points have always to be arranged by aid of the telephone.

On one of his journeys, Allen almost fell to his death. Part of the road was so bad that they thought it would be safer to dismount and lead their mules across.

It was fortunate that we did so. Pattison's mule made it across alright, but my beast slipped as he came down the side. I held on with all my strength, but it was no good. He rolled and disappeared over the steep bank. I stood breathless as I listened to the moans of the poor beast as he smashed through the brush falling slowly towards the raging waters below.

34

The mule was snagged in rocks only fifty feet below so Allen was able to climb down the cliff face. He rescued his saddle and his bags but could not save the mule. Pattison took his possessions and Allen had to walk back fifteen miles to get another mule. Torrential rain set in and Allen crawled on his hands and knees through several mudslides. He was almost washed off the ledge by sheets of water rushing down the mountain face.

> It called for every ounce of strength and courage I possessed. In many parts I could only keep my feet by holding the overhanging vines, or working my way through with a pole. But I kept at it and eventually reached La Pampa after dark. A pretty spectacle I was!

It was stories like this that captured Monica's imagination and deepened her already great admiration for her father. But perhaps it was his medical service that inspired her to become a medical missionary.

Before he left England, Allen spent several months doing hospital training for basic field medicine, so that he would be prepared to help in remote areas. Many of the mountain outposts and mining camps in Peru had no doctor or nursing services at all. Although Allen had only rudimentary medical training, he bought medical supplies and, in the absence of any other support, he was able to help treat many of the mountain villagers and miners.

As I happened to be located in the medical rooms, I was transformed in the eyes of the men into the new doctor. After the first day I had instant callers. Never a day passed without a steady flow of patients. Over and over again I explained that I was only a quack, but the patients continued coming and some even wanted me to stay for a proper appointment. Malaria was the most common malady and I found several new cases each day. In all cases, but one, I found quinine to be effective. In addition to my own medicines I had access to the medicines and books left by the late doctor, which I also put to good use. I was surprised over and over again by the results that I achieved. Of course there were some failures as well. But I ended up treating quite a few diseases. All of this might seem amusing, but the experience gave me to realise how very valuable is my little medical knowledge. Now on all of my travels I take my medical case and I am always putting it to good use. I advise this of every missionary.[24]

Allen extracted teeth, poulticed boils, removed ticks, dressed leg ulcers, and prescribed for 'rheumatism, coughs, constipation, diarrhoea and biliousness'. Even if he did feel an unwitting imposter, his work was clearly appreciated by miners and villagers alike. He would also travel out to the mining 'outcamps', such as Camp 4, so named because it was four leagues from the Santo Domingo mine. There, accommodations were even more limited, and the same hut might be shared with many, including on one occasion a couple with a baby, who shared the only bed:

Every available yard on the floor was occupied by myself, five other men and four dogs. I wanted to sleep but it was almost impossible for the baby cried all night and the Captain gasped for breath the whole time.[25]

36

In the morning they would sometimes wake to find their mules bleeding and ravished by vampires.

> Their backs might be bleeding quite badly. This is due to the blood-thirsty vampires – a bat that inhabits these parts and attacks both man and beast at night. One does not feel them while they are sucking out the blood and only realise they have been after they have left. They never fail to tap a good blood vessel which accounts for the stream of blood which flows when the bat flies away satisfied.[26]

The gold mines were also dangerous places. Injuries and deaths were not uncommon. And the gold attracted bandits from far and wide. A gang of outlaws from Bolivia was known to be in the area when Allen was there. Although there was a generous reward on their heads, Allen had no desire to meet them.

> This afternoon in St Domingo, we saw an American being put in a shallow grave without any ceremony or shedding of tears. 'A crude funeral' I said to the manager [of the Santo Domingo mine]. 'Yes' was the reply 'but that is all an outlaw is worth'. Then I was told that this man was one of the gang of notorious robbers who had just come across from Bolivia to hold up the next consignment of gold that went out. He has been working at St Domingo in order to get the necessary information. But he had attempted to take the gold himself.

This outlaw had apparently tried to take the camp using several revolvers, firing more than 100 shots before he was captured. Then somehow he tried to attack the cashier with a dagger that had been concealed in his boots but the cashier drew his revolver and shot him dead.

The remaining gang members were suspected to be waiting over the pass, mounted on the best of horses. Brave as he may have been, Allen was nonetheless glad instead to meet twenty-five soldiers on his next mountain crossing, on their way to escort the next consignment of gold. There were often soldiers passing through the region as they came from the interior where an army was kept to prevent the Bolivians from stealing Peruvian territory.

As expected, Allen did not have many kind words to say about the Catholic missions. He described the friars as 'generally bad men' who saw the 'Cheericho' natives as savages and treated them as little more than beasts. The friars would throw bananas to them from the wall of the yard where they were 'kept' and watch them scrap for them. The Cheericho, as Allen refers to them, were generally regarded with great fear. Allen met one man whose father had been taken by them and killed. But there were other stories of white men who had gone to live among them.

> There is a remarkable character up there named Bobby Crawford. He was an Irish sailor who ran away from his boat at Mollendo. He married a Cheericho and lives among them. He trades with the natives and is said to have an annual income of between £4000 and £5000.

Allen also stayed for a time with a childless couple from Italy who had 'found a Cheericho boy and brought him up from the river'. The boy was about ten years old and the couple were raising him as their own.

The lad has been going to school here and speaks Spanish well. He can read and write and is not at all backward. He compares favourably with the smartest child here.

On another occasion friendly natives took them to visit a Cheericho temple in a remote area. It was quite difficult to reach and had not been seen by many white men. The Cheericho were described as sunworshippers and they wore a tin dish in their upper lip. Allen met a man called McLaren who had lived for five months entirely among the Cheericho. He 'treated them kindly and got on with them better than most men'.

Many of Allen's preconceived ideas were being challenged. He began to suspect that 'the savages', as they were generally referred to, might have more moral fibre than some of the Christian men he was living and working with.

During my earlier travels in New South Wales, I was often brought face to face with the low moral conditions of labouring men, especially in those places where they are separated from the influence of Christianity, from pure and noble women and other uplifting faces. And during the years that have lapsed since, I have always hoped that if I got to know such men in other parts of the world that their lives would be better than those of my countrymen. But my experience on the Tambopata [Peru] has in this respect been sad and disappointing. The men here come from all parts of the world. Some have spent their early years in Christian and refined homes and others have never known such inestimable blessings. Most of them have travelled widely and many have led wild lives. I have laid myself out to know their inner lives and thoughts. I mixed among them and as far as possible was one of them. To some extent I succeeded in my object, but it has left me exceedingly

39

sad at heart. I am nearer pessimism today than I have ever been. To see a community of men, fine looking, brave and strong whom a stranger might trust and honour – but men who can talk of nothing but lust and live for the same. After my years among missionary men, such company is overwhelming.

And how is it that the pioneers of commerce are generally men who look for every opportunity to degrade the innocent natives?

With Ethel planning to join him in six months (March 1908), it was probably with some relief that Allen prepared for a more sedentary life near Cuzco.

A civil marriage in Peru

Allen refused to be married in a Catholic church, and it is clear that the local priests were equally reluctant. He ascertained that there was provision in the laws of Peru for a civil marriage and, with much opposition, Allen and Ethel were married by the mayor in the first civil marriage in the records of that country. Ethel arrived five days before the union was to take place in what she described to her mother as 'the worst country in the world'. In the only letter that we have on record from Ethel, she writes of her first impressions.

> It has some splendid sunsets, beautiful buildings, a lovely cathedral and elaborate churches. The shops are very, very much better than I expected to find them. Although window dressing has yet to be learned! The prices of things are about three times as much as in England. The city has some really wealthy people, and strange to say that some of the most important people here are English or North American. In fact, there is quite a colony of English-speaking people here, exceedingly nice people but not out-and-out Christians and some are Roman Catholics.
>
> The streets are filthy and for those intending to visit Arequipa it would be well to bring as much Eau de Cologne as possible, and to certainly practice the art of looking up and not down. But one is

constantly obliged to look up to where one finds a blue sky and lofty snow clad mountains.

The situation, climate and surroundings of Arequipa are ideal, but in this beautiful spot which God has made are found people whose sense of morality has been blunted, whose habits and mode of living are to an English girl most repulsive and depressing.[27]

Considerable legal obstacles were placed in their way and Allen had to engage a lawyer to help them navigate a reluctant system. Ethel saw the achievement of a civil marriage as their first act of mission work together.

What a five days we have had. Allen did nothing but trot about with documents for signing and visits to the lawyer. I am just tired of signing documents, but the lawyer was an exceedingly nice man – very liberal minded – a treat to find such a man in this stronghold of Romanism.

When you realise that marriage here can only take place in a Roman Catholic church and that the priests can demand what they will, you can tell what life here must be like. We find, however, that there is provision within Civil Law, but that it is never used and the people are kept in ignorance. To be married here by Civil Contract has no precedence. The mission felt that and that to get our marriage through would do much to open the eyes of the people. It was a daring thing to do here but we have gained a victory and now the people know what has been kept from them. The English people have all rallied to our side. That has been our first missionary work. In the eyes of the Roman Catholics we have been guilty of a heinous sin.

On the day they were to be married, Ethel rose at 6am, still uncertain if she would end the day married or not. She packed a trunk and dispatched their luggage in preparation for their intended journey for Cuzco. At 1.30 they had to appear before the judge in the High Court of Justice, together with their English entourage, which included their new friends the Browns, and Mr Ritchie, a fellow missionary who had arrived from New York on the same voyage as Ethel.

> I don't think I have ever been in a filthier and dustier room, with dirty and faded hangings. The Judge was so different from our smart English Judges. We were there to swear that everything we had signed was correct. When we arrived there was other business taking place for which they were casting lots. Four dice were put in a box, shaken and then the Judge drew. Number four had it! Our party were highly amused. Mr Brown said they were casting lots as to who would have me. Mr Ritchie said it was he. However it was only a question of land dispute and our business soon followed. After we had all done quite a bit of swearing (a good occupation for missionaries) the Judge granted us permission to be married.

From there they had to return again to the lawyer's office to collect yet more papers to present to the alcalde (the lord mayor), and did not receive confirmation that they could be married until around 3pm.

> I had just two hours to dress and be down at the Municipal Buildings by 5.30pm! I wonder how an English bride would feel if she did not know she was to be married until the afternoon of her wedding day.

When her carriage arrived at the municipal buildings there was a large crowd waiting. Not only had all of the English community turned out to support them, but so had a great many others.

There was also a great crowd of office men and many others curious to see a Civil wedding. I think they were rather surprised to see an English girl all in white appear. The room in which we were married was lovely – very long and part of which was shut off by a palisade. It was rather like going into a church. We all marched in. The seats were arranged against the wall and Allen was told to sit on one side and I on the other. The other members of our party, including our lawyer sat alongside. The lawyer then read Allen his duties and then he read mine, all in Spanish. Then Allen had to cross to my side and I to his and then we were married. The ring had no part to play. But when Allen put it on everyone smiled, especially the Acadie. The lawyer and all were exceedingly nice and wished us all happiness. Then we drove off to the office again.

You never saw such a carriage and pair as we had. It was a broken-down sort of four-wheeler, and it was quite necessary to put travelling rugs on the seat to keep our dresses respectable. The team was a pair of scraggy mules which had certainly seen the wear and tear of life and upon whose bones one's wardrobe might be hung, so decided were the points. I would have loved to have sent you a snap-shot but we did not have the Guild Photographer with us. Oh how we laughed! One certainly can be happy under all circumstances and the details do not seem to matter!

The Browns had a very beautiful house with splendid grounds and sweeping verandas. They befriended Allen and Ethel and had invited them to have a religious wedding ceremony in their large drawing room on the evening of the civil union. The room had been beautifully decorated with flowers, and most of the local English community were invited. Ethel wore a veil with her white gown and carried a wreath of orange blossoms. Mr Brown gave her away and Mr Ritchie conducted the service. Then they all enjoyed a feast, so kindly prepared by Mrs Brown.

> What a bond of love and friendship there is between all the English-speaking people. The kindness we have had shown to us has just been grand, and from those who only a few days ago were strangers. Allen and I came away at about 10pm and were simply pelted with rice.

Ethel joked that their wedding breakfast consisted only of cocoa, bread and butter. It was certainly a taste of the more simple life that was to follow. They were anxious to reach Cuzco where they planned to spend several months doing mission work before setting to work on the farm.

> I am finishing this letter on my birthday [22 March 1908]. We have been down at Tingo now for a week, going into Arequipa most days as we had a lot of shopping to do and mission affairs to see into. So we have had an exceedingly busy but happy week. We are leaving for Cuzco on Wednesday morning, so we will have two busy days packing as Cuzco is a dreadful place to get things.
>
> We have to go two days by train and then two days by mule! So I am expecting a lively time. I tell Allen that he will have to tie me on as I can't even ride a donkey! Oh the pleasures of travelling in Peru![28]

Allen took his bride back to live in the mountains. They were not allowed to teach Christianity overtly, but proposed to live a Christian life and 'hoped that, by example, some might find the Lord in their own tradition'. Life was very difficult.

45

I also grew up listening to Monica's accounts of her parent's story:

> Once my mother arrived Dad stopped the more dangerous travelling.
> Mother never really adapted to the high altitude. They were living at well
> over 10,000 feet above sea level. She used to say it took half an hour to
> boil an egg and two hours to boil a potato. It just was not Mother's way
> of life. She was so tired and hardly ever got out of bed. She had a lot of
> difficulty breathing.[29]

Ethel was completely unprepared for life in Peru, and wrote to her parents to tell them how she was so 'dismayed at it all'. She never got used to it, and must have doubted her choice daily. She was very weak and got even weaker when she fell pregnant. Monica always said it was a miracle that Ethel survived the pregnancy. The baby was never expected to live:

> My older sister was born while they were there. They called her Hope
> because they didn't think she would live at all. They were just too high
> [up]. It must have been very difficult having a pregnancy. Hope was only
> five pounds when she was born. She was about eighteen months by
> the time they had to leave, because she just didn't grow up there. When
> they left she was probably still five pounds!

In July 1911 they set sail for New Zealand. Allen loved Peru, but knew it was impossible for them to stay with the failing health of his wife and daughter. It was a very long journey that took them via Cape Town and Australia. The monotony of the voyage was broken by games, concerts, fancy-dress parties, and even cricket matches. Allen and Ethel enjoyed the concerts and the games, but did not join in with any of the dancing or the drinking.

> Nearly everyone, even the Christians, play at cards and dance. I feel
> quite puritanical among them.[30]

Allen stuck to his principles! No matter how extreme they might seem today, it must be remembered that these philosophies were more widespread then. The temperance movement was gaining favour and became powerful enough to achieve a total ban on the sale, manufacture, and transportation of alcohol in the United States (from 1918).

There were many other theologians on board and Allen again made many friends. On one terrible occasion he was called upon to take a funeral.

> This afternoon a very sad accident occurred. Mrs Davis was carrying her
> baby down the stairs when she fell and injured the baby severely. There
> was very little hope and it cast gloom over all. The child was a lovely
> little girl of 12 months. Just previous to the accident Babs (Hope) was
> playing with her and they kissed one another so sweetly.[31]

The baby died in the night and the captain asked Allen to assist with a service the next day. Then the little body was weighted, wrapped and lowered down a plank into the ocean. The mother was out of her mind with grief. It affected everyone deeply and Allen did what he could to support them for the rest of the journey.

Ethel was sick for much of the voyage and was often confined to her cabin by the ship's doctor. An outbreak of whooping cough also affected many of the children on board and Hope did not escape. Her coughing and crying were a constant source of conflict with the less than sympathetic passengers in the next cabin. After months at sea, nothing could describe Ethel's relief on finally reaching New Zealand to start a new life. She hoped that it could only be more civilised than the one she had left in the mountains of Peru.

Monica's early years

Ethel was certainly happier and healthier in New Zealand. Hope also started thriving, although she was always very short. I met Hope many years later in 1982 just before her second marriage, at the age of seventy-two, to a delightful man who travelled around London on a large tricycle. This was the easiest form of transport with his club foot. Hope struck me as a much more outspoken woman than Monica. She trapped me for hours with her monologues, but I did not mind because she had so many incredible tales of her own. To me she was as close to Agatha Christie's Miss Marple as anyone could be. She was very shrewd and had the same determination as Monica. Although they adored each other, I sensed there may have been some sibling rivalry as well. Hope's first marriage was also to a missionary, and they worked in China and Africa where she wrote both romance novels and historical textbooks. She was also a most unlikely smuggler of documents for the anti-apartheid movement in South Africa. When she returned to England she became a lecturer in Latin at Cambridge University. In her later years, when she moved to London, Hope became a Quaker and a good friend of actor Paul Eddington (who was also a Quaker), famed of his leading role in the BBC television series *Yes Minister*. I remember her as a small, rotund but very bright old lady, who delighted in showing me the sexy underwear, fortunately not in situ, that she planned to wear on her second honeymoon. She and her new husband had some happy years together before they both eventually succumbed to cancer. When I met her, Hope joked that she hadn't done so badly since her parents never expected her to live.

They all seemed more suited to New Zealand, where Allen's missionary work continued and Monica was to be born. In those days a major focus of missionary work was to help save people from the perils of alcohol. The family remained strict teetotallers. I find this amusing because Monica enjoyed a good drink in her later years. Allen certainly had his work cut out for him in New Zealand as Monica later reflected:

My father took Hope and Mother out to New Zealand to help a group of British people who had left England for a new start in a new country. In England they had struggled, drinking, smoking and gambling and doing other things they shouldn't. They had settled in a place called Kawhia in New Zealand, which was so out of the way it was quite hard to get to. Well, the idea was that they would be so far away they would not be able to find the drink again. But when I was born in 1913 the doctor was so drunk he could not even deliver me properly. So they found it again all right![32]

The family moved to the South Island and stayed for a time before leaving New Zealand for Australia. It is not really clear why they moved on. This may have been a directive of the mission society, as it is unlikely that Allen gave up on the drunken New Zealanders. I am sure it was more likely to have been a calling to return to his homeland. His mother Frances was still

50

alive and had not yet met her grandchildren or his wife. Monica had fond memories of her grandmother Frances in Parkes, but most of these came later when she was an adult returning there with her own son as a refugee from China during World War II. By all accounts, Monica was a happy child who loved and appreciated being around other people, and did not appear to take herself too seriously. Although she describes herself as much less scholarly than her sister, she was clearly very bright and learned easily. She was far more athletic than Hope and was particularly good at gymnastics.

It was not until 1923 that the family finally returned to England. We can only imagine how relieved Ethel would have been. She hated Peru, and probably never really felt at home in Australia or New Zealand. Monica, on the other hand, just loved it all:

We stayed in Sydney until I was about eight. Then we moved to Tasmania where we lived right on the water's edge. It was a beautiful home. We watched all the boats passing by. By then my father thought that we would never do anything if we stayed in Tasmania because it was just too pretty. So we packed up and got on a ship and took six weeks and two days to get to England.

We stopped at every port. Dad wouldn't let us do any schoolwork. No, he said, 'Never do any schoolwork! It is better to learn from all the people you meet. Look around you and really see where you are and what is going on. Write it all down. Join in and take every opportunity'.

I found an old man on the upper deck. He was first class, and we were all tourist class. He liked to have somebody to read to him. Oh, he was wonderful. He really just loved me. I just went up there every day and read all the books that he wanted me to read. So I was able to sit in first class all the way.

This may well have been the start of Monica's love of travelling. She was always reminding me that her father said that 'travel is the best education', and it must have caught on because I now love it just as much. Although she had not been to England before, it seemed to be a homecoming of a kind. Perhaps this was because of her mother's reminiscences. She told me sentimentally many times, 'I still remember seeing the white cliffs of Dover for the first time when we landed in England'. Sometimes at these moments, she would break quietly into a few bars of the song 'The White Cliffs of Dover'. In her later life, she would continue to return to England almost every year until she was about ninety and her medical insurance became an issue. Even then, I am sure she would have gone if her children had not been so worried about the idea. But as a young girl, it seems that she was filled with a mixture of wonder for this new culture and a realisation that despite their best intentions she and her sister were considered to be different, unruly and even undisciplined. Having said this, I am sure that they were exceptionally well behaved.

We stayed with Mother's people. I remember my aunt, Mother's sister, said that they had been very worried about us coming. Worried but also fascinated to see what sort of strange children might come from Australia. We were coming from a strange country they knew little about, and they had no idea what we were going to be like.

Once they met us they were very concerned that we had not learned English manners! We were used to enjoying ourselves and our own company. We just didn't say the right things, and we didn't do the right things, especially around adults. They kept having to tell us off. All the time. It was very difficult at first.

The girls seemed to have had a strong bond and perhaps this was made stronger as they were scrutinised as alien creatures together. There is also a sense that because they were together, this did not bother them all that much and instead they found much to laugh about in this new strange land. They seemed to settle in naturally, and seeing their mother's happiness at being reunited with her family must have helped them feel more at home as well.

Mother was so happy to be back in her home country. She was born in England. We also got to know her sisters, our aunts and our other grandmother. All four had exactly the same voices. And when Hope and I were upstairs and the aunts were talking downstairs you had no idea which one was talking. They had exactly the same accents. A Birmingham accent it was, I think. And we thought the whole thing was so amusing.

There were lots of other little things that we found quite odd. My grandparents had special wheel chairs I think they were called 'bath chairs' or something like that. A person stood behind and wheeled them around the seaside resort with a rug over their knees. We had never seen anything like this, and we thought that this was all so funny. We really did.

Once again, Allen had arrived in England with no job and an uncertain future. Unemployment was a considerable problem at the time. They were still too poor to have a place of their own, and they had to stay with Ethel's family (the Pulleys) to begin with. Although Allen had no work he was ever the optimist in Monica's eyes:

> My father had no job, but he did not see that as a problem. He just said that if millions people in England could still survive and find a job he didn't see why he couldn't too. He got a job temporarily at the United Kingdom Alliance. Talking at meetings against drink.

It is not really clear how long they remained with the Pulleys or whether Allen was paid for his temperance work. In his obituary it is said that Allen 'knew more about gambling than anyone in England'. His later work for the Anti-Gambling League brought him into frequent contact with members of the House of Lords, tipsters, and 'big' bookmakers. He had just finished compiling the annual report for the society the week before his death in April 1947, and had collected 'amazing figures of the money spent on gambling in England, and the manpower engaged in promoting that evil'.

Allen's calling was difficult and confronting. He was the likely target of protest and abuse. It must have been very difficult for Monica to see her father so ridiculed for his beliefs. I suspect that she was both proud of him and embarrassed at the same time. She wanted and needed to see her father as a hero, and it must have been undermining to see his struggles. This may have been one of the first challenges to her early images of her father, and may explain her later steadfast determination to preserve her desired version of reality. From our vantage point it is easy to admire Allen's perseverance and conviction, but it might have been more difficult for Monica at the time.

He was eventually appointed as the pastor at the Congregational Church at Oldham Road, Manchester (in September 1927), presumably through his connections to the London Missionary Society. Excerpts from the church notices from Manchester Congregational Church 1927–1928 reveal his progress:

In July 1927: 'A special church meeting held on June 1st decided to invite Rev. H. Allen Job to the pastorate, and we are glad to announce that Mr Job has accepted and hopes to commence his pastorate in September. Mr Job will be our seventh minister in 77 years and comes to a church that, notwithstanding the changes in the district, is as strong and virile as ever, and great hopes are entertained of further progress under the new ministry. The Rev. Job has had an interesting career. Born in Australia, he studied at Harley College London, and went out as a pioneer missionary to South America. Since then he has had experiences of congregational pastorates in New Zealand and Australia and after a period as a Temperance Organiser, returns with zest to regular ministry all the better equipped by his training and experiences for our particular sphere and opportunity.'

In October 1927: 'Our new pastor commenced his ministry on September 14th, under very encouraging conditions, the sermons were appropriate to the occasion and the day concluded with a very impressive communion service. Mr Job visited the Sunday School and spoke at the Brotherhood meeting where there was a very large assembly of men. The new ministry will, we believe, be a great power for good in the district.'

In December 1927: 'We had a very interesting experience on Sunday evening, December 4th. Our pastor had invited questions from the young

55

people and they responded readily. The discourse on December 4th was responding to these. There was a fine congregation, the questions showed keen interest and the Minister's response met with great appreciation. Altogether it was an interesting innovation.'

In May 1928: 'The Annual Business Meeting of the Church was held on March 28th and was remarkable for the best attendance remembered by anyone present. Reports were presented showing progress in every department of the great work of the Church and tribute was paid to the earnest and successful labours of the Rev. H. Allen Job since he succeeded to the pastorate.'

And so it seems that Allen found his niche. But there were still challenges, with reported hostilities and vandalism. He angered other congregations in the area because he was regarded as 'too down to earth' because he welcomed all comers to his church. But as ever, he persevered and became very popular with his own growing congregation.

This meant a new life and a new school for the girls in Manchester. Monica always remained very modest about her accomplishments, even in her school days. She always appeared more interested in having fun than being studious, but she clearly did well academically in spite of this, or possibly because of it in many ways. It seems that she had a very sensible and balanced approach to her studies with a clear idea of just how much she needed to do to get where she needed to be, without interrupting the things she would much rather be doing. She was passionate about sport and excelled at gymnastics. She much preferred to be outside playing, and was the less serious of the sisters. Even so, her leadership qualities were already clear.

She was a Girl Guide for many years and much admired by the other girls.

Finally, we went up to Manchester because Dad got a job there. And I went to a new primary school. My sister Hope was always fond of reading, right from the beginning. And I was more interested in playing games. Hopscotch. On the streets. I don't know if you play it any more now. Hope was a real scholar. She was really interested in it all. I wasn't. But I had enough experience with travel, which I agree is a wonderful education. We learned so much on that journey between Australia and England, because everywhere we stopped we had to mix with people, see if we could talk to them and understand them. We were always learning as far as Dad was concerned. Not in schools. Yes, 'meet the world' was his idea. So that was what I always did.

·I thought our new school in Manchester was hilarious because the children were so well behaved. They were much better than we were. In Australia I always had to stand out of class and get the strap on my hand because I had been naughty or talking in class. It was a great thrill you see, because once you got the strap you were counted as a hero. You didn't wince or move your arm. You were strapped two or three times. Even the little girls. I was only seven when I first got the strap in Australia. Then you sat back into the class as a hero. It was terribly important. But they were much too good for all this in England. We had to learn to toe the line.

I remember the wooden desks with a hole for an ink well. We used a pen with a quill. There were no fountain pens back then. And you had to make the strokes going up very fine and the strokes coming down very thick. I was quite good at writing.

Monica enjoyed her school work and did not find it difficult at all. It is hard to tell through her modesty if she really did take this more seriously than she let on, particularly in high school when her ambitions were clearer and stronger. It was already evident then that she had an exceptionally retentive memory, one that sustained her until the end. I always marvelled at the details of her recollections, even for shared memories that had already faded for me.

I did very well and won a scholarship to a private high school. Hope went to a state school. She was doing very well. I had been quite determined I was going to go to this very expensive fee paying school. It was quite famous and rather 'upper crust'. We were relatively poor people because Dad was a minister. I won the scholarship simply because I could make up all sorts of stories about where I had been. I was a great one for pretending I knew lots of things, when I probably didn't. So I won the scholarship when there were only two given. It took me right through six years of high school. I never found school work very hard. I thought it was funny in some ways. It never worried me at all. I found maths very easy, but I was not so good at English literature. I learned chunks of it off by heart so I could always quote things. And that seemed to get me through.

Inspired by her father, Monica said that she always knew she wanted to study medicine and become a medical missionary. This idea must have solidified in high school. The family were still quite poor and her only option was another scholarship. But scholarships for medicine were very difficult to get. So she had to be creative. Again, we have to admire her tenacity, drive and lack of doubt or intimidation. We can certainly see where she got this from:

58

My father was never afraid of anything. He always kept on saying to us 'Where there is a will there a way', and we were always all quite determined. If I decided I wanted to do something, I would do it. I already knew I wanted to do medicine, and Father said I had better win a scholarship then, because we had no money and there was no way to do something like that without money in those days.

So I knew I had to find another scholarship to do a medical degree. I knew that I would probably never get one, so I looked through all the possible scholarships you could get and there was one given for somebody who didn't drink and didn't smoke, but went to church regularly. It was called the Sam Gamble Scholarship. I applied for it and I think I was probably the only one who did, because everyone else was either smoking or drinking then. So I got six years of a medical degree free.

Although I am sure Monica loved her mother dearly, Ethel never seemed to feature as strongly in her recollections as Allen did. He was obviously a man of deep convictions, but although the nature of his work must have required a confident personality to some extent, it does not sound as though he was a brash, loud or outspoken person. He was obviously someone Ethel was prepared to follow halfway around the world despite few financial prospects. It is much harder to get a sense of what Ethel was like and how she might have influenced who Monica was becoming. Monica rarely referred to Ethel as anything other than 'Mother', although Allen frequently earned the less formal title of 'Dad'. I always had the impression that she was more emotionally connected to her father.

Allen later moved to the Twickenham Congregational Church (1934–1943) with great success, his 'outstanding personality drawing many to his congregation':

During his ministry many were enthralled with his tales of adventure from far flung places. Mr Job quickly made an impact on the area. Mr Parker had left a small but stable fellowship, and now it began to flourish. Work with children and young people was particularly successful.[33]

He remained there for many years, until he later returned to his temperance and anti-gambling mission, eventually being appointed secretary for all of England. During the war that followed, Allen offered the church hall as a refuge and feeding centre. Ever dedicated to the service of others, he was always a hero to Monica.

A woman in medical school

Monica seemed to approach her medical training with much the same spirit of enthusiasm and fearlessness. There was never any sense that she might be at all intimidated by the establishment, or by the social class, gender or intelligence of her largely male peers. As one of so few women, I once asked her if she experienced any prejudice or intimidation. I was surprised by her answer. She said that it just never occurred to her that this might be an issue, and because she did not make it an issue she did not experience it. She delighted in the company of her male colleagues and they delighted in hers. They all just 'got on with it'.

Her answer implied that although there clearly were strong social inequalities between genders, she was somehow able to dismantle this on a personal level so that it did not affect her or those around her. She seemed to be telling me that by focusing on an issue we sometimes create bigger problems, and make things worse. Instead, she believed that we should just get on and do what we want to do regardless. She felt that with that approach we take the power away from the issue, and can still bring about change, but more quietly and without conflict. Thus, by seemingly ignoring gender issues she may not have been so much denying it, but rather rising above it and thereby destroying its potential to in any way darken her world. This was before the World War II but clearly after the suffragette movement had gained momentum, but Monica has on other occasions acknowledged that she was not one of 'those blue stockings women'. Although she was a beneficiary of the women's movement, and was clearly aware of the struggles, she always insisted that she was not one to make a fuss.

Without wanting to read too much into this, it is fascinating to reflect on these things. It still strikes me that here we have a young woman, poor and born in the colonies, who, in many ways like her father, turns up at the door of the medical school with a sense of expectation and unquestioning entitlement that must have been highly unusual in most other women of her era. Perhaps it was because she was from the 'outside' and because her background had engendered a strong desire to return to the colonies and help others. She saw a medical degree as the best way of doing this. But it is still interesting that she did not choose to be a teacher or a nurse, which would have been more in keeping with the times. Allen was a father of only daughters, so would things for Monica have been different had she had brothers? In any case, as she said, gender just was not an issue for her. If anything, she used it to her advantage:

> There were only six girls and sixty men in that class. There were very few women doctors. Very, very few. But I noticed by the time I finished my six years this was changing. The first year of medicine was all physics, chemistry, botany and zoology. Well! It was rather nice, because whenever we went to open a bottle of medicine or anything, one of the men would help us. They loved helping us, you see. We were thoroughly spoilt.

62

We went to every dance you could possibly imagine because there were so few girls to ask. I was quite popular. Tom Dinsdale, who I didn't particularly like, knew my father was a minister. So he started raising money for our church because he hoped to make a friend of me. But he didn't do any good by that![34]

During her time at university, Monica was also actively involved in her other interests. She became president of the Student Christian Movement, chairwoman of the Student Volunteer Missionary Union in English Colleges and Universities, and was an English delegate to the World Student Christian Federation Conference in Bulgaria. Monica had already decided she would put her medical degree to work helping the less privileged through the missions, and her convictions were strengthened when she found that it was the community work that she enjoyed the most.

The studies were heavy going. In the second and third years we did anatomy, pathology and physiology. After that we went into purely clinical work. I found it rather exciting, particularly our work in the community. We went out to the elderly, we went to prisons and we worked with the poor. We talked to people and helped heal them, or tried to.

We had virtually no antibiotics when we started. There was a lot of tuberculosis then, and [the patients] were just sent to lie in the sunshine. Except there wasn't much of that! Manchester had very heavy clouds, all the time. It rained every day. This also meant that so many children had rickets as well. Infectious diseases were so common. Diphtheria was one of the worst. Antibiotics came in during my fourth year. It changed everything. Before that all the maternity wards were filled with puerperal sepsis. Nearly everybody got it. It was dreadful. They often died. 'Childbed fever' they used to call it. Then it suddenly changed. The whole thing transformed with the introduction of sulphonamides. And what a difference! Suddenly the wards changed. It was absolutely another world. Extraordinary! And all in a very short period. Then penicillin came in, around the time I was finishing. I think I impressed them when I mentioned it in my final exams. The whole idea of treatment was changing. Before that there didn't seem to be any such dramatic treatment for anything.

I first heard Monica's stories of medical school when I was sixteen. Having just finished high school myself in 1981, I was waiting for my results before deciding my own future. In her generosity, Monica took me to Europe as her travelling companion, and it was during those travels that I got to know her more and my own plans to study medicine, not to mention my own love of travel, were inculcated. I cannot say that I was set on it from an early age, as Monica was. Actually, when my father first tried to tell me that Grandma was a doctor I did not believe him. At four years of age my nursery teachers had given me cause to believe that nurses and doctors were the gender-specific names for those that helped sick people. His news was very puzzling.

Monica's eyes always shone when she recalled her days of medicine, and I think this played a large part in my decision. When I finished school it was exciting to have the future as an entirely blank slate in front of me. I felt I could put anything on it. Still waiting for my exam results, I knew I wanted to go to university, but I hesitated to be too specific in case I should narrow my horizons too soon. I am equally determined when I set my goals but I tend to follow my heart more than my head when opportunities arise. Listening to Monica there came a moment when suddenly I just knew in my heart that medicine was for me too. When I look back, I cannot imagine doing anything else.

I think Monica was as nervous as I during the wait for my exam results. We were dining in a hotel in London when my father called me from Australia with the news. He could hardly speak and started by telling me that the numbers were so low that he had to call the authorities to see if there was some mistake. I was already feeling sick as he explained that he had been looking at my state ranking and not my aggregate score, which was so large that he also could hardly believe it. Neither could I. Although I had always done well in school, I had no way of knowing how I might do in the state ranking. Still in happy shock, I returned to the dining table to tell my good news. I had never seen Monica look so proud and that was the best moment. So, with the same sense of anticipation, wonder and adventure of my ancestors, I set off on my own path. A door of the universe had opened to me and I felt my own calling to go through. How could I not?

Monica, who always loved people, seemed to enjoy the clinical side of her studies most. She had very fond memories of her hospital attachments, even though this must have been quite difficult at the time. In those days, the hospitals were a more hostile environment for staff, students and patients alike. Order was a priority over communication. The hierarchy was strong and medical students were at the bottom. The patients seem to have been only slightly above that in terms of being heard. Working in paediatrics as I do today, where there is now every focus on dismantling intimidation and promoting a 'level playing field' for communication, some of these old attitudes now seem unthinkable.

We went to Manchester Royal Infirmary for our clinical training. It was a very big hospital, and it is still there. We lived in the hospital for three months. The beds were in large wards and each had a matron who sat in the middle. All the nurses were scared stiff of her because she saw everything they did. It must have been terribly hard for them. The doctors didn't like us either because we interfered with what the nurses were doing and we didn't know how to make beds properly. Nothing we did was right. But we still got through somehow. I think the worst exams that I ever sat were the oral exams. Going into the room, up to the bed with the doctor, and trying to work out what was wrong. Oh, we were scared of those. You haven't got time to think.

· The hospitals were so dreadful to work in because everything had to be so horribly spick and span. The patients weren't allowed to get their beds untidy. I worked in the Children's Hospital as a nurse to get some money in the holidays. Oh, I was so tired. The beds had to be absolutely perfect the whole time. Children want to jump around and play, but they weren't allowed to. Those were also the days when the new vaccinations came in. Nobody had ever been vaccinated before. You got the most dreadful pox. I think I still have the marks on my arm.

It has all changed so much. I remember when my grandson Stephen was ill and I went to hospital to visit him just a few years ago. It was completely different. In the early 1930s you weren't allowed to sit and talk to a patient. And the bed had to be perfect all the time.

I became quite enthralled with her stories. My own medical training in the 1980s had echoes of this past, with the preclinical subjects in the first three years and clinical attachments after that. Mine was one of the last generations of Australian doctors to go through this, before a more modern hybrid version of the North American 'problem-based learning' style was introduced in the 1980s. My own training was still dominated by long lists of details and rote learning. There was still very little applied knowledge. That all happened later on the job. Now there is much less focus on facts and figures and more focus on communication, personal development and practical approaches with integration of information. As ever, there are upsides and downsides. The level of detail that Monica had to learn was far beyond anything that I encountered. We just have to look at her *Gray's Anatomy* textbook to see that. Many of the disciplines that I studied did not even exist in her day, including my own speciality of allergy and immunology.

In her second year, when she studied anatomy, Monica was allocated a cadaver, just as I was fifty years later, in 1983. This cadaver was with us the whole year, which was generally how long it took us to dissect it in detail, learning each section as we went. In my own day we had one body between six of us and we started at the hands and moved gradually from there, gently and respectfully nibbling through the layers with our scalpels. We named our cadaver Basil, but we were very respectful about this. So we were quite upset when, six months into the year, we returned from our winter break to find that Basil had lost his head. Decapitated for the dental students. I am not sure how Monica started her dissections, but her cadaver was a woman. In giving her body to science this woman had modestly requested that her stockings not be removed. So, to comply with this request, when they got to her legs they respectfully rolled her stockings back up after each day's dissection. But of course

67

none of this happens today, and medical students, at least at my university, no longer do any dissection like this.

Monica made lasting friends. Over the decades that followed, the regular letters and occasional visits to these friends kept her in contact with her Manchester roots long after she left Britain. This was incredibly important to her. She spent so many of her early impressionable years in Manchester, it is not surprising that she always partly felt England was home. Several of her women colleagues went on to prominent positions. One became a very successful surgeon, which was also extraordinary in those days. Even now, surgery remains a specialty largely dominated by men. Over the decades that followed, Monica stayed in contact with many of these former student friends, particularly her best friend, Muriel Bennett. In 2006, when she was reflecting on her old friends from medical school, she said:

> Of the six women in my year I made one very, very good friend, Muriel, who lived in Manchester. She died last week. She is the last of the people that I knew at school. She used to write and tell me about the others. But now they have all died. I only got a letter from her daughter this very week. It knocked me out, because I realised that there is nobody left of my generation in England. Absolutely nobody. So I don't think I will hear another thing about Manchester.

This was deeply troubling for her. Everyone she had known was gone. There was no one left who knew her then. There was no one left to connect her to the Manchester that she knew. In her typical way, she was private in her grief, but I could tell she was devastated. She was alone in her past now.

But she was not alone in 1936, and it was in those years in Manchester that she met my grandfather Stanley Prescott, a lecturer in physiology. He fell in love with her immediately.

Love at first sight

but she was not alone or idle, and it well in those years. Monica became one her grandfather Stanley Hopwood.

At the time he met Monica, Stanley had already completed a bachelor degree and then a masters in science specialising in physiology. Still only in his mid-twenties, he was a Wild prize-man, a lecturer in physiology, and the subwarden of Lancashire Independent College. .

Although Monica grew to love Stanley deeply, at the beginning of this relationship Monica made herself out to be almost an innocent bystander. Listening to her and reading between the lines, I am sure that she was in love with, or at least attracted to, a man called Tom Bromley before she met Stanley. He was a friend of Stanley's and it sounded like she was disappointed that Tom already had a girlfriend. There was a pallet-knife painting on the wall of her flat until the day she died. I had always admired it, and I later discovered that it was done by Tom Bromley, so they all remained friends. She said he was the one who invited her out to meet Stanley and I think she had secretly hoped that the invitation was really from Tom.

It was not in Grandma's nature to describe her emotions or say that she was in love. Monica was always much more likely to describe affection directed at her, rather than describe her own feelings for others. I say this because without this knowledge you might get a false impression of her feelings from her words alone.

I met Stanley while I was in medical school. He was a lecturer in physiology and pharmaceutics. I had already done physiology at that stage and so he did not lecture me. But he passed through the medical school a lot. And he saw my fair curly hair. And that was it. He decided that he had to marry that girl. So that is how I was caught.

He was a resident of Lancashire Independent College, which was a theological college that took in other people as well. Men only of course. He was actually a tutor there and stayed in residence because his people lived in the Cotswolds. Stanley had a friend at his college who knew me. Tom Bromley. Stanley found out what church I went to and got Tom Bromley to invite us both to some scrap meal somewhere in his rooms. So of course I went, not knowing that I had already been caught. Stanley had decided that he was going to marry me and I hadn't even seen him. And I thought that Tom Bromley was much nicer that he was. But he'd already got a girl.

So much to my surprise, Stanley walked me home. We had no cars then, or so very few. He walked me home and then he made an appointment to see me again. It was during that time my parents went to live in London, and I went in to residence at Ashburne Hall. The hall was almost exactly opposite where Stanley was staying. So he was on my doorstep the whole time. He was quite determined. He knew he was going to marry me. That was all there was to it. I didn't really like being caught like that. I had no time to look at him without knowing that he wanted to marry me. I couldn't stand back and see him.

Of course, I had heard her tell this story before, but this is the only version I have recorded verbatim. Previously, I had heard only more romanticised versions without such a clear indication that this affair was, at least initially, very one-sided. I can't say that I liked this more candid version as much. Perhaps, like Monica herself, I preferred the romantic idea that this was mutual love at first sight. On this telling of the story, Monica almost sounds annoyed that she was 'caught' against her will and did not have a chance to 'fall in love' the way she may have dreamed of doing. There is no doubt that she came to love Stanley deeply, but in the beginning she was probably overwhelmed by his passionate enthusiasm. So I am reluctantly inclined to believe this version, which is probably more realistic.

Stanley was clearly a very focused and driven man. Although he was quietly spoken, he was the sort of person who when he did speak he always said something insightful and worth listening to. He was acutely intelligent and ambitious, but he also had a very cheeky sense of humour. Obviously he was both inspired by and single-minded with Monica. He was very tall and slim and the sort of man who became more attractive and distinguished as he got older.

Stanley's people – the Prescotts

Stanley Lewis Prescott was another remarkable person. As with Monica, it is valuable to have an appreciation for what he was like and where he came from.

I was only thirteen when he died, so my own recollections are those of a child and young adolescent. My impressions and memories are of a gentle and wise person, who was quiet yet determined in his intentions. It is so very appropriate that the motto on our family crest that was later granted when he was made a Knight Bachelor is 'Gentleness is the Hallmark of Wisdom'. This was aptly chosen and epitomises Stanley. He was surprisingly passionate and I hope that his wicked sense of humour is apparent in the parts of his letters I have included later in the story.

My English relatives have reminded me just how remarkable Stanley's behaviour was for a 1930s Englishman. At a time when people were far more private, as Monica always remained, it was unexpected that he was able to express his love so ardently and explicitly to her, and to tell his parents about it so enthusiastically as well.

It may sound odd, but Stanley had an almost oriental bearing, perhaps not surprising for his many years living in China. I can't quite work out the reason for this impression.

It was something pervasive, evident in the way he moved, the respectful way he approached others, even in the way he wore his clothes, although they were Western. I remember his crisp white shirts, always worn with a white singlet underneath, and the high-waisted pleated trousers that were the fashion in the 1950s. Never any casual attire in my memories. He was quietly spoken and quite possibly shy. Although this is my adult interpretation of my childhood impressions, it seems to reflect those of others. In a biography, G. C. Bolton also commented on Stanley's mandarin-style leadership:

> Prescott left the University of Western Australia thriving and well nourished. His leadership was perhaps underestimated because of his preference for operating through a quiet diplomacy at times verging on mandarin subtlety. [35]

He was noted for his diplomacy and was very patient with me, but I do recall he was always reminding me to slow down when I was tearing around the garden. He would always say *Man man di*. I still need to pay more heed to that.

I believe that his family origins are all important in understanding Stanley. His father rose to respectability through 'hard work and a wise marriage', and it seems that this was at the core of Stanley's approach to life. Both of his parents had a strong influence, but my impression was that his very dominant mother may have played a greater role. That may also be because she lived longer, into her nineties, with more opportunity to exert her influence. Parts of the following family information come from records kept by Stanley's younger brother Malcolm.

Their father, 'Jack John' Prescott (1873–1950), was one of five sons born to a farmer, Benjamin Prescott who 'owned and worked a small holding of good quality land of 9.5 acres'[36] at Butterwick in Lincolnshire. I refer to Benjamin as a farmer, but all of the historical documents appear careful to avoid that term, possibly for its lowly connotations at the time. In a time when class was all important, 'owner of small land holding' would have been a preferred and more accurate description.

Although the sons were all apparently destined to follow Benjamin's occupation, Jack was described as being good at his books, and under the influence of an encouraging mother (Mary Prescott, nee Lewis), he was persuaded to stay longer at school and continue his studies. As it was, this is sure to have had a profound effect on his prospects and those of his future family. The land was left to Jack and then to Stanley's mother, and sold towards the end of her life to the farming tenants, to help with nursing-home costs. Jack was ultimately the only one of the boys to have children. Two of his brothers, William and Joseph, died young. The other two, George and Tom, died in the 1940s but they never married and remained childless.

In 1888, at the age of sixteen, Jack was apprenticed to Elijah Brackenbury of Bardney, Lincolnshire, chemist, druggist and grocer, for four years to learn his art. His father Benjamin had to pay the then considerable sum of £25 for this opportunity. The terms of his apprenticeship were altogether different from any modern workplace agreements and are quite fascinating:

His master faithfully shall serve, his secrets keep, his lawful commands everywhere gladly do. He must not play at cards or dice tables, haunt Tavern or Playhouses nor absent himself from his said Master's service day or night.

And in return Elijah Brackenbury 'would teach the Art of Chemist Druggist and Grocer' and 'find sufficient meat, drink, lodging and all other necessities except wearing apparel and medicine'.[37]

Jack went on to study at Owen's College in Manchester to become a Member of the Pharmaceutical Society (founded in 1841) and did further studies in Edinburgh to complete his qualifications in 1897. He then moved to London to study as a chemist's assistant while also studying to qualify as an optician at the Northampton Institute (later the City University). He was: 'admitted by Redemption to the Freedom of the Worshipful Company of Spectacle Makers and having been approved by the Examiners and Court of Assistants granted Diploma of Fellowship',[38] a company founded by Royal Charter in 1626.

It was when Jack moved to Peterborough that he met his future wife, Jessie Lamplugh. Curiously, as with Monica's family, religion played a part in this union as well. Although the Lamplugh family boasted a former Anglican Archbishop of York (Thomas Lamplugh, 1615–1691) the family was now firmly Wesleyan. Jack had also been a loyal and practising member of the Wesleyan Church. His youngest son (Stanley's brother Malcolm) later became a Methodist minister. In his own account of these events, Malcolm later wrote:

It was at the fashionable and flourishing Wesleyan Church at Wentworth Street Peterborough that he met Jessie Mary Lamplugh. She was a Sunday school teacher, with a fine professionally trained contralto voice. She was the younger daughter of Thomas Crosby Lamplugh and his wife Mary Jane. Thomas Crosby was a leader in church and city, a magistrate and city and county councillor who became the mayor of Peterborough in 1905. He had built a fine house 'Eastwood' on the Broadway with spacious grounds including a coach house, green houses and a bowling lawn.

When John ['Jack'] asked permission to become engaged to marry his daughter, he refused in a kindly way. John was a man of no means and slender prospects and the age difference of 30 to 21 was too great. Lamplugh warned his daughter that she could face a lonely old age and long widow-hood.

But is seems that Jessie was just as headstrong as her father, and by all accounts an intimidating woman. Jack was described as a handsome and considerate man and Jessie remained determined.

At the second time of asking Thomas Crosby Lamplugh relented. It was agreed that John would find a suitable business to buy and that they would marry once he had settled in it.

There is another small story that is worth mentioning about Jessie's parents. Thomas Crosby Lamplugh married Mary Jane Rogers in 1872. Her family line went back to a Rogers who was martyred by Mary Queen of Scots, but that is not the story I want to tell. The strange story of this couple is that they were both born in 1848 and both died within an hour of each other in 1927, neither aware at the time that the other was also dying. Their family always liked to believe that 'so great was their love that they left this world together'.

So before Jack could be married to his 'aristocratic' fiancée, he had to become established and successful. He found a business premises in the market town of Tetbury, Gloucester, with living accommodation over the shop. It is reasonable to assume that Jessie's father lent him the money for this purchase. Jack took his cousin Jenny Lewis as his housekeeper. This shop at 23 Church Street became the setting for the lives of John and his family for the next forty years, until 1946.

From the beginning Jack was involved in the small Wesleyan congregation that met at the bottom of the Bath Hill, which apparently later turned into a petrol station and a meeting house for the Exclusive Plymouth Brethren. The foundation stone of the old Methodist Chapel in Tetbury, now an antiques centre, lists Jack as one of its founders. Much later Jack became recognised as a local lay preacher and an elected member of the district synod. However, shortly after he had arrived in Tetbury, he had a visit from the local Anglican vicar:

'You are a good churchman I hope, my man?'

'No, sir, I am a Wesleyan.'

'Oh you wretch, I shall never come to this shop again.'

Not only was he not a churchman, he was not a Tory and not a Freemason. He had come from a very different world in which his father and brothers were fiercely independent.

They touched their caps to no man and were formed in part by strong nonconformist and puritan influences. The world to which he had come was one of rigid class distinctions – aristocracy, gentlefolk, landed

78

or otherwise known as 'the gentry', middle-men, and trades folk and the labouring classes. The county clergy counted as 'gentry'.

It was also a closed society that was suspicious of 'incomers'. So there was a great deal for Jack to come to terms with. This was also likely to have been more of a life change for Jessie when she eventually joined him two years later. They were married in Peterborough on 27 June 1907. A local paper wrote of the bride as:

enjoying the popularity which comes to her as the daughter of one of the best liked public men in Peterborough [and] her own service to a hundred good causes in the city.

To celebrate their wedding, Jack gave Jessie a fur muff, and Jessie gave Jack a gold Albert watch, so at least he would be properly dressed.

Stanley Lewis Prescott was born on 21 March 1910, two years after his elder brother, John Lamplugh Prescott. He was a mischievous child who delighted in playing tricks, particularly during family visits to the Lamplugh home in Peterborough for Christmas and other family gatherings. Dissolving spoons was apparently a favourite trick.

The family lived behind the shop, which was extensively renovated to make room for the growing family. The shop itself must have been very beautiful with solid mahogany counters, sets of narrow drawers and shelves of green and white bottles. My uncle Nigel has some of the lovely old syrup jars and medicine bottles in his study today. In a time before commercial medicines, Jack made pills and prepared his own mixtures, tonics, liver salts and hand creams. He was interested in old-fashioned and herbal remedies. It is most likely that growing up in this environment influenced Stanley's interest in the medical sciences.

In those days apothecaries were traditionally consulted about ailments and treatments and throughout his time Jack's advice was sought, not least as to whether a Doctor should be consulted and the cost justified.

The local doctor, Dr Sedgewick, was chauffeur-driven in a Rolls Royce and was afforded a commensurate respect. Some of his more unusual requests, such as for leeches, would be sent to London and delivered by 'fast rail' to the station.

Among Jack's valued customers were King George V and Queen Mary, which led to its royal appointment as pharmacy of HRH the Prince of Wales. Monica told me that the royal crest remains above the door, although the shop was eventually sold to become a veterinary clinic. In Jack's time Tetbury was still a prosperous agricultural centre and so he also prepared liniments, drenches and cough balls for horses and pastes for sheep. He was also the first to provide an optical service in the area. Among his other diverse activities, Jack was a justice of the peace and as was appointed an absentee magistrate.

Jessie was a fundamental life-force in this family, and was obviously an ideal counterpoint for Jack:

They were complementary. He could be anxious, diffident and hesitant, at times burdened by responsibility or fretted by pettiness. He could feel hemmed in by a narrow world: 'Life should be bigger'. Jessie Mary was a strength and immensely loyal. She was direct and outspoken and folk

could for a time be in awe of her but she never forgot her father saying:
'If you are too busy to be kind, you are too busy'.

I certainly feel those simple words are more relevant to us today than ever.

Her singing was a great gift and given generously in Choral Society, concerts and worship. She worked to establish and finance the first two District nurses in the town...She visited almshouses and the workhouse and took comfort to those in need.

As with Monica's family, the Prescotts' faith and spiritual community played a fundamental role in their lives. Although they were of different faiths, this probably contributed to Stanley's enthusiasm in becoming a missionary with Monica. I also suspect that this was mixed in at least equal measure with his ardour for her. For Stanley's parents, the chapel was immensely important, as his brother later reflected:

Father [Jack] once said that it kept him sane. It was there that they heard rumours of angels and saw the meaning of their lives and the world's life and found a gladness and a reverence. It was there that they were given a sense of belonging to a great company of humble and faithful people, on earth as in heaven.

Jack had married well and had established himself through hard work in a well-regarded profession. Stanley therefore grew up in a respectable family, with a father esteemed in his local community and a mother born to local 'gentry'. The boys were all very proud of who they were. They went on to excel at their chosen professions, and both Stanley and John (junior) were later admitted to the Order of the British Empire (OBE).

However, there remains a sense, from what Monica told me, that Stanley may have somehow felt an 'outsider', at least in the early days. This may have been because his family's religious and political positions were not those of the conservative establishment. This too may have contributed to Stanley's drive, giving him something to prove. It may also have contributed to his willingness to leave Britain for a new life in China and the colonies. Monica was so clearly different from most young women he was likely to meet. She was fiercely independent and strong-willed, traits that we can clearly see in his mother Jessie, although they were altogether different in personality. I think Monica had a carefree and spontaneous quality that I am not sure was strong in Jessie's nature.

After schooling at Tetbury Grammar School, Stanley studied physiology at the University of Manchester, becoming a member of staff in 1932. It is difficult to get a clear picture of his thoughts at that age, as there are no letters from him on our records until a few years later in 1936. He was already showing his academic and leadership qualities, as subwarden of Lancashire Independent College and the university's Wild prizeman in 1934.

Stanley did all this in his own unassuming way. Although Jessie was forthright and outspoken, Stanley's personality was more like his father's, quietly spoken but with deepness of conviction and sureness of mind. On Jack's death, on 25 June 1950, the obituary in the local newspaper told more of what he would have been like, and I can see very definite reflections of Stanley:

It was almost paradoxical that a man of quiet disposition should engage himself in the hurly-burly of public life, yet Mr Prescott's high sense of duty prompted him to do this, coupled with deep convictions and a charm of personality that enabled him to carry out these duties with distinction.

Mr Prescott was one of the members of the Urban Council, that, following the war, set about putting to rights the extension of the water and sewage facilities in the town and carrying out the earlier housing schemes. Simultaneously Mr Prescott did a good job as a magistrate, as one of the governors of the Grammar School, a president of the Literary and Debating Society, together with official position or membership of other organizations.

A leading figure in the Methodist denomination, he was a tower of strength in religious work, his Christian character permeating all the public activities of a man who made a lasting impression on the community in which for so long he lived, moved and had his being.[39]

Jack did live to see his grandchildren in Australia, including my own father. He and Jessie made the voyage to Australia in 1949, after Monica and Stanley had settled in Melbourne. But by then Jack's health was already failing. Malcolm says of the last days of this father:

When I saw him last, near the end of his story, Jack was ill but strangely confident and at peace. He was cared for devotedly by Jessie Mary until he died.[40]

Just as her father had warned her, Jessie lived many years beyond Jack, twenty-eight in fact. She eventually died on 31 December 1978, also surviving her son Stanley.

Meeting the family

Very much in love and with clear plans to propose, Stanley was extremely proud and excited about introducing Monica to his family. It is amusing to see Monica's trepidation at this prospect and her perspectives on the encounter with 'his people' in Tetbury:

It was a different world because they were from a very respectable family. I certainly thought so! England was very much divided into the upper and lower classes in those days. His father was a pharmacist, but you could never have called him a shopkeeper. He had the royal crest above the door because he supplied the royal family.

I went there with Stanley on the train. Well! I was almost sick on the way down because I had never met them before at all. I was not used to country people, and they were upper-crust country people. The chemist shop was at the front of their home. There was a long corridor down to the house and there was a lovely sitting room at the end. There was also a beautiful garden at the back.

When we opened the front door, I could see Mrs Prescott right down the end of the hall. Jessica Prescott. But they called her Jessie. She was a very dominant woman. She stood there waiting for me to come down, standing very straight with her shoulders back. She was always saying 'Put your shoulders back Stanley, put your shoulders back'. I didn't know how I was going to get down that corridor. It seemed like such a long one. I came to her finally and she just put her arms around me and gave me a hug.[40]

Intimidated though she initially was, Monica soon felt that she very much belonged to the Prescott family. I am sure that Jessie would have liked and approved of Monica. I never have had any impression to the contrary. While some mothers may have been intimidated by a young, independent woman entering professional life, this does not fit with what we know of Jessie. Although Monica was from a different background from theirs and did not come from a wealthy family, I feel that this would also have been very much in accordance with Jack's more liberal philosophies. I am sure they thought Monica would be a most suitable match for their son.

With her more humble background, there were some things that Monica found difficult to get used to at first:

It was all very strange for me. They had a maid. There was a washbasin and a jug with water in the bedrooms. There was a chamber pot under the bed for you to use at night and I didn't know what to do with any of these things. I really didn't. Tom Bromley, Stanley's best friend, had also stayed there and he didn't know what to do either. He didn't want the maid to see his chamber pot in the morning, so he just emptied the thing out of the his upstairs window. But the handle came off! Really!

Her first meal with the family sounds almost comical. Not only did she have to contend with her unfamiliar surroundings and intimidating hostess, but her beau's effeminate brother started stroking her hair at the dinner table:

85

It was a very frightening time for me. The first night we sat down to have a meal, and were served by the maid. Well, I was not used to a maid to start with. But then Stanley's older brother John saw my lovely curly fair hair and he got up from his seat and came around to the back of mine while we were having our meal. And he ran his fingers through my curls. I didn't know *what* to do! I wasn't used to this sort of life. It was terrifying. I had never even met him before. John was just a bit fey, and he never married. I don't know what you call it now, but he was a very lovely person. You know, he built his own harpsichord from scratch and played it for the BBC. He later became quite senior in the civil service. When he was older he also received an OBE from the Queen, for his many years of service to the British Government. Very knowledgeable. But it took me a while to get used to him. At that stage, when I first visited, I did not know how to react! Their brother Malcolm, who was a lot younger, was still at boarding school near Bristol.

Stanley had seen the agony that I was in with John curling my hair, Mrs Prescott being so definite and a maid that I wasn't used to. So he said he would take me for a walk. So we got out of the house, and I was so relieved. We walked past a paddock, although they didn't call them paddocks there, they were 'fields', and a cow suddenly sneezed right beside me. I nearly died. Oh, I had never heard a cow sneeze. It is a terrible noise. I threw myself into Stanley's arms for protection.

At least in retrospect Monica is painting herself as a helpless heroine with Stanley as her protector, even though we know she was anything but helpless. But this small incident paints a nice picture of an early intimacy growing between them. It was something that had stuck in her mind, so it must have been important to her in some way.

The embarrassing moments of her first visit were not yet over for Monica:

> That night after I went upstairs to go to bed, I realised that I had left something terribly important in the sitting room. So I crept down the stairs and opened the sitting room door. I stepped in and there were Mrs and Mr Prescott kneeling at the foot of their chairs saying their prayers. Night prayers. I backed out quickly and tore up the stairs. I didn't care what I left behind. I was so nervous I hardly slept. They lived a completely different life. Mrs Prescott's father, Mr Lamplugh, was the Mayor of Peterborough and everyone knew that family. We later also gave our son, David, Lamplugh as his second name. They were such a famous family and I knew nothing about English gentry. Nothing at all.

They took Monica to chapel with them during her brief stay:

> All the wealthy people of the villages went to a church in those days, and most to the Anglican church. In those times people were either church or chapel. The Prescotts were very respectable people, but they were chapel people. Methodists. The church and the chapel were in opposite directions. It was quite segregated. We passed all the Anglicans going to their church. The Prescotts had been chapel for a long while. Oh yes.

I find it amusing that, while the Prescotts were all very proud of Jessie's contralto singing voice, Monica thought it was painful and embarrassing:

> Mrs Prescott sang very loudly in church and I felt so embarrassed standing next to her, hearing her voice wavering over the top of

everybody else's. In those days every pew was owned. You paid for your pew and had your name on it. You daren't sit in a pew with someone else's name on it. But there were some without names and you could sit in those. When I came here to Perth, in the cathedral, people still had pews. That's all gone now. It is extraordinary the things that change without you realising they have changed.

Now I am Anglican I go to the cathedral of course, so when I went back to Peterborough on a holiday recently I went to see the Anglican church. A lovely church. But it did seem that I was going in the wrong direction! I felt I must be doing something wrong, going to the church not the chapel.

Monica came to adore her new family. She always spoke of every one of them admiringly. It is not clear how long they had been 'courting' when Stanley first took Monica home to his family. Presumably Monica had already committed herself to the relationship sufficiently to agree to this visit with its considerable implications. It was uncommon to travel to meet a man's family unless the intention of engagement was clear to all. We can wonder what role meeting Stanley's people had in solidifying the relationship. In any case, I am sure Stanley was relieved that it was not scary enough to undo it either!

China

Forging a new path

Stanley leaves for China

Until he met Monica, Stanley had not planned to leave England. But he soon did: as soon as he learned that she had already planned to go to China as a medical missionary. So, to a large extent, Monica's plans were instrumental in everything that happened thereafter. It is difficult to know if Stanley's fortunes would have been different and what he would have done had he not met Monica. No doubt he would have stayed in England and done well, but he may not have had the same unique opportunities as he later enjoyed in the new world. From Monica:

> I still had contacts with the London Missionary Society, the LMS. They had already agreed to take me. When I met Stanley he had never even heard of the LMS. But he was keen and he went out to China first. I still had one year more of medicine to do. The men would generally go first and spend a year or so getting used to the language. Everyone had to go to the language school in Peking, or Beijing as its called now. The women followed a year later, and they *never* caught up with the language the way their husbands did, you see. A great shame. It was a great pity that it was different for me in that way.[1]

So Stanley went out to China a year before her as Professor of Physiology at Cheeloo (now known as Qilu) University

Hospital and to learn the language while Monica finished her medical training. It seems that such long separations so early in engagements were still commonplace. They were to get longer yet for so many as the war approached.

Stanley wrote regularly in the years that followed. Although his letters to Monica were all lost, the letters that he sent his parents fill several volumes in our family archives, and I have selected small fragments of these to tell his story. He began his chronicles on the SS *Naldera* in October 1936:

This is written in anticipation, but I know that as you read this, the blow has already fallen. That we have parted at last for some years. Don't weep for me. And if you must weep then weep with happiness and joy and not with sorrow. I am doing the only thing that I feel that I can do. In going to China I am obeying something stranger than reason, something deeper than feeling. I am merely obeying the voice that you have always been listening to, and to which you have always taught me to listen. Oh God! I hate to hurt you so. It is so hard to take my leave. I shall be lonely and depressed. But I hope that you will be glad to know that your son has been called to do good work.

I want you to know that I have dreaded the journey and the parting terribly, yet I have found a wonderful peace in doing the work that I have been called to do.

Think of me sometimes and pray for me always, that I may face life as a man and live up to the standards that you, my parents, have shown me. It is difficult to say what I want to say. But thank you for my life, my hope and all that is mine. And perhaps to others in China I will be able to pass on some of what you have taught me. Please remember that the work I shall do out East is the work that you started.

One last request. During the days that Monica will be with you, help her with her temporary loss. Regard her as your daughter for so she is. She means all the world to me, and it is strange knowing I have to hurt her before she can join me in China. Much more I would like to say, but you know me and you know my mind. You know how much I love you. Help each other in your loneliness and when we meet again in six years' time, how happy we will be in our fulfilment.[2]

Stanley arrived in Shanghai on 13 November 1936, only twenty-six years old and probably quite bewildered. He found a typewriter somewhere for this letter:

Here I am at last in Shanghai – thrilled, interested and amused! We had an easy voyage from Hong Kong. The approach to Shanghai is not beautiful. Buildings, warehouses and wharves. It is very difficult for friends and relatives to get down to the docks. I waited a bit, but could not find anyone there to meet me. So there I was, in the wickedest city in the world, without a friend. I felt quite depressed, but decided to laugh as it was such a complete muddle. After making many enquiries in 'dog' English I at last found the missionary home representative. He is Chinese and never wears his hat labelled 'Miss. Home' if he can help it, which was why I missed him. He helped me through customs. So far no duty, but the wooden cases need to be examined on Monday. They have confiscated my binoculars until I can get a permit from the Minister of War (China) to have them! I understand that it will take the best part of a year to get them back![3]

He made his way to the Mission House where he was to spend his first night. Professor Reade, Director of Physiology, Lester Institute, sent a car for him to join them for a Chinese tea party.

In an era when Chinese food was not much known in Britain, Stanley had never seen or tasted anything like it. His quietly deferential manner caused his hosts to comment that he was 'almost Chinese, right away'.

> I had my first Chinese meal complete with chopsticks. I managed these
> for the first time in an expert manner and received the approbation of
> all the guests. It was a great meal, eating in rapid succession – some
> twenty courses of dainty Chinese dishes, several courses on the
> plate at one time, and drinking it with delicately flavoured jasmine tea.
> I can make no attempt to describe what we ate. That must follow
> later when I become acquainted with the food and the names.
> Needless to say my imagination took full control. I ate with relish,
> bowing and kow-towing in the best possible manner. As you will
> guess this was a wonderful introduction to China and the thrill has
> not yet left me.

Returning to the Mission House, strictly no smoking, he retired at nine o'clock to 'smoke himself dry' in his bedroom until it was time to sleep. The next day he moved to the Reades' house for the rest of his stay. He had more social outings and engagements in his first weekend than he had probably ever had in all his life before then. The large expatriate English community lived very comfortably, at a level he had not experienced before. He even started playing tennis.

> They have a wonderful house and I wish I could give you an idea of how
> kind and generous they have been. Prof. Reade is a man after my own
> heart. I shall hope to do a small fraction of the great work that he has
> done. Already he has helped me scientifically, mentally and spiritually,

and staying in their home means a lot to me. The standard of living is something that we shall never be able to keep up, but serves as a useful introduction to Chinese and English dinner parties and manners.

I am too thrilled to describe or even indicate my impressions. I have fallen on my feet and I am very, very happy.

The following Monday he went back to the docks to collect the rest of his luggage.

The duty on incoming goods is terrific, up to 80% and I was fearing a bad time when my boxes were unpacked. I went down to the docks calling for the Mission Home Rep on the way. As luck would have it, or maybe providence, I got a good customs official and chatting to him, on the way to my boxes, I told him I was going to Cheeloo. He had many friends there so taxed me lightly at only $20 to pay (£1.50). So once again I have fallen on my feet.

In the next days he visited the Lester Institute, St John's University, and met many people from the Mission Society and several senior government officials. He also visited a small local village, which had been founded fifteen years earlier by two Chinese Christians with the intention of introducing modern agriculture and rural industry. He described it as very simply done but an astounding success. With money that would normally have been spent on parental graves, they had built a village hall, school, library and dispensary, all in a simple but modern style. He was impressed to see how this was all achieved by the local people, largely without the mission societies. He was inspired and considered all of these experiences to be of great use in his future work.

Ten days later he made his way to Cheeloo University in Tsinan, now known as Jinan, where he and Monica planned to make their future home.

And so on to the Cheeloo University, where I trust that I shall live out the rest of my life. There again description fails and continually I wonder at the greatness of the minds that conceived the idea, and then gave reality to the ideal. It is a wonderful place and one could dwell for hours on the beauty of the campus and the various buildings. Buildings that must and do inspire wonder and worship in the minds of the students so that they can look back to the 'home' where their minds first learnt of the problems facing China and of the solutions. Even I, newcomer though I am, have come under the spell of its beauty and its order. But the real proof of the work here can be seen in the faces of the students.[4]

I have taken the following descriptions of Cheeloo and Tsinan from a Christmas card Stanley wrote sometime later (in 1939), but which captures something of the place and its spirit:

Cheeloo University is situated outside the south wall of Tsinan city. About five miles to the north of the city is, or rather was, the famous Yellow River. To the south, only a quarter of a mile away, are the foothills of the Shantung mountains which reach their greatest height at Tai Shan. If you can imagine flat country stretching out for the distance of a whole day's journey, you can imagine what a relief these hills are for a traveller journeying from Peking to Tsinan. As the Psalmist turned his eyes to the hills for inspiration, so we living under the influence of this range sense a different atmosphere from that which can be felt in any other town, city or village on this vast mud flat. We can sympathise with the minds who for countless centuries have endowed these hills with Spirits to be

96

worshiped. They too have felt the awe and reverence of these wonders of nature.[5]

Stanley seemed impressed by the commitment of all the young doctors, teachers, scientists, preachers, nurses and midwives who had left their homes and families to help in China. He was touched by the quiet appreciation of so many of the Chinese he met queuing for hours in the outpatients area for help with their ailments, many with conditions such as leprosy that he had never seen before. He saw so many bright with hope and then with amazement as they responded to their treatments. While his Christian ethics were strong, he was equally intent on the science, research and education that would be needed to improve health and living conditions.

It would take too long to describe the hospital, besides the pictures do this better than I. But I was struck by the efficiency and the perfect up-to-datedness of the methods employed, and the hallowedness of the asylum of healing that the patients experience after the squalor of their homes. I would like to dwell on the research work into disease and cures, Chinese drugs, nutrition, social conditions and all the lines of work that must be done before China is pulled out of the morass of poverty and oppression. But time does not allow and at this stage I would be foolish to attempt to. I am thrilled by it. Its Christian spirit has captured me completely.

It is going to be a great life, and I am thoroughly enjoying myself, but just longing for the time when Monica will be out here. All the staff are friendly. The campus, the labs, the life and our new home and the general conditions are much better than I could have imagined.

97

From there he also travelled widely in North China, gathering impressions and meeting the local people.

The real China is not seen in Shanghai, but on the Shantung plains, on miles and miles of flat dusty country intersected by cart roads that with age and long use have sunk below the surface, and dotted with small mud villages and ancestral graves. A horizon as flat and extensive as the sea. The land in winter looks almost like a desert. So also the people. Poor and ill-nourished as their land in winter. They tend to worship the past, and their land has not varied with the years. Still bearing children to pestilence and famine. Even their own manure is valuable, and after careful drying is spread with due economy over the decreasingly fertile land. Ploughing, sowing, reaping, thrashing is all done by hand, living on the edge of the abyss of starvation and death, such that to a small village environmental change may mean the death of whole villages and families, can one wonder that they are fatalists and hope to placate angry Gods by ancient custom and ritual. Each mother knows the pain of foot binding, but if this is not done, who will support the girl when she cannot be married? Some have questioned their cruelty to animals – I was with a friend and stopped a man to ask why he loaded so much on the raw back of a donkey. His answer was to shift his own load and to open his shirt and show his back of sores and blisters that had been caused by his own many loads. What can Christianity do for such as these? It depends on what it means. If it means just being told about the Love of God and the brotherhood of man, I doubt very much whether any would understand. No, Christianity divorced from educations and economics can probably do little for these people. Changed economics and education could save these people.

And China has since transformed herself. As now, more than seventy years later, I travel the same flat plains in a high-speed bullet train, I see highly structured farming collectives between some of the largest and most industrialised cities in the world. I feel sure that Stanley would be astounded and impressed by all that has been achieved by China, her people among the most industrious in the world. So organised, so efficient, so productive and so many. Arguably among the greatest nations on earth in many respects. What impresses me most is that, despite the modern congestion and pace of life, the people on the streets seem to have maintained a sense of serenity, smiling easily as they continue to ride through the choking cities on their bicycles. Yes, China is a country with many problems still, but which nation is not?

Although Cheeloo campus was to become his home, Stanley first had to journey to Beijing and spend at least nine months there at the Peking Language School so he could return to Cheeloo fully conversant in Chinese and begin his real work. Before he left, he spent as much time as possible meeting people and getting a global picture of Cheeloo University and the city of Tsinan. He gave lectures in English and began to plan a restructure of the Physiology Department, knowing he would become head upon his intended return in September 1937 at the beginning of the academic year. But by then he had to be fluent in both spoken and written Mandarin.

He was full of frustration at the policy of many of the mission societies that men should precede their wives, often by many years, into the field.

There are many things that make life hard here, but what is the worst is waiting, sometimes anxiously, for Monica. When she arrives I think heaven will nearly be here, because it is such a wonderful place. It seems such a shame that while all the missionaries in the field say that it is better for man and wife to come out together, the committees still arrange for the men to come out first. Some have been here waiting for three years unmarried. I don't know how they manage. I hope that someday this can be altered.

Do you remember last Christmas and the excitement of bringing Monica home, and all of the joy that we had in her and each other's company? It seems so long ago, and when you read this Christmastide will be over, Monica and her parents will have left you, and we will be in 1937. The year that Monica and I will meet again and settle down into that wonderful state of companionship and love. I hope that we will be able to make such a great success of marriage as you have done. We accuse the Chinese of ancestor worship, but perhaps I am almost Chinese in that. I have felt so much that I am carrying on the work of so many before me, as you have carried on your traditions. And so the world goes on. Pray God, that if we have children that they may have as fine a home and nearly as fine as parents as I have had, Pray God that I shall be as good a husband to Monica as Dad and Grand-da have been, and that when we are middle aged we can look back and treasure in our hearts the things that must mean so much to you. Coming abroad here has been such a wonderful experience. I feel that I have arrived where I belong.

Peking College of Language Studies

On New Year's Eve, Stanley set off on his journey north to Peking (Beijing) to begin his Chinese lessons on 4 January 1937. The teaching methods were somewhat different to the approach today:

> All day, so far, we sit and listen to Chinese with no English words, and only by acting does the teacher show us the meaning. It seemed very strange at first, listening to lectures instead of giving them, and so much more easy as far as the mental effort is concerned. We shall do this for the next three weeks before we are allowed to speak in class. The idea being that we are learning like children do; to hear the word in the mind before they learn to speak it. It is a splendid method and I am a good mimic. Those who cannot mimic are not getting on well. I have another advantage that I learned to write some of the characters in Tsinan. Later we will be split into smaller groups and allowed to speak.[6]

Stanley continued to study the characters on his own as well and found them absolutely fascinating. He loved their history and the stories behind each. I have shown his notes in Mandarin to my Chinese friends, who tell me he was studying the traditional characters that few of them could understand any more.

The characters are all pictures really, or rather were, and each represents a word. Altogether there are about 40,000 of them. A well-educated Chinese scholar will know about 5–7000 and we will learn about 3,000 but can probably hope to get by with about 2,000. I am completely fascinated with the Chinese language, but unfortunately it is hard to pass that fascination on to others!

He also came across Americans for the first time. While he took the time to understand the colloquial differences, he could not comprehend some of their more fundamental religious attitudes.

This college is largely American and we Britishers are quite out-numbered. I am gradually learning Americanisms and now I can usually answer them when they speak to me. It was quite queer at first, I could not understand so many of the words they used. For example they don't know what a gramophone is, for some reason they call it a 'victrola', and so on. So it seems that I am learning Chinese and American at the same time.

They are much more fundamental in the doctrines than we are. The other day I was enlarging on the social reconstruction that is taking place in China, and that in another ten years we should see a new China take her place among nations. I was interrupted by several people saying it was not important because they believed that the second coming of Christ was due anytime now so we should not bother with social reconstruction. What can I say! What I did do was blush and shut up. Also making another mental note of their peculiarities because if the second coming is due then why the blazes are they bothering to learn Chinese. And also if the second coming occurs before I get married I should be mighty peeved with the Almighty!

He soon discovered that he had 'little in common with such forms of Christianity'. Later, when challenged again on his views on the second coming, he confessed that he did not believe in that particular interpretation of the scriptures, and that it was harmful if it induced the very form of fatalism that we should be trying to avoid. Of course they did not like that at all. He tried to point out that the major critics of missionary works in China were claiming that substitution of Buddhist fatalism and magic with Christian fatalism and magic could achieve nothing. Stanley firmly believed that the missionaries should learn from the mistakes of past arrogance. His frustration with the fundamentalists continued.

In a lecture on the 'Origins of the Chinese', the lecturer mentioned the theory that mankind probably arose in Tibet, and half of the Americans burst out laughing because they thought it was a joke, and one of them asked me afterwards if I thought that the lecturer might have actually believed in evolution. So here we are in the twentieth century still quibbling over whether Genesis is a literal account of creation or not. I have never met people who are educated in other things but don't know the first thing about biology and don't seem to have thought about their religion from an intellectual perspective. And yet with this poverty of thought they are here as missionaries to save China. What will the effect be! It cannot be good for this nation. And it certainly makes our work harder. The Chinese may see us as all the same, but it has taught me one thing: that at Cheeloo my main task will be to make sure that while the students in Christian Studies learn the fundamentals of the religion, they don't get caught up in fundamentalism.

It was also from the Americans that Stanley learned of the scandal between Edward and Mrs Simpson. He was careful not to mention this in his letters to his parents until they mentioned it first, as he had been told that the 'American scandal' was initially banned in England. He was amused to think that England seemed to be following so many countries in getting rid of her king.

Stanley continued to work hard and he excelled in his Chinese studies. His memory was exceptional and his teachers complimented him on his progress. He tried to help his fellow students, particularly a fellow Brit he called 'Lance, the Tetbury evangelist'. He lived happily and frugally in the hope of saving some money for his and Monica's future together.

Tonight you should have seen me, sewing on buttons, stitching up the seam in my trousers, mending a tear in my pyjamas, and washing thirty handkerchiefs. The laundry costs three cents a piece, so I send out the big stuff and wash my own handkerchiefs! I don't manage to get them a very good colour and I don't have an iron, but they dry quickly on the radiator. I have also darned a few socks with more or less success! It will be good to have Monica here for many reasons!

And I don't think I am smoking as much these days. I am seriously thinking of giving up as an example to the opium addicts!? Don't worry about me not taking care of myself, I am too anxious to get married to take any risks!

I am always amused at mother's advice not to have children too soon! At present we are hoping not to have any for the first two years. As an expert on the subject I hope to arrange this but even the experts fail sometimes. Poor Monica is finding life a bit trying right now. She seems terribly afraid of her final exams and she wants to get out here quickly.

Sometimes my heart aches for the time when Monica and I will be in our home together in Cheeloo, and both settled into our work. But the days are passing rapidly and I have time only for language study, and no time to feel depressed or lonely. I feel that I want to wait until Monica joins me so we can start everything together. I am so keen that we be real partners.[7]

By February the cold weather was almost over. Blue skies every day. Stanley was enjoying his studies and the life around him, which he found endlessly fascinating. He was acutely aware of the potential of the nation that was now his home.

I am sitting writing in my little room, with the window wide open, and everything seems quiet and lovely. The weather is the most perfect I have seen. In the distance I can hear the cries of the street sellers carrying around their wares, and the blind men tap as they wind their way through the crowd.

Last night a beggar died on the road near our College. He stayed there for quite a while because no one seemed to be responsible for his removal. People seem so casual, yet life is so hard that the luxuries of sympathy and compassion seem to hardly exist. But things are already so much better than they were. Only the other day I saw a policeman hold up the traffic – mainly rickshaws and carts – while some children crossed the road. This may seem ordinary to you, but in China it is quite a surprise.

This is a great country, the millions of its hardworking people toiling from dawn to dusk working only by hand. When China becomes mechanised what will be her labour problems? What will her place be in the world economy? Until then the uneven distribution of raw materials and standards of living are factors in the unrest.

105

China seems to be climbing the ladder again. She is awakening from the Medievalism that we once had. In the cities the new culture of the West is dawning and threatening to drive out all things Chinese, but in the little villages the old ways hold true. Writing as I am 10,000 miles from home in the heart of a foreign land, yet I feel at home. I love the Chinese people – they are gay-hearted and humorous. And yet capable day-by-day of enduring great hardship. While the West has much to teach China, we also have much to learn from them.

I have met a fair few Chinese now and I am struck by their friendliness. They are a great people and it is a great land. This is a nation awakening to the realities of the modern world. Those at the top awakened long ago, and now it is spreading downward the poor sections of the community. When the new spirit has grasped every Chinese, the world will stand astonished at what this country can do!

And I think he was right. As I write this now, I am sitting looking out of my window in China. I see skyscrapers for miles across the most industrious nation on earth. Now, so much of the world's clothing and commodities are 'made in China'. They would hardly have imagined that then.

The English mail arrived twice a week and brought good news of Monica's proposed trip to join him. His joy is clear at the prospect of their December wedding:

Today I am feeling quite excited – Monica's passage has been booked on the SS *Corfu*, sailing from London on July 30th, and arriving in Shanghai on September 8th. Nearly six months have passed since we parted and now only another five months more. Monica says that there is always the chance that she might fail, but in my heart of hearts I know that she will be with me in September. I am quite confident and hopeful. We will spend nearly a month together before she starts at the language school. And then time will fly until Christmas, which is when we hope to marry, if all goes well on the 21st of December. What fun! Then I shall be finally seeing the pyjamas that you say King George would not mind sleeping with. Do you think his brother the Duke of Windsor would be more particular?![8]

The story of Monica's father's plight when he had arrived in England without ever having owned a pair of pyjamas had become somewhat of a family joke. Apparently Jessie also bought Monica pyjamas for her wedding, as they suspected that, like Allen, she did not possess any.

This has been a hard time for both of us and yet the time has not been wasted. Our love has been tested and shown that its enduring qualities are real and great. Although apart in body we are united in spirit, and in that union we have learned more of each other and had revealed to us something of the greater qualities of the love that unites us. It is a strange paradox, yet so much of life is a paradox.

Stanley was not one to pay too much attention to fashion, so it is amusing that he took the time to make some practical suggestions.

Judging from my experience of the climate I think a polo neck would be the best for Monica. I have suggested dark green, a suede golf jacket and a heavy green skirt. A green beret to match. I think that should suit her rather well as long as the colours blend. I shall also need another polo neck. But in exactly the same shade as I have now. Please on NO account send me a RED one as I might be mistaken for a communist or a bandit!!

As expected, Stanley did exceptionally well in his first exams. He celebrated his twenty-seventh birthday on Sunday 21 March, as well as his exam results. He wrote his whole paper in Chinese characters and received the top mark of 98.5 per cent. Most of his contemporaries did not fare nearly as well. Despite Stanley's efforts to help his new acquaintance, Lance failed badly and disappeared without saying goodbye to anyone. He owed many people money and Stanley felt disappointed and foolish for spending so much time helping him. But his disappointment with Lance was overshadowed by his joy at doing so well with the language he was growing to love. He also arranged for a private tutor when he left the college. His talents and leadership potential did not go unnoticed by his peers or his seniors.

> Did I tell you (and this is for your eyes only) that the hope is that after my first term I shall be made Dean of the Medical School. At least I have been told confidentially that that is on the books, so soon I will need to work in with the high Chinese Government circles so that I can carry the position. It is still a murmur and I somehow think that it is too good to be true, but then there is only one more step to the President of the University, but that I can never be because I am not Chinese.

Perhaps this was half said in jest, perhaps not. These words were more prophetic than he could know. Even then, at twenty-seven, he was setting his sights high. But I doubt that even he would have suspected that within fifteen years he would indeed be the 'president' of a university. Only it would not be in China.

> These twenty-seven years have been wonderful. I am glad that Monica will be spending part of the Easter holidays with you because I know

how much she loves you, and loves being with you in my home. It seems as though I have always known her, because she means so much to me. I have also told Monica that if she is hard up to borrow some money from you and that I will pay it back as soon as I possibly can. Please remind her of this, as she will be embarrassed to ask.

Oh Mother and Daddy, I wish you could know how terribly happy I am, and how certain I am that I have fallen on my feet again! China is a wonderful place, and I feel that I have come to the place that as a youngster I used to dream of when I should have been learning French! Do you remember when I was a child and could not sleep and Daddy would come in and sleep with me? Who would have thought that now I should be Professor of Pharmacology in a Chinese Medical School, a missionary, and soon to marry the finest girl in the world, who at that time was in Australia!

It seems such a long time now since I arrived in Shanghai with no one to greet me, and my first dismal introduction to the mission home. And since I watched the lights of England drawing away in the distance. I now hardly remember the days when the sea was terribly rough and most people were lying like corpses on the deck and wondering if I too would be sick. I look back at the days when I wondered if I should come here as a missionary. I remember my days of doubt and indecision, before in faith, I took the plunge. Today, knowing something of China, I am absolutely confident that this is my work and that the vision of beauty and love and goodness will help keep my hand on the plough and work along the small furrows of this land of promise and hope.

The time was passing quickly, and Stanley took his weekend breaks to visit local sites and villages where he would meet and converse as best he could. He loved to watch the women grinding the corn by hand between flat millstones and to watch

109

the children playing. The infants were often still suckling from their mothers while they worked. At that time, it was common for women in the villages to breastfeed for at least four years. He was always impressed by the wisdom in their simplicity and the happiness he felt in everyone he met. Their contentedness was humbling. He began to wonder if he could learn far more from them than they could from him.

As his studies progressed, Stanley became more involved in other university activities in Peking, including the Biochemical Society. He also had a chance to converse in Chinese on his first official social outing after arriving in Peking. He went as a guest of Dr Maxwell, Professor of Gynaecology at Peking China Medical College, to the annual dinner of the Chest Society of Peking.

> The Chinese were in their dress suits which consist of a flowing gown of royal blue and a short black jacket of black silk. It was a colourful assembly. After dinner we listened to a lecture on the relationship of the cultures of our own Stone Age and the corresponding period in Inner Mongolia. It was a great do and I met so many interesting people. We had great time talking in Chinese.[9]

He was doing outstandingly well at Chinese; he was the best in his class, and probably all the college based on his teachers' comments. Many were urging him to go on to do a masters in Chinese. The mission chairman was not so keen on the idea. This was probably because he was the only one in North China with a degree in Chinese, and then only at bachelor level. In his final exams Stanley received 98 per cent. He was always a very understated person and quite humble, so I believe him when he says he was proud but not boasting. I have shown his Chinese writing to my Chinese friends and they are most impressed with the neatness and accuracy of his work. They are quite amazed that any Westerner could have achieved this, and particularly in such a short time.

I did excellently, getting what the Americans call a 'grade A+', which rather reminds me of pasteurised milk! And once again I came top. I am not boasting, but really feel that I have done very well in language study and the speed with which I learn the Chinese characters is the envy of all the students, even those who have been there for five terms already. But still there is much to learn. My friends have said that it is a good thing I am leaving College because I would get a swelled head if I stayed much longer, and that it sets such a high standard for the others to keep up! I might sound a bit conceited about this, but I really have done excellent work and I will not be resting on my laurels.

Meanwhile back in England, Monica was preparing for her final exams, with the added pressure that if she did not pass, she would not be able to travel to China to be married, possibly having to wait another year. Knowing Monica, I can't see that it was ever likely, but the uncertainty must have been difficult for her.

Monica seems quite well, perhaps still a little nervous about the forthcoming exams. She was honoured to get a letter from you. I know that you always wanted a daughter, and now you have one, and she is far nicer than I could ever be. Monica said she would like to have another weekend with you during the term. Her mother was a wee bit jealous (this is private) when Monica told her. Mrs Job has the fear that Monica

would prefer to visit your home than hers. Such are the complications of
the jealous mind. So when you do write to Monica again, don't
press her.

In spite of her own mother's jealousies, Monica did go and stay
with Stanley's parents, and enjoyed her stay immensely. She had
a growing bond with Jack and Jessie Prescott, with a particular
admiration for Stanley's mother. Ethel Job probably had good
reason to be jealous. Jessie Prescott was a strong and dominant
woman, in every way different from Ethel. Monica did not seem
to have the same relationship with her own mother, and I never
heard her talk about Ethel in the way she did Jessie.

Stanley planned to return to Cheeloo University in Tsinan
on 10 June 1937 to make preparations for Monica's arrival. He
was to stay there for a month or so before joining the mass
exodus of expatriates on their summer vacation in July. He had
been very much looking forward to his return to Tsinan. With
a great many friends there, he already described it as 'home'. He
was still waiting to unpack his 'best stuff', which he was saving
for his 'married days'. But he was not to know that it would be
many years before he would open those trunks again.

He enjoyed life there even more now that he was conversant
in Chinese. However, he was becoming increasingly impatient
for Monica's arrival, at the same time wishing he could have a
weekend with his parents in Tetbury. His brother Malcolm had
just decided to study theology and become a Methodist minister,
so Stanley had much advice to give on the subject. This and
his language study helped him carry on and 'not be upset like a
child because "I can't have it now"!' Most of all he was happy
to be reunited with the friends that he had made in Tsinan

before leaving for Peking. He enjoyed a month settling back into the community. I found this amusing note in his letters, an advertisement in pidgin English from the Tsinan Store, where he bought his supplies:

Gentlemen, we beg to inform you that we have commenced business three weeks ago. Owing to the cheapest price and honest manner. The members of the Tsinan Club are all cheerfully to buy our goods. We express much thanks to them. But somebody disunderstand. Why we sold in so cheap price. And say we may not be a Chinese shop. Oposing to this. We would kindly to explain. Our shop was establisher by the employees of this club. We do not bend soley upon profit on account of small expenses in our shop. We settle the price of all goods cheaper than anywhere. All kinds of goods are newly arrived from Shanghai or Tientsin. With full guarantee for the most refreshing. For returning our sincerest thanks to our customers. We discount the price by 5% from the price list. We hope after you receive this letter. You kindly come to take a view of our shop. We believe that this will remove all mistrust. Thank you for your past favour and in the hope of a continuance of your patronage. We are your faithful servant. The Tsinan Store.

I just loved reading that and had to include it here.

A Chinese summer by the seaside

It was a tradition every summer for all the expatriates in the region to migrate en masse to the seaside to Peitaiho Beach in Hopei, North China. There they would stay for two or even three months. Stanley had never seen so many missionaries. There were many hundreds.

> Well here I am at last at the summer resort. In a wee little bungalow within twenty-five yards of the sea, and only six other bungalows in sight. The sea, which is so warm now, is frozen up to thirty miles out from land in winter. It is hardly believable. It is safe swimming and there are no sharks. Anyway, I am caution personified. I left Tsinan by train at 8.15pm on Wednesday night and arrived here by Thursday at 2.30pm after two changes. It is strange how one gets so content and used to such long journeys here. On the train coming up here there were people from all nations here. British, American, Chinese, Japanese, White Russians (but no Reds), Germans, French and Swedish.[10]

He found that life on the whole was much better than in England. The conditions, the food and the weather, even the simple things like fruit – bananas, strawberries, peaches, apples, oranges, apricots and a host of others that he had never seen before he came to the East. He had a very social time, making new friends and spending time with the many he had made already.

On 7 July 1937, Stanley received a telegram from Monica announcing her exam results. He was so filled with excitement and nervousness he could barely open it. But when he did, his joy knew no bounds. Then he could hardly wait to meet her ship in Shanghai. She announced that she had done well in her exams and would be sailing on 30 July as planned. She would visit with her family before leaving, but again spend some of her holidays with Stanley's parents.

As you can imagine, Stanley's letters were particularly excited and effusive around this time! They were also filled with information about the people he met and the stories they had to tell. It sounded like a very relaxing pace of life after his intense study. He was basking in the sun and in the anticipation of his reunion with Monica. Idyllic. Or so it seemed. The letters that soon followed began to reveal another story.

Their paradise was a very precarious one. Although unrest was brewing to the north, it was difficult to predict its significance. There had been civil unrest in China for centuries. Many believed that this was the reason a nation of such potential wealth had not advanced while other nations had developed during the industrial revolution. The conflict between Japan and China was also not new, and for several years there had been reports of skirmishes following the Japanese invasion of Manchuria some six years before. For those on the ground, it was also difficult to know how accurate the information was. Although the expatriates still had fairly reasonable access to international news, largely through the BBC, the news of events to their north was fragmented, conflicting and less reliable.

Stanley and the others were clearly aware that all was not well. For security reasons they also felt they could not directly express their thoughts or concerns in their letters. It was important to remain neutral and not interfere. Their sanctuary and safety depended on it. More than ever, they felt the need to stay and help the Chinese. In one of his letters, written from his beachside bungalow only weeks before the full-scale Japanese invasion, Stanley was more candid than he had been before about the 'difficulties'. He indicates that he is unable to comment, but he makes it equally clear that there is more to be said on the matter:

> At present there is some unrest here in North China, but God grant a peaceful settlement will be found, and the great work of reconstructionism can be continued. You will notice that I make no further comment on this situation. That is wise on my part.[11]

And a week later, only days before Monica was due to sail, Stanley wrote with a little more caution and a change of plan. And it would not be the last. Clearly the letter could not have arrived before Monica departed.

> I expect that you have heard the bad news of North China, but it may not come to anything serious. The only difference is that it will probably mean that Monica will not go to Peking, that we will stay in Tsinan and get married rather sooner. Of course it is possible that the mission will delay Monica's sailing in which case I hope that she will send me a telegram. But I hardly think that things are as serious as all that. Anyway trust me to look after her.[12]

On 23 July he wrote again saying that from the news they had heard, all seemed to be settling down. Again, news was fragmented and clearly unreliable. But by 29 July it was clear that they did have major cause for concern, and Stanley was still choosing his words carefully:

I am afraid that we are in for a dust-up in North China. But don't be worried because we are safe in Peitaiho Beach. It is a bit worrying because I shall have major difficulties in getting down to Shanghai to meet Monica, but I shall probably go by sea. I expect that I shall be in Shanghai with her until the trouble is finished. I don't know what the British papers are saying about it all, but however bad, it will be localised in the North, and we shall be quite safe, so please don't get anxious or excited about this.[13]

He was clear to repeat that Britain was neutral in this matter so they should not be in danger from either side of the conflict. He was not to know that soon he would be learning Japanese as well as Chinese. With Monica sailing the next day he was clearly churning with mixed emotions of excitement, joy and concern.

By 5 August they were completely cut off at Peitaiho Beach. No news and no contact with Shanghai or Tsinan. Letters were written but much delayed. Still in their precarious paradise, still on the beach finding it hard to believe there was a war raging around them. By now, Stanley felt it would be increasingly risky to leave their haven, and that it would be difficult to make it to Shanghai alive. Love made him determined. On 11 August, still in Peitaiho Beach, he wrote:

For a long time I have thought that it would be impossible to get to Shanghai, but after much rushing and hurrying around I have managed to get a passage on a coal boat. I am leaving Peitaiho on the 18th of August so will be in Shanghai in plenty of time. If things look very serious then Monica will be taken off at Hong Kong and I shall go down to Hong Kong by boat to meet her there.

At Peitaiho everyone is very anxious as to what the future will be and whether or not they will be able to return to their stations with the end of summer. I don't know whether we will be able to get back to Tsinan and Cheeloo for some time, because after Tsientsin that will be the next danger spot. But the Shanghai international settlement should be quite safe. Unfortunately all my possessions, except the bare minimum, are still in Tsinan and when I shall see them again is hard to say. But we are safe.

As for the future and the views of the people on this incident, I make no comment because of policy, except that it is an important struggle for Far Eastern supremacy.

I left England a pacifist. It is difficult to remain one, and yet I still feel that meeting force with force will never solve the issues of the world. Japan has shown a great lack of insight into the psychology of China. With peaceful means she could have won China commercially, by war she may get the territory but will always be suppressing minor revolts. One cannot understand why this should have broken out when all the signs of friendship between the two nations were becoming apparent. All we can hope is that out of evil good will come, and that all the dead Chinese and Japanese will not have died in vain. Poor Monica is arriving at a dreadful time, but we shall be safe in Shanghai.

The day of peace will come. We may not see it, but God grant that we may be strengthened to help that day come quickly. Russian communism, Nazi fascism, England's prevailing democracy, American isolationism. All futile. All useless. Unless we find the spirit of a new world, the spirit of peace and love that can give strength to a plan for the good of the whole of mankind.[14]

But an escalation of the fighting around Shanghai destroyed Stanley's plan. The coal boat he was planning to take would not sail there. No one would take him there and I am glad because I don't think he would have made it out alive. There would have been no reunion, no marriage, no children and no grandchildren. A week later, on 19 August 1937, he wrote:

Well as you can see, I have not gone to Shanghai because of all of the fighting there, and the fact that there are no trains and no boats that will go there. But I am hoping tomorrow to catch a small boat from near here down to Hong Kong. It is only a small chance. I will probably have to sleep on the deck. As I said it is a small chance but I am hoping and praying that it will come off. In any case Monica will never be allowed to go to Shanghai. Her boat will be stopped at Hong Kong. And there we will stay until it is absolutely quiet again. I rather expect that we shall marry there and stay with the Methodist minister there, carrying on language studies.

It has been a nerve racking time. I am safe. My only anxiety has been that you at home and Monica at sea will be worrying. As soon as I can get to Hong Kong I will send you an 'airmail' to tell you that we are safe. If you don't get that letter then I will still be here in Peitaiho and Monica will probably be in Hong Kong.[15]

Monica's sister Hope and her husband Arthur, also missionaries, were somewhere in the region, Stanley was not sure where. He said he was hopeful that they too would be evacuated to Hong Kong and that there might even be a family reunion.

They finally had some word from Cheeloo University to hear that it was safe but cut off from all sides by the fighting around Tsinan. He was worried for his Chinese friends still there and when, if ever, he would come back. For so long he had been dreaming of returning there to his house, Wesley Bungalow, with his new bride. Those dreams seemed shattered. All his possessions and his future plans were possibly lost to him.

The way forward will unfortunately be across the bodies of the dead
and dying.

That August letter was also the last received from Stanley in North China that year. And it marked the beginning of his family's most anxious years.

Monica's journey east begins

Having just completed her exams and with an exciting future ahead of her, Monica was euphoric as she began her journey on the SS *Corfu*. Full of the excitement of seeing Stanley, she was unaware of the perils that lay ahead. Before she left, Monica had a portrait photograph made into postcards to be mailed to Stanley over the course of her journey. With the unrest in North China, many of these did not reach him.

Again, the only surviving letters that we have are those that she sent to her parents. Her first letter was sent from the Suez Canal on 11 August. It was unbearably hot. The canal still. The boat just gliding gently past scenes of sand, sand and more sand. Everyone lying around the decks in a stupor; the swimming bath empty as no one could raise the energy to dress or undress. She had a cabin to herself, but slept on the top bunk to catch more of the breeze. This was quite unlike her last major voyage. No on-board entertainment was organised. No concerts. No games. No competitions. And no Sunday services. But Monica rather liked this lack of structure. She enjoyed the company of her fellow travellers and they made their own fun.

She was so clearly unaware of Stanley's plight, still writing of how she was looking forward to seeing Cheeloo and starting their life there. Her journey seemed uneventful, with stories of the people she met and the places she saw. The only entertainment they had was a 'Gully Gully man' who came aboard in Port Said and did 'tricks with chickens' before diving from the top deck as he departed.

With no land to look at for most of the 1,300-mile journey down the Red Sea, she and her fellow passengers just lay perspiring in their deckchairs. They came alive when they passed Hells Gates, and mused that the name felt appropriate. In Colombo she went ashore to meet the local missionaries and visit the old Methodist Church, apparently one of the oldest in Asia, built in 1816. They had tea and listened to the gramophone. One of her hosts was taken to hospital with dysentery, but Monica somehow escaped.

When Monica had left England in July 1937 to meet Stanley everything seemed relatively calm in China, or at least not out of the ordinary. She had her satin wedding dress ready for their planned winter wedding in the north, and described herself as completely in love. She was excited about her mission in China but had received no word from Stanley. If the boat had news of the dangers ahead, it had not yet informed its passengers. Monica continued to describe a peaceful and uneventful journey.

> We are now nearing Penang. I will post this letter from Singapore when we reach there in two days' time. Nothing very exciting has happened apart from the fact that we have been inoculated against cholera.[16]

The excitement was yet to come. She was quite unaware that she was about to be romanticised in the newspapers as a wartime heroine.

The growing unrest in northern China almost prevented Stanley and Monica's reunion. Japan and China had fought intermittently since Japan occupied Manchuria in 1931, but full-scale war did not begin until mid-1937, only shortly after Monica left English shores. The war was the result of decades-long Japanese imperialist policy aimed at the political and military domination of China to secure its vast resources. This was also fuelled by Chinese nationalism and a rising spirit of self-determination. Many believed that full-scale war was triggered when the Japanese assaulted a crucial access point sixteen kilometres outside Beijing, the so-called Marco Polo Bridge Incident. The word 'incident' was used to describe the conflict, as neither country officially declared war until 1941, and Japan wanted to avoid intervention by other countries such as Britain or the United States, which was still a major steel trader with Japan.

China was unprepared for open war and compared with the Japanese had little military–industrial strength. Further, it was a nation divided by its own civil war against the Communists. In 1937 the Japanese disembarked 80,000 soldiers on the Jianxu coast with the intention of conquering Shanghai, where Monica had planned to meet Stanley. After a battle of more than two months and countless casualties on both sides, the city fell to the Japanese on 13 October 1937. During the eight years that followed, Japan occupied most of China and killed millions of Chinese. Most Western historians believe that the casualties were at least twenty million,[17] including approximately three million soldiers as well as nine million civilians and another eight million non-military casualties who died in the crossfire.[18]

Stanley sent telegrams to their families in England, to alert them to the dangers in Shanghai, and to explain that Monica's boat would not be able to reach there. This was also picked up by both the English and Hong Kong newspapers, clearly before Monica was aware of it herself.

War May Stop Her Wedding

On board a liner bound for Shanghai, where she hopes to be married, is Dr Monica Job of Crumpsall Manchester, bride-to-be of Dr Stanley Prescott who is now working in the heart of the war area. Miss Job has just completed a university course in medicine to enable her to help her future husband in his life's work. A close friend to the couple told the *Daily Mirror* yesterday 'The wedding was planned for Christmas, but I do not know if this will be possible to take place in view of the disturbances in Shanghai'.[19]

It is interesting that Monica is portrayed more as an accompanying person in 'the life works of Stanley Prescott', when we know that she was in fact the reason he was there at all. Some of this was because he left for China first, but I don't think Monica discouraged this view either. Although it may be more accurate to say that he had followed her life's goals to be a missionary, Monica was more than happy to assume her role as supportive and accompanying wife. I think it was very important to her that Stanley be placed in the role of her hero. She loved and admired him, and this only grew with each passing year.

Crumpsall Girl Doctor To War-Stricken Shanghai To Get Married

Crumpsall bride-to-be, just through a University examination which qualified her to help her future husband in his life's work to help the sick, left Manchester three weeks ago eagerly looking forward to reunion and marriage at the end of a 12,000 mile journey to Shanghai.

Today, Monica Job is on the high seas, ignorant of the fate of her lover, Dr Stanley Prescott, a former Manchester University lecturer, in war-torn China where he has been stationed for a year. It is not even certain that she will be allowed to land in China and the Manchester friends of the couple are anxiously awaiting news both from Shanghai and the liner.

Their hope is that, as a doctor of medicine, Dr Job may be able to join her fiancé and help him in tending the victims of the latest war – with perhaps a hastily arranged marriage amid the explosions of bombs and boom of guns.

'When Monica left England everything was calm' the Rev. William Hodgkins, minister of Oldham-road Congregational church at whose home the lovers met, told a *City News* reporter. 'The storm burst a few days later. Dr Prescott is a Professor of physiology right in the heart of the struggle and with the whole country in the thick of what looks like being a long and bitter war his position will be grave and extremely delicate.'

In such circumstances it is difficult to see how the wedding, which was planned for Christmas, can take place. It would be a tragedy, if after travelling half way around the world, Monica should have to cancel the ceremony.

Dr Prescott and Mr Hodgkins were fellow tutors under Dr Grieve at Lancashire Independent College and it was while the doctor was visiting his friend at Crumpsall that he met his future bride. She was studying for her medical degree, which she obtained shortly before she left China. She was an active worker at the Oldham-road church. Dr Prescott went out to China, leaving his fiancée to follow him when she finished her examinations, so that she could continue her work in Chinese hospitals.

The ceremony was to have been conducted by Dr Job's brother-in-law with her sister, Miss Hope Job, as one of the bridesmaids.[20]

125

It does seem odd that the sense of tragedy was focused on the risk of cancellation of the wedding rather than the imminent possibility that both parties might die in the conflict. But perhaps the newspapers did not want to entertain that scenario.

A few other uncertainties are revealed in this account. Hope, Monica's sister, was clearly already in China, also as a missionary in the area. But although Hope is referred to as 'Miss', she was already married to Arthur Hay, another missionary, and they had a son, Michael, in 1937. Arthur was the intended officiary of Monica and Stanley's wedding. Hope's later romance novel, *Five Cloud Valley*, was set in China before the war and between the lines tells something of her own experiences. I discovered this lovely novel in Monica's library in 1985, but I have so far failed to find the book again. Hope and her family all survived the conflict. I know little of Michael apart from that he went on to make nature documentary films, inspired by his subsequent childhood in Africa, and for some thirty years headed the highly regarded *Survival* wildlife series for Anglia Television in the UK. In the clipping, Mr Hodgkins is claiming credit for introducing Monica and Stanley, whereas Monica recalled that this was engineered by Tom Bromley at Stanley's request. I suppose that both could be true.

It was not until after the SS *Corfu* left Singapore that Monica and the other passengers were told that it was too dangerous to continue to Shanghai and that the ship would be diverted. Then began some of the most worrying days of Monica's life. She had received no mail and no telegrams for many weeks. As she heard more of the fighting and devastation in North China, she became more and more worried for Stanley. Knowing Stanley as she did, she was convinced that he would gallantly try to reach her in Shanghai, and this made her even more worried. Almost seventy years later Monica remembered her journey:

> Stanley was to meet me in Shanghai, but as we approached they told us that because the Japanese had taken North China, all ships had to be diverted to different ports. I did not know what was going to happen. We were told we would be stopped at Hong Kong instead, and I was really worried for Stanley should he try to reach me there. But if he was waiting for me in North China, I was worried I would have no idea how to find him, or how to get there.[21]

When she first heard the news, she had received no word from Stanley and had no idea where he was or what was happening. For the days that followed she felt sick with worry. She wrote him no more letters and she later told us that she truly thought he might be dead.

Meanwhile, Stanley was having a worrying time of his own. Unable to travel by land, and with no ships to take him, he relied on the local Chinese to help him to travel the 1,300 miles to Hong Kong. This was done by night, in small Chinese junks and trading boats, past the Japanese warships. Clearly he did not have time to write letters during this period, but several weeks later, when things had settled down, he wrote how, after much wrangling, he had managed to catch a small Chinese sailing ship to cross the bay of Peitaiho. This took him to Chin Wangtao where he caught a coal boat to Hong Kong. His skills in Chinese language were probably what made all this possible. After a very rough and difficult passage he managed to get to Hong Kong on Sunday 29 August. So against all odds, Stanley arrived just in time to meet Monica. His journey was also chronicled in the newspapers, in the rather sweet sensationalist style of the day:

Defied 1,300 Miles Of Peril To Win His Bride

Japanese battle ships and planes stopped steamers from sailing and trains from running, but they could not prevent Dr Stanley Prescott from claiming his bride-to-be.

He was in Tsinan, in the heart of the North China war area. His bride–to-be was at Hong Kong, 1,300 miles away.

No ship would take him, so he journeyed down the coast in Chinese sailing junks, slipped at night past the Japanese warships at Shanghai, and arrived in Hong Kong after weeks of peril.

Dr Prescott and Dr Job had arranged a Christmas wedding, but cables to their homes yesterday told that they had decided to be married immediately. His bride recently sailed from England after completing a special university course to help her husband in his work.[22]

1,300 Mile Dash To Win A Bride

Braving the perils of a 1,300 miles sea journey down the Chinese coast, and slipping past Shanghai in the dead of night, an Englishman whose sweetheart had been held at Hong Kong dashed to her by sailing boat and won himself a bride. A cable received from China at his home in Tetbury, Gloucester, tells of the happy ending to the romantic adventure of Mr Stanley Prescott, son of Mr and Mrs John Prescott, of Church-street, Tetbury.

Mr Prescott, unable to get to Hong Kong by land because of the war, travelled by Chinese sailing boats and then by coal boat for 1,300 miles to Hong Kong.

He left England last October to take up a position on the staff at the Christian University Hospital at Tsinan, North China. His fiancée Dr Monica Job of Twickenham, London, sailed some weeks ago to meet him, but was not able to reach Shanghai as arranged and was forced to disembark in Hong Kong.[23]

128

I think you get the idea. Even without the hyperbole, this was clearly a very brave and perhaps slightly mad thing to do. But I am sure that he did not hesitate. Stanley was fast becoming a hero to Monica. He was not a man of machismo, but she always described him as a passionate and 'ardent lover'. I wonder if her own father was altogether that different from this: always a little unusual but greatly admired by Monica.

Only the day before she was due to land, Stanley tried to send word to Monica. She had received none of the letters he posted over the past months, and sailed into Hong Kong not knowing what to expect. But there he was waiting for her. She wrote to her parents the next day:

I am sure that you will be happy to know that Stanley and I are together at last and what is more, we love each other even more than before. It was lovely seeing him there on the wharf as we sailed in this morning. He managed to get all the way down from North China on a coal boat. It is amazing the things he manages to do. I am staying at the Mission House on the mainland and Stanley is putting up at the Soldiers and Sailor's home on Hong Kong Island.

It is wonderful to be able to write to you on the same page as Stanley. We are as happy as the day is long. It is queer being refugees though! They even give us a 10% discount in the shops!

Stanley is just as he was when he left England, and as soon as we met we forgot the eleven months we had been apart. It is wonderful that after all the things that might have happened, we are still together. I expect that it will be some years before I see you again, but we have got some very happy memories to live on. I hope that we will be able to get some good snaps of the wedding. It is a great life and in spite of the troubles we are very happy.[24]

Not yet married, they could not stay together. I am sure that after more than a year's separation, living on an island while Monica was on the mainland was not to Stanley's liking!

> I was advised before I left Peitaiho by the Missionaries Meeting to get married straight away. And as Monica has no objection !!! we are getting married on the 15th of September. Monica looks a lovely as ever, and is quite happy again. She has had quite a worrying time and, as she could get no news of me and thought I was dead. We have sent a wireless letter to you which you should have by now, and so all your anxiety is over.[25]

On this occasion he was more than happy with the advice of the Mission Society. As for the future:

> We are not sure, but it will be in China, I hope and pray. Should Cheeloo be blown to the skies, which I very much doubt, then I shall probably become the Methodist Representative at the Medical School here, and possibly made the Head of the Methodist Mission in China. But it is settled that we will certainly stay here until the troubles blow over, which will mean at least Christmas and probably until this time next year. I will take a temporary post at the Medical School and Monica will start her medical work here.
>
> And of course there is the wedding – Monica looks even lovelier than she did when I left, and a year's separation has certainly made the heart grow fonder. The pyjamas will be much in evidence at the honeymoon and the cufflinks will also look well. At present I am getting a few clothes together and trying to find a place where we can have a future home.

God bless you. Pray for us and for our love, that married we may mean as much to each other, as much to our children, as much to our friends and acquaintances as you have done.[26]

Monica recalled seventy years later:

When we found ourselves stranded in Hong Kong, we thought the only thing to do was to get married straight away. I had my wedding frock with me. It was a long-sleeved satin one. Beautiful. Long. It was for a winter wedding. But it was mid-summer in Hong Kong. Rather warm! There were no air-conditioners in those days. They just had big fans going round and round. Very effective but not the same as air-conditioning. That was all there was.[27]

They were married on 15 September 1937. Most of their wedding party were unknown to them because of the spontaneous nature of the event. The only one that Monica knew slightly was one of the bridesmaids, who had shared her voyage from England. No cameras were allowed in the church, but a Super 8 movie that was shot of this event shows them arriving and departing. We then see them on their honeymoon, both playing to the camera in 'pre-talkie' movie-star poses. Monica looks so happy and light on her feet skipping before the camera and tossing her curls as she removes her hat to pose. Stanley looks quite gleeful and cheeky posing in a Panama hat and lighting a cigarette. I am still startled by his resemblance to my brother Stephen, his grandson.

Wedding Bells: Morning Ceremony
At The Methodist Church

The English Methodist Church was the scene of the wedding yesterday morning, when Mr Stanley L. Prescott and Dr Monica M. Job were married. The Rev. D. B. Childe officiated at the ceremony.

The bride, who looked exceedingly charming in a gown of oyster satin, wore a filet of silver brocade. She carried a sheaf of gladioli and lilies. She is the daughter of the Rev. and Mrs H. A. Job, who were formerly in mission work amongst the Inca-Indians in Peru. Dr Job's Father is now the congregational minister at Twickenham, Middlesex.

Mrs D. B. Childe acted as the matron of honour and the bride was given away by Mr E. Loyd Jones. Miss Janna Smith, who acted as bridesmaid, wore a blue organdie dress, and carried a bouquet of golden lilies, whilst Miss Barbara Conibear, as train-bearer, wore a pale pink dress and carried a posy. Mr A. P. Granville presided at the organ and played the bridal march from Logengrin [sic] and Mendelssohn's wedding march. The hymns were 'O perfect love' and 'Fill thou my life'.[28]

Monica always kept a copy of the prayer booklet of the wedding service, for which they had chosen the hymn and prayer. I think it is very beautiful and was a perfect choice for them and their situation. Knowing their stories, before and since, I believe that that these words are, in some small way, an embodiment of how they lived their lives. It seems partially to capture the concurrent innocence, faith and yet selfless determination and hope that I have tried to portray in my descriptions of both of them:

> *O perfect love, all human thought transcending,*
> *Lowly we kneel in prayer before Thy throne,*
> *That theirs may be the love which knows no ending,*
> *Whom Thou for evermore dost join as one.*

O perfect life, be Thou their full assurance,
Of tender charity and steadfast faith,
Of patient hope and quiet brave endurance,
With childlike trust that fears neither pain nor death.

Grant them the joy that brightens earthly sorrow,
Grant them the peace which calms earthly strife,
And to life's daily glorious unknown morrow,
That dawns to eternal love and life.

Most of us are not very religious these days, so to many people such words might be gratingly unfamiliar. But this was then a world more coloured by religious devotion, and this was an integral part of their culture and their way of life.

They were ecstatically happy together, as they both reveal in their first letters home to their families. This first is from Monica, now as Mrs Stanley Lewis Prescott:

> This will be the first note from your daughter-in-law. We were so glad when your cable came yesterday and we were so happy knowing that you knew that Stanley and I were together at last and I can't tell you how happy I am. We have had a wonderful time and yesterday exceeded everything I could have imagined. The whole day was lovely and the service very beautiful. I will certainly do my best to make Stanley happy. It won't be a very hard task as I love him so much and I am very happy in having you both for parents. It seems quite strange being called Mrs Prescott and I did not recognise the name at first.[29]

And from Stanley:

Your newly married son salutes you! Yesterday at 11am Monica and I were married at the Methodist Church in Hong Kong. Monica stayed the night before with her bridesmaid Mrs Childe and I stayed as usual at the Sailors and Soldiers home. The ladies at the church decorated it beautifully, with heaps of flowers and completed it royally with a strip of red carpet from the door to the communion rail. At 9.30 I fetched the licence from the law courts, changed, packed and complete with best man arrived at the church by 10.45. I chose a pale grey palm beach suit and we both had button holes. By five minutes to 11.00 all was ready and then we sat up the front – waiting – It was a wonderful five minutes, in which all the past that had led up to our love passed through my mind. All the worries of whether I should get to Hong Kong or where Monica was, were all distant memories. I thought of you and all that you meant to us. Then suddenly the organ music changed to the wedding march. I stood and faced the communion table. All was peaceful and quiet except for the music, until I was aware that Monica, looking more lovely than I have ever seen her, stood by my side. I can't describe the service, except that it was the most perfect service I have ever attended. There was no hitch or pause, and we were declared before man and God to be man and wife.

We had tea with the Childes and then Mr Childe motored us up to The Towers where we are spending our honeymoon. We have a lovely room with a marvellous view and a private bathroom. We unpacked and went into town for dinner, returning around 9.40pm. After a lovely hot bath and donning mother's pyjamas we retired for the night.

After the uncertainty in the preceding weeks, married life seemed blissful, and for a few days at least they put the war out of their minds. And Stanley was now paid a 'married stipend'!

Well we have survived the first week of married life! We are happy and having a wonderful time. I had no idea that married life could be so nice. It is also restful, peaceful and enchanting after my grim weeks in North China and the uncertainty of my voyage to Hong Kong. But now we are together forever, and our worries are truly halved and our joys doubled.[30]

They stayed at the Towers for several weeks before moving on 30 September to their new home at 3 Conduit Road, next door to the British Admiralty and directly below the Japanese Consulate. They joked that they were in interesting company. Monica was enjoying her new surroundings and learned to love the Chinese people too. As the other expatriates and missionaries were being evacuated from the Chinese mainland, Monica met more and more of Stanley's new friends, including many from Cheeloo. And so, slowly, their community grew. Monica also started picking up some of the Chinese language although she never had the same grasp of it as Stanley. There was a cholera outbreak around this time, but apparently only three expatriates succumbed and Stanley and Monica remained healthy.

Stanley found an appointment at Hong Kong University, while he also continued his Chinese studies. And Monica started her medical service in Hong Kong. As she started her language studies, Monica described Stanley as being at the 'top of the school, while I am still in baby-class'. He was now reading Chinese textbooks on physiology. And loving every minute.

During those months, both Monica and Stanley made many lifelong friends. In the decades that followed, the destiny of a number of their medical friends was significantly influenced by these early connections, as Stanley later selected the founding professors of the medical school at The University of Western Australia. In 2007 Monica recalled:

> We were caught in Hong Kong for months. Fortunately the Baptists ran a hospital in Hong Kong and I went there straight away and started my six months of hospital duty. That was also where we met Dr Gordon King. He was a missionary in China too, also based in North China in Tsinan where we were going. We were all stranded in Hong Kong together.
>
> Many years later [in 1953] when Stanley was appointed to start the medical school in Perth, Stanley invited him to be our first professor of Obstetrics and Gynaecology. He had also looked after me when I first became pregnant with your father, David. I later also became friends with his wife and always followed the success of their three daughters. Two became doctors, and one of them, Allison Kennedy, married Justice Geoffrey Kennedy, a former Chancellor of UWA. Those children did very well.[31]

Coincidently, many years later I also found myself studying medicine at UWA in the same class as Gordon King's grandson Christopher, son of Alison Kennedy, and Monica would always smile at the symmetry of that. She remained very good friends with Gordon until the day he died, by which time he had become remarried to a lovely Chinese lady, Bektoe.

Just when things seemed to be settling down for Stanley and Monica, there was another unpleasant development. For reasons unclear, Stanley was recalled to Peking, this time by the Japanese.

Although Stanley had always professed to being a pacifist, he also knew that war had been inevitable, and he was developing a deep resentment for the actions of the Japanese against China.

I have made no comment about the war so far. But it is such a ghastly business. Because of the damnable policy of the Japanese, war was the only thing that could happen. Their opium smuggling and general bad feeling towards the Chinese was something that had to be stifled somehow. Even though China might lose in the end, what else could she do? My feelings are heart and soul for the Chinese, and my hope is that the Japanese will be beaten. When one remembers what China was doing, how she was becoming a fine nation, one's heart bleeds for the people and feel real hatred for the Japanese. I need say no more, but if you hear anything against China then deny it, because China was the innocent party, and I am now Chinese at heart.[32]

He was flabbergasted, confused and angered by the cable that he received from the Japanese administration now occupying Peking, recalling him to North China. It seemed entirely illogical and against the aim of the British Government to keep its people in British territories such as Hong Kong.

The only snag now is that now that our plans have been settled, we have just received a cable to go up to Peking – now under Japanese administration, to return to the language school. This seems to be absolutely mad, after everything. Tomorrow I am going to see the Chairman of the district to discuss it with him. What will be decided I don't know, but at present I am very tempted to refuse to go. To refuse an order is asking for trouble, but it seems to be positively mad. What the mission will say I can't think, but I don't think they will sack me for it, and all things considered I don't think it can do any harm. What makes me so wild is that after giving me carte-blanche to make my own arrangements, which I have managed to do after much hard work, and

137

get everything arranged that we should be expected to go immediately to Peking for no reason at all.[33]

A week later they were still awaiting the outcome of this issue. Stanley had written a letter declining this offer but was yet to receive a reply. Meanwhile, they had a surprise encounter with Monica's sister and her husband, who had fled from China. Arthur and Hope had more stories of the Japanese atrocities and Chinese suffering. The Chinese were no match for the ruthlessly efficient Japanese Army. Most of the Chinese killed were unarmed civilians. Stanley was rapidly abandoning his pacifist ideals.

On Tuesday, much to our surprise, we met Hope and Arthur on their way back to England. Arthur has resigned from the mission – he seemed to have problems with the language, and to have been stationed with very shallow minded people, so much so that they could not stick it any longer. From what I hear, I can't blame them. They looked tired and I felt terribly sorry for them. It must be a terrible disappointment for them. It would be for me now that China has become such a real part of my life.

China seems to be having its full quota of suffering at present. The brutality, senselessness, harm and poor spirit of the damnable Japanese makes me writhe with anger and indignation. It is some satisfaction for us to know that the English papers are backing China. I am now of the firm belief that sooner or later the Japanese military will have to be slaughtered to the last man before there is any hope of a decent nation arising in Japan. It may mean war for England and America, but that would not be so horrible as the inhuman slaughter of innocent country Chinese people. But it is no good getting worked up about the Japanese. My job is to learn more Chinese and prepare for the day when the way back to China will be open for us again. Whether Cheeloo will stand or be bombed to pieces, we will be ready to return, perhaps to the ruins to build again and perhaps to build more wisely than last time.[34]

It was Hope and Arthur who brought the cinefilm of Monica and Stanley's wedding and honeymoon, the one I know so well, back to England with them.

Sadly, as the months passed, more and more of their mission friends began to leave, returning to their homes or bound for safer places. By mid-November there was still no reply from North China to Stanley's letter, and they were hoping that it had been forgotten. They did have news from Tom Bromley, Stanley's old friend and Monica's first crush, saying he was engaged to marry to a girl called Connie Clegg. Monica made no further comments on this, but I know that she always remained very fond of him. In the three years that followed, she received news of their wedding and the birth of their first child.

Monica also heard regularly from her best friend in medical school, Muriel. They continued to write regularly to each other all their lives. Several years later Monica said:

I heard from Muriel every month after I left England. She is a real gem. I wonder how many people in this world have such a good friend.[35]

Although they barely saw each other, this correspondence continued into their nineties. I am sure that the eventual loss of her friend many years later contributed to Monica's own decline.

Finally, Monica and Stanley received a letter of support from the chairman of their district, countermanding the Peking request, and saying that they were right to stay in Hong Kong until the unrest was settled.

But there was also bad news from Tsinan in late November. The Japanese were advancing on Tsinan, and were now only five miles from the centre of the city. With the city being shelled they were even more worried about of the fate of Cheeloo University and Stanley's Chinese friends. He was expecting to lose all of his possessions, but that was the least of his concerns. It was only a matter of time before the city fell to the Japanese.

> If Cheeloo does open again I can lecture in Mandarin now, but now
> I will probably have to learn Japanese instead. Perhaps I will end my
> days as a Professor of Oriental Studies at an English University yet.
> We shall see.[36]

I think he would have loved that, but he had much greater things to do.

Another tragedy stuck much closer to home. The Japanese were setting booby traps in luggage being sent out from the Chinese mainland. This they discovered when one of their professors received his luggage from Shanghai. It was the first violence that Monica had seen first-hand.

> He was unpacking his luggage the day before yesterday, sent down from
> Shanghai. After he had taken out his clothes he saw something hard
> lying in the trunk. He just tapped it to see what it was and it exploded.
> It blew his right arm right off. He was operated on the next day because
> his abdomen was full of shrapnel. But he died yesterday evening and the
> funeral is today. He had taught in China for 15 years. Poor man, after
> escaping from Shanghai he was still killed in the peace of Hong Kong.[37]

The university closed for his funeral, another bleak reminder that the war was close at hand. Hong Kong also went into blackout for hours at a time as the harbour lights searched for enemy planes. Each day they would read the paper, but things in China seemed much the same. Talk of peace, but no peace. Talk of Japan's economic downfall, but as yet no sign of it.

> And so day passes day, with still the same news of Japan's cruel and relentless bloodshed and China's hard stand, with her back to the wall, fighting for the last trace of freedom and liberty. We just live and hope that all that has been done for good during the last years will not just be tossed aside.[38]

Around this time, their pregnant Chinese amah disappeared. She left with her people when her labour pains began and they thought that she was going to the hospital as planned. But she had not been seen since. No one seemed to know where she was and they feared that a dead baby might be the result. It is still not clear what happened.

Their lives stayed very much in waiting mode. They enjoyed regular mail from their families, but the news from Europe also seemed worrying. They busied themselves with their friends, their studies and their letters home. Waiting. Monica enjoyed watching Stanley sitting at this desk writing Chinese. By then he could write more than 2,000 characters and she could write 200. Stanley passed his Chinese physiology paper, written all in Chinese, with 90 per cent. At social outings she would love seeing him speak Chinese 'as easily as a fish can swim'. Monica could understand some of the conversations but was still able to contribute nothing. The days continued much the same.

They loved the people and the community that had developed. Stanley did find that many were more 'British-minded' and perhaps not as 'deadly-keen on China' as he was. But he still very much enjoyed their company.

> And again the afternoon sun sinks to its rest. From the window I can see a faint haze gathering over the mainland hills, and the reflection of the sun on the boats in the harbour. The curli [coolie] in the garden is watering the flowers and tea is being set. Monica sits sewing by my side. And another day of work and leisure, happiness and memories draws to a close. But what has this day meant for the wounded and the dying. Please God, that soon the sun will rise on the new, and love will dwell where hate has lived, and peace be our hope as the world grows out of childhood and realises that life is all we have and that without love, that life has no hope.

And then, some news came about Cheeloo. News that inspired them to travel north again.

> We received a letter from the North China Chairman (Rev. Howard Cork) in Tientsen telling us that Cheeloo would be open again very soon and that after Christmas we were to go North and await the opening so that we could start our work straight away.[39]

This time they were very pleased and very excited and began making plans on how they might get away after Christmas. They had just decided to go when another letter arrived from the South China chairman, which actually seemed to have been written at the very same time as the first, ordering them to stay in Hong Kong another six months. The mission administration seemed to be in chaos, and Monica and Stanley were not sure which to believe.

> The missions are in a terrible muddle out here. With so many people
> kicking up their heels to get out, the Missions are still trying to send out
> new men. Still, that is their business, not mine. Personally I think that
> they would have been advised not to send new men until they could
> know what the future is going to be.

Stanley wrote to each of the chairmen for clarification. And although they were still awaiting Reverend Cork's confirmation from North China, the South China chairman's advice was then to obey the North China command. Once confirmed, their plan was now to go to Tientsin (now called Tianjin) and to wait there for further instructions. They were pleased to know Dr Gordon King was also being sent back into the field. They started changing money and packing for the Arctic weather in anticipation, even though there was still no confirmation that Cheeloo might open any time soon. They were sad to be leaving Hong Kong, but glad to be returning to China, which Stanley now saw as home. They were not sure what they could do in Tientsin. More waiting probably. But this was where Stanley was to learn Japanese. Later in the war, his Japanese would make him invaluable to US intelligence in the South Pacific region, when he went on to serve under General MacArthur.

Once it was decided that they would leave for Tientsin, they wrote to reassure their families they should be safe there with British troops stationed nearby. They also explained that as all mail had to go via Siberia there could be a month or more without letters. There was a very large party at the Hong

Kong Language School to farewell them, with equal numbers of Europeans and Chinese. With all their boxes and trunks packed and sent down to the small coastal boat the night before, their rooms looked bare and they did not even have a chair to sit on.

Through typhoons and icebergs

On 4 January 1938, they began their journey on the SS *Huper*. Their friends came to see them off, and gave them parcels to take back to family and friends who were still in China. The language school was sad to see its star pupil leave and sent a delegation with a large basket of flowers.

Monica and Stanley were surprised and pleased to discover that they had been given a first-class deck cabin, and Monica was thrilled to be travelling 'in grand style'. It was spotlessly clean and she was impressed to have a window instead of the porthole she had on her last boat journey. They were also invited as the only passengers to share the table of the captain, chief engineer and the first and second officers. Unfortunately, Monica was soon in no state to enjoy any of these pleasures. As soon as they left Hong Kong harbour and the boat began to toss, Monica felt sick, which did not bode well as conditions only got worse. It was a much smaller boat than the *Corfu*, at only 1,600 tons; it did not fare well when they sailed into a typhoon.

> I was so sick. It was awful and Stanley was rude enough to say I looked like a cow giving birth. But he was kind enough to hold my hand.[40]

Their boat continued its long journey north and they broke their journey at Shantou. There they saw the effects of the war. The town was desolate. All the shops had been closed down and the people had vanished. Monica described seeing great wide streets, with no sign of life. They were very saddened by this, and glad to leave the emptiness.

> But we sailed out to Shantou only to run right into the North West Monsoon. I shall never forget it. We almost gave up hope of getting to our next port near Foochow [now Fuzhou]. The boat pushed and pushed but the wind and the waves were against her and in spite of all her efforts, at times she stayed still or even went backwards with her propeller going around in the air! The propeller, which was out of the water 52% of the time, would reach the water again and with a lurch we would push on. The wind was terrific and almost lifted the boat up. We only averaged four knots/hour so we could have walked the road just as quickly.

Needless to say, Monica spent most of the trip with her head in a bowl. She could not imagine how hard it must have been for the hundreds of Chinese who had been sleeping on top of the luggage on the open deck at the stern. Eventually they reached the estuary twenty-five miles from Foochow. They could not enter. The Chinese had laid booms across the river, so they anchored there to load wood and other supplies. They stayed the night while the monsoon dropped. After that it was fairly smooth sailing north for another week on the open sea towards Shanghai. The temperature was also steadily dropping and it was bitterly cold on deck. It must have been almost unbearable for the many Chinese without shelter on the deck.

> We are very well guarded, with an armed policeman on every deck. One is right outside our door. It must be very cold. They are wearing big

leather helmets pulled over their ears. We have still got some Chinese passengers. I would never have thought that it was possible to sleep or even to live under such terrible conditions.

The last part of the journey was even more exciting as we had to plough our way through about ten miles of ice. It was amazing to see a whole sea of ice. Once we got stuck and had to go back through the channel that we had made, then find another way in again.

On Sunday morning we left the open sea and went up the river with mud houses on either side. At 4 pm we reached Tientsin [Tianjin] and to our great surprise and delight, the Craddocks were there to meet us. We had no idea they were even here.

They went to live temporarily with Dr and Mrs Craddock, while they awaited further instructions. There was absolutely nothing to do. Everyone was restless and uncertain and no one seemed to have any idea what work to give them. So Monica went to work at the Mackenzie Memorial Hospital, doing both ward rounds and antenatal clinics. She enjoyed returning to her medical profession. This and all her work in the following years was either voluntary or covered by a meagre missionary's stipend. They heard that Dr Gordon King had returned to his work at the Tsinan Hospital, but with Cheeloo University still closed the mission saw no reason to send Stanley back there yet. Monica found Tientsin dirty and dusty, but enjoyed the way of life. It was amazing how everyone in the expatriate community was connected and they kept coming across people they knew. They were amused when one of the new people from the Peking Language School said that they were still talking of Stanley there!

Stanley also found a copy of the eleventh edition of the *Encyclopaedia Britannica*.

The latest edition is the 14th, but the 13th is considered best because it is
not Americanised like the latest edition. The 11th edition consists of
29 volumes and my job will be to also find the three extra volumes to
make it up to the 13th. All 29 volumes are leather bound and in Indian
paper, and at just £3 we are very pleased with it.[41]

Until I read that, I had no idea where the century-old leather encyclopaedias that now sit in my study in Australia had come from. They are dated 1911 so I still wonder what interesting travels they had in the twenty years before they came into Stanley's possession. And now I also know why several do not match.

Monica and Stanley were excited to see Dr Ingle, a surgeon, who came with news from Tsinan on his way to Shanghai to meet his wife. Tsinan had seen difficult times, and had fallen to the Japanese. Many people had been slaughtered. The Japanese now occupied the city and an uneasy calm had returned. Cheeloo was safe. Their possessions were safe. But some of their friends had lost everything in the 'trouble', as they politely referred to the massacre. It looked like the Japanese were settling in there and not showing any signs of moving on. Although the hospital was still permitted to run under the Japanese, it seemed likely that the university would remain closed.

We hope that as soon as the warm weather comes we shall be able
to go to our real home. They need me to do some work in Blood
Chemistry and to supervise the Biochemical and Biological side of the
hospital. Monica will work in Antenatal.
    This is great news and we are terribly thrilled at the prospect of
going back HOME! For it is our home.[42]

Chinese New Year was more sombre than anyone could remember. No one was in the mood for celebration. At the mission, all the Chinese helpers were given a holiday but they came back early of their own accord to make the dinner saying that they did not have the heart to rejoice that year.

Once again, their glee at the possibility of returning to Tsinan in March was short-lived. Until the fate of Cheeloo University was known, the mission chairman felt that it was more appropriate for them to return to Peking after all. Now that they were almost there, they relented and saw this as an opportunity for Monica to start her Chinese studies in earnest.

Monica was beginning to think they would never settle down as they set off yet again on 17 February 1938, this time for Peking.

Peking under Japanese occupation

For once their journey was uneventful. Stanley was reunited with the old friends who still remained, and Monica settled in easily. Their life moved into a happy routine and Stanley enjoyed life so much more, with Monica at his side, than he had the year before. Another major difference was the Japanese presence, which was very much in evidence. But conditions were stable and everyone tried to go about their lives as though their new 'friends' were not there. Concerned that their mail was being read, many now felt it was safer to refer to the invaders as their 'friends' in their letters, although they were anything but.

Monica had very fond memories of her early days in China. As when she was a child, she delighted in other people and other cultures. She always said she found the Chinese people she met very friendly and accepting. There was never any sense in her recollections that she felt ill at ease or alien to this culture. Admittedly, she had arrived into a country and a city that had been occupied by the British for a long time, so there would also have been much that was familiar. Although the intentions of the missionaries were only good, it is obvious to us now that many aspects of the British occupation were misguided and ill conceived. However, at least at that stage, she gave little impression that she or her compatriots were viewed as invaders or occupiers. Having said that, the Chinese were far more bothered by their more recent invaders, and seemed happy to tolerate a few Westerners, at least at that stage.

Most of their letters from that time are filled with happy accounts of their friends and social life. Monica's letters are also packed with her first impressions of life in Peking. The busy streets, the wonderful people, how strange it was seeing rickshaws everywhere. When they went to a 'picture theatre' for the first time, it was exciting to make their journey by rickshaw. The only motorcars belonged to the Japanese. Monica made many of her own dresses, frocks as she called them, but was also pleasantly surprised to find that she could buy almost everything she needed. In the evenings they would visit friends, talk and listen to the gramophone.

In addition to her own Chinese language studies, Monica also started teaching. She gave English classes every day at the YWCA, with over seventy Chinese students in her classes. This was something she greatly enjoyed and it was a chance to make many Chinese friends. She became quite an English scholar, claiming to be learning more than her students. Before long she even had them reading Shakespeare.

The Chinese Language School and the London Mission were both in the centre of Peking, on either side of the Forbidden City, the language school just to the east, and the London Mission just to the west. So every day they would enjoy the walk around the northern walls of the Forbidden City and across the bridge of the beautiful Beihai lake. My first journey to Beijing was in 2004. I was invited to give medical lectures there myself. This was before I had read any of my grandparents' letters and knew any details of their travels. I remember walking

151

five kilometres from my hotel without a guide to find the Forbidden City. I walked the back streets and eventually found Beihai, walking all the way not even knowing I was retracing the steps of Monica and Stanley.

I like to think that Monica and Stanley would be both pleased and proud to know that I have returned to China many times since, to give invited lectures at many hospitals and universities all over China. I am in fact just near Shanghai as I write this. Unlike Stanley, I can never hope to lecture in Chinese. I find that the modern Chinese are very interested in history and relationships, and they are always excited and amazed by the story of my grandparents. They are still pained by the collective memories of the Japanese invasion, and remain eternally grateful for the help and support they received from their Western friends.

In 1938 things were very uncertain for everyone. Although the Japanese occupied many cities, they still could not control a country so vast, particularly the rural areas, where many Chinese remained in hiding and organised strategic assaults on the Japanese.

> At the moment everything is vague and shadowy and we don't know what the future will be. We have heard of Germany's ultimatum to Austria, and we are wondering what will come of it. War seems to be in the air today and we all wonder how it will end. Japan is having a hard time here subduing the Chinese mobile units. We get very little news and what we do get is in duplicate, with the Chinese claiming raids with damages to Japanese planes, but Japanese news claiming no raid and no damages. So something must be happening somewhere, and soon we will learn the truth.[43]

152

Other mission workers came and went, but it was clear that the missions were in growing confusion. Without knowing clearly what was going on in the field, it was difficult to know where to deploy workers to help.

Many of the Irish Presbyterians who came out on the SS *Corfu* with Monica also ended up at the language school. But within a few months they were deployed for their work in Manchuria. So there was another mass exodus, leaving Monica and Stanley still wondering and still waiting. But during this time they received a wonderful surprise gift. They had a visit from a mission friend, Dr Smilie, who offered his lovely house on the coast at Peitaiho the whole summer, while he went back home on furlough. With the high rents for the summer houses, this was a very generous offer. Dr Smilie wanted them to have it as a honeymoon present and he was even going to send his cook up for them too! Monica could hardly believe his kindness. This gave them something to look forward to in a time of uncertainty.

Stanley celebrated another birthday in China. It was two years since Monica had given him his engagement ring, which I now have, as it is engraved with the same initials as mine (SLP), and she described him on his birthday as 'just as handsome as ever'.

The time seemed to pass quickly, but they were still focused on a future when they might be able to return to Tsinan.

> I always say 'back in Tsinan' as if I have been there before! I keep thinking I have, as although I was in England last year my mind was always in Tsinan and I feel as if I know the place.[44]

As far as they could tell, each Japanese 'victory' seemed to be followed by stalemate. To the 'neutral' expatriate observers it seemed that neither the Japanese Government nor their army officials had a clear plan when it came to the details. And when they made each conquest, they did not seem to know what to do with it.

> It is pathetic. All the waste of materials, money and lives, and in the end they will not be any better off. 'Bamboo grows quickly and the oak grows slowly. The Bamboo is hollow with no heart at the centre. The oak has a heart which is dense and hard.'[45]

Now that Stanley had a firm grasp on the language, he was gaining a deepened understanding of the philosophies and culture of the Chinese. He felt that many of the missionaries before him had not taken the time to understand and appreciate the culture and language deeply enough.

> Gradually I have begun to delve into the 'mind' behind the language, to learn something of the real philosophies and the great works of Confucius and other great Chinese. Now I have an even greater enthusiasm for it. There is so much to be done and studied. But each day I make a little progress. One of the great mistakes of the Methodist Mission is that in the past the emphasis has not been put on upon these studies.[46]

In May the dust storms came and conditions were not as pleasant. For the first time the war touched Monica and Stanley more personally when two fellow missionaries were shot dead. One of them, Dr Wyatt, was well known to them. His wife and daughter were also at the Peking Language School. It was a dreadful tragedy. In a terrible misunderstanding they were actually shot by the Chinese.

> A party of four missionaries were travelling in a lorry from a Japanese occupied territory, to a Chinese territory and were unfortunately mistaken for Japanese. They were shot at and two were killed. The other two were wounded and captured, but allowed to go as soon as it was seen that they were not Japanese. It was a terrible mistake and the sort of thing that is bound to happen in war-time when people are moving about on dangerous ground.[47]

Everyone was sobered by this event, and very sorry for the families of the men killed. It emphasised that the missionaries should be better advised to stay in the safe zones and not try to continue as though there was no war.

> At present there is a tremendous battle being waged to the south, the result is still undecided, and in no way means there will be an end to the hostilities. Perhaps this slaughter in the East will make the West realise a little of the absurdity of war. And yet people still seem so blind and stupid. On the other hand when an enemy attacks what can one do but defend.

They had news that things were still stable in Tsinan and they should plan to go there in the autumn after their summer vacation at Peitaiho Beach. It was still not clear if Cheeloo would reopen, but they were getting so sick of waiting they were planning to go anyway. Stanley was doing so well in his Chinese exams that he was reaching the point where he was ready to give his lectures in Chinese. He had just written an essay in Chinese on 'The Function and Action of Respiration', but the thought of lecturing was still a bit daunting.

> But when I think of lecturing in Chinese my heart gives a thud and my stomach turns over. It is one thing to read and speak the language, but quite another to lecture. I have got to the stage now that I have to break the ice, but the first plunge will be cold!

They also received word that Stanley's brother, my great-uncle John, had an audition with the BBC and was accepted. They were looking forward to hearing him broadcast. John was an extremely gifted musician who had built his harpsichord for the performance. Having started his career as a university librarian, John had entered the civil service and was already progressing quickly through the ranks. He went on the work for the Monopolies and Mergers Commission (MMC) and later received an OBE for his lifelong service to the British Government.

Things became more festive and relaxed as the academic year came to an end, and their planned departure for Peitaiho Beach in mid-June. There were concerts and parties. But although it might have sometimes seemed that there was no war, it was never far from their minds.

> Perhaps soon we will come to realise that culture is greater than territory, and other men are as important as ourselves. Perhaps one day it may even dawn upon the nations that life is better than abundance, that markets, capital and pomp are small compared to freedom of the soul. I feel at present that this country is like an old sage whose life has been

spent with books and culture, whose children are unruly and naughty and very destructive. But time will advance and this nation will grow up.

Men may want to rule the world, but what shall it profit any man who in gaining the world shall lose his soul?[48]

Honeymoon at Peitaiho Beach

Arriving at Peitaiho Beach, they had even greater appreciation for the generosity of Dr Smilie. The bungalow was perched high on cliffs falling straight down to the sea. The coastline folded around them so that they had a view across the bay to the mountains in the distance. Although not visible from their windows, the Great Wall of China began just five miles to the north. There was a lovely wide stone veranda around two sides of the house where they would sit for most of their meals. All the rooms faced the sea with spectacular views, and the gardens were beautiful. There was a rocky beach below the house, and the main swimming beach was a short walk away. They swam every day and had private Chinese lessons. Stanley tanned easily and became incredibly brown. He often joked that one of his ancestors might have included a Spanish sailor. His father, Jack, always said so.

> I am writing this letter and watching the gorgeous sunset at the same time. There is a slight wind blowing and the sea is slightly rippled. The bungalow faces north so it's beautifully cool and we get the sea view and the mountains all at once.[49]

But there were a few drawbacks that Monica noted:

There is no running water so it has to be carried by a special man who does nothing else all day. And so there are no baths. Our biggest wash is in a basin. We have no flush lavatory, so we have to wander along to an outhouse. We use oil lamps and they are quite hard to read by and give out too much heat. However, it is surprising how well we can do without modern comforts.[50]

Within the month over 1,000 missionaries arrived at Peitaiho Beach for their holidays. Monica was in her element and made many new friends.

This year practically every missionary in China is here! It is the best place I have ever been to for meeting people. Many of the people here are strangers to me so I have been able to make a lot of new friends.

The Americans gave her 'ice coffee' for the first time:

Cold coffee with great blobs of ice cream. I found it sickly, but the Americans are able to eat any amount of such mixtures!

Monica missed teaching, so she got involved in the Sunday School. With so many families, there were plenty of children to look after. Her medical skills were also required on several occasions. One of the mission wives had a miscarriage and Monica went to see her twice a day. She administered ergot and kept her in bed for a few days. There was also a woman suffering from menopausal haemorrhage, which Monica described more as flooding. Monica put her to bed, applied pressure and tilted the bed up at the foot with bricks. She visited daily to see her patient improve. There were infected insect stings, children with fevers and other assorted ailments that also needed her skills. Monica ran a cholera injection clinic and inoculated hundreds of people, each needing three doses. There was also great effort to raise funds for the refugee children in Tientsin.

And there was an outbreak of dysentery in Peitaiho. Because everyone's food was prepared by Chinese helpers, the health of each family was dependent on the hygiene of its helpers. It was generally accepted that good servants were more expensive, but worth every penny. Monica and Stanley remained well and they were certain that this was due to the high standards of Dr Smilie's Chinese helpers. But many were unwell and there were several deaths, including one of the mission children. He was the only child of one of the families in their group. Although they transferred him quickly to the Tangshan Hospital, there was little that could be done in time and sadly he died there. It was a devastating loss.

Stanley continued his Chinese lessons and was now highly respected by all the Chinese they knew. He was rapidly becoming more Chinese in his ways as well. The Chinese began to regard him as one of their own.

> Stanley has a wonderful gift for getting on well with the Chinese people. Teachers, Cooks, Boys and Amahs all come to him for their troubles and look upon him as their friend.

And so they spent the summer.

In August they finally made plans to go to Tsinan. Dr Gordon King and many of the other Cheeloo Hospital staff had joined them at Peitaiho Beach, so they were able to make more definite arrangements. With the mission heads also there, their plans could receive final approval. There were rumours that Tsinan had been recaptured by the Chinese, but this turned out to be untrue. Rather, there had been another outbreak of violence, but it was contained more quickly. Wesley Bungalow, their home in Tsinan, had been searched. Because it was empty the Japanese had suspected that Chinese dissidents might have been hiding there. But nothing was damaged. They would go to Tsinan anyway.

Now, with many of the railways shut down, the problem was how to get there. While they had been in Peitaiho, the local train lines had been closed down at least three times. They had also heard that sections of the lines to Tsinan had been bombed by Chinese guerrillas on 11 August. Chinese renegades would often destroy their own infrastructure to sabotage the Japanese. The damage must have been extensive, as it took almost two weeks to repair. With news that the trains were running again in late August, things were looking up.

The next problem was the coal supply. Each year families had to purchase their own coal supplies, enough to last the whole winter. This was the only way to keep warm through the bitter cold and to heat their meals. But the Japanese had commandeered most of the coal supplies and would not sell it back. Without coal, winter in Tsinan would be unbearable. Stanley put it so nicely:

Our friendly islanders have taken all of the coal for their work of making friends with the Chinese, and there will be little left for us, if any.[51]

161

In Tsinan they were already rationing supplies by only having one hot meal per day. If there was no coal left in November they would all have to leave. But it was a risk they decided to take. By the end of August, Peitaiho was fast becoming deserted, and they left for Tientsin on 31 August.

As chance would have it, they travelled with Mrs Mackenzie, mother-in-law of Eric Liddell, the famed British Olympian whose story was eventually celebrated in the film *Chariots of Fire*. They passed stations that were burned to nothing, and the train was stopped several times because of fighting further down the line. A train full of wounded soldiers passed them. There were many delays, but that was now a way of life. Stanley and Monica got off the train in Tientsin at 7pm, and were later very glad they had. Many of their friends, including the Craigs, were continuing on to Peking, another three hours down the line. But after Monica and Stanley left the train, it was raided. The Craigs later recounted a horrifying night, hiding under the carriage seats to avoid gunfire. The train did not make it to Peking until 8am the next morning, twelve hours late, and the Craigs were glad they were among those who lived to tell the tale.

In Tientsin, after three months without running water, Monica rejoiced in her first hot bath! They paused there a few days to gather supplies, while their cook and house servants, who had been with them in Peitaiho Beach, travelled on to Tsinan to ready their house, Wesley Bungalow. They had two main Chinese helpers. Mr Ma Ru was the cook from Wesley Bungalow who had come from Tsinan to help them at Peitaiho. Then there was Mr Lai Hsi who usually worked for Dr Smilie, but was 'on loan' to Monica and Stanley for the year until Dr Smilie returned from furlough. In a very uncertain world, they decided to split their possessions, leaving half in Tientsin and taking only half on to Tsinan. That way they might still have something if things went wrong. They left their luggage at the British Commission in Tientsin, where it would be secure until they felt it was safe to call for it.

The following day, with great excitement and some trepidation, they set off to Tsinan on what they hoped would be their final journey for some time. Yet again there were many delays. As Monica described, the Chinese were much better at dealing with this than the foreigners:

> The Chinese are the most patient people. When our train was delayed for three hours from Tientsin I don't think any of the Chinese people got out of the train to find out what was happening. They just sat and waited. They don't worry about anything over which they have no control. Stanley and I, like the other foreigners, were up and down all the time seeing if there were any signs of starting, but the train didn't go any sooner for us who exerted ourselves![52]

We still have a lot to learn from the Chinese.

> The Chinese often look upon us with pity in their eyes. They must think we are fools sometimes. And even if they don't think we are fools, they often make us feel we are.

In Tsinan at last

They finally arrived in Tsinan on Sunday 4 September 1938. Their train came in many hours late at 11.30pm, and there was no one to greet them. With so many unscheduled delays, train timetables meant little and the car that had been sent to meet them had turned back hours before. It was extremely dangerous travelling at night. The guerrillas were more likely to attack under cover of darkness and the Japanese were also on heightened alert at night. With other missionaries already killed in the conflict, to arrive in the middle of the night was terrifying. Monica and Stanley were also not to know that the local Japanese had now enforced a strict curfew in Tsinan and closed all the city gates at 9pm. Armed Japanese closely patrolled the city walls and the city streets.

Eager to get 'home' and rather than risk staying at the very dubious railway hotel, they decided to try the journey to the Cheeloo campus. To improve their chances as much as they could, they hired two horse carts, sending one ahead so that they would get at least a few seconds' warning if it was attacked.

Our horse cart is something like a red cab, but with unstuffed seats and venetian blinds instead of windows, and a horse that the knackers would refuse.[53]

They had been worried enough on the train, but travelling by road was even more dangerous. It was the most terrifying half-hour journey that Monica had experienced so far.

> I wish I could describe it more fully. It was like travelling in an English Stage coach in the middle-ages with the same dangers likely to confront us. We took one cart and sent our luggage ahead of us in another, so that it would be attacked first if such should befall us.[54]

They were stopped by Japanese soldiers several times. Monica was terrified. I think they both were. This was the first time she had guns trained on her. As they passed between each sentry point, Stanley tried to reassure her that the Japanese were trying to frighten them and show them they were in control, but would not hurt them. At least he hoped not.

> We were held up many times by guards as we went along the city wall. Our friends in the watchtowers had their toys pointed straight at us.

Monica and Stanley now wished they had stayed at the railway hotel instead of making the journey to Cheeloo in the dark. They were stopped yet again at the city gates, which were already closed for the night. The Japanese guards spoke some 'schoolboy Chinese', and Stanley had learned some Japanese. Again Stanley's dedication to language paid off. The Japanese were not known to be all that kind to foreigners, but his oriental politeness and the mandarin-style subtlety for which he was lauded in years to come, earned them safe passage through the gate. The sentries kept a close watch on them and they made their way into the university campus as the clock struck twelve.

They fell into the arms of waiting friends, who had been worried for their safety, and who offered them a bed for their first night.

> We were so glad to get to a peaceful bed and a quiet sleep, after so many anxious moments in the latter part of our journey.[55]

When they awoke the next morning to the sight of the wonderful gardens of Cheeloo, Stanley was overwhelmed with joy. Now with his adored wife and in the place he thought of as home, he was the happiest he had been, telling his family that it surpassed both his memories and Monica's dreams.

Before they arrived at their house, Wesley Bungalow had been cleaned, painted and the floors varnished.

> Last night we slept in our own home for the first time, in our first double bed, which is beautifully sprung. Today we have finished unpacking all of our luggage, and I see things that I had forgotten I possessed. I have worn one pair of shoes for the last year and now I have dozens at my disposal! Tonight we are writing at my desk in our study and the world seems at peace. Tomorrow we shall go down to the hospital to look around and probably start work on Monday. Altogether we are about fifty foreigners here, and it is a wonderful community to work in. Our garden is a thing of beauty. A lovely lawn and a willow tree. We wish you were here to see our little house. It is great fun and at last we have the home that we have longed for.

Monica and Stanley lived comfortably in China, certainly more comfortably than Monica ever had before. Monica was so happy with her new home:

I wish you could see our home. Mother would love to run a house like this. It is all on one floor and the walls are all freshly distempered in cream, the woodwork newly painted white and the floors gleaming with varnish. Everything is spotlessly clean, bright and sunny. From the windows we see our garden ablaze with colour softened by a cut lawn and trees through which we can see the mountains only five miles away. A prettier sight one couldn't find. It is perfect. Stanley and I are sitting at our desk for two, where we get our many letters written.[56]

The house was actually on two levels. They had all of the downstairs rooms, and shared the house with Miss Nunn, who had the upstairs flat with her own entrance. Monica would affectionately call her Nunnie. I would be amused if there was any connection with my husband Craig Nunn's family, but as far as I know there is none. There was electricity, but it was never on during the daylight hours, so they could not use any electrical devices during the day. If Monica did any ironing it would be in the evenings. During the day Lai Hsi would still do some of the ironing with what Monica described as a cumbersome iron contraption that was filled with hot coals.

And now I will give you a glimpse of the campus so that you will understand what sort of place it is. On entering the campus you might imagine that you are entering a park like Kensington Gardens. There are long extensive avenues of trees and large expanses of grass. In some places the gravel paths are lined with thick fir trees. In the centre of the park is a big stone church, which is very beautiful and nestles amongst

167

trees and hedges. Hidden also among the trees are the University buildings, all except the Medical School and many houses. But they are all well spaced and almost hidden by the trees and vegetation in the summer. Our house is the last on the row, forming the boundary of the campus furthest away from the entrance and nearest to the mountains. The campus is quite extensive and it takes about ten minutes to walk across it. The entrance to the campus is on a main road, and on the other side of the road is the city wall, with a big gate. Just the other side of the wall is the Cheeloo hospital, the Medical School and about eight houses. The Ingles and the Shields live there. Although we only have to cross the road and go through the gate to get to the hospital, the gate is controlled by the Japanese. They close it if there is any sign of trouble and we can't get through.[57]

The shops and markets were further down the main road, about a thirty-minute walk. Ma Ru did most of the shopping, just once a week. Although Monica was initially uncomfortable having servants, this was a way of life in China. They provided employment, accommodation and a living for a Chinese family. Perhaps this was how she rationalised the inequity of their situations. The relationships with the Chinese were complex. They regarded them as friends and colleagues. They trained and worked with Chinese doctors. They also had paid Chinese servants. Although the British Empire was losing its strength, it is clear that a residual sense of false superiority still permeated the colonies. This was part of a collective consciousness and did not reflect either Stanley's or Monica's personal feelings. Certainly, Stanley had a very high opinion of and enormous respect for the Chinese people all his life. Monica also had a great love of the Chinese and this made it much harder when the Chinese were later forced to take sides against the British and Americans, and help the Japanese push them out.

Chinese families lived in separate quarters at the other end of the back garden of each house. In Wesley Bungalow, Ma Ru cooked and ran the house, assisted by his wife and eldest daughter. Mrs and Mr Ma already had five children. Lai Hsi was a very good, quick, hard worker. Nothing was too difficult for him. But whereas Ma was 'quiet as a mouse', Monica found Lai Hsi always made a terrible amount of noise. They were there all the time and always on duty for the family. Monica and Stanley paid them well and they also paid for the education of all the Ma children. This meant a lot to all of them. The Chinese family formed a strong bond with their English family. They had no word for Prescott so they gave Stanley the nearest name they could, which was Pu!

Pu Rai Go was the closest Chinese sound to Prescott. So that was what we were called. So Stanley was Pu Sian Sheng [xiansheng] and I was Pu Tie Tie [taitai]. When he was born, David was called Da Wei.[58]

Monica was fascinated by the Chinese work ethic, which at the time was quite unlike anything she has come across before.

If you tell them what has to be done by a certain time it will be done, but you cannot control the speed or the order of doing it. If they feel tired, they sleep, whether on duty or not. Nature has its way with them and they do not fit in well with routine work. One is liable to go into the kitchen fifteen minutes before the guests arrive for dinner and find nothing done, and the servants asleep in the back. But if nothing is said and the guests arrive, you can sit down with confidence that everything

169

will be served just as you like. They are amazing for saving their energy. If they know that a job takes five minutes to do, they do not even think about it until five minutes before it has to be done.[59]

Again, there was much to learn. Seeing China today, I am afraid that these were lessons lost. Sadly that natural freedom of time has been lost to the modern and Western ways of industry. It seems we have all made the world too crazy. In the photographs that Monica showed me of the Chinese family, she explained that the boys all had hats and the girls were bare-headed. Traditionally the girls all had fringes, as a sign of virginity. They used to keep this until they were married and grew it long. This custom was becoming less common, but it used to be possible to tell by her hair if a woman was married.

It was also soon revealed that there had been another reason Monica and Stanley chose to spend three months on holiday at Peitaiho before starting work in Tsinan. They had been waiting to share this news until things were more certain. Perhaps a little sooner than they planned, but certainly at a most respectable time into their marriage, they were expecting their first child. With a new baby on the way, having servants to help her was a luxury Monica would have never had in England.

And sometime in March you will be grandparents! We did not want to tell you until we had arrived safely in Tsinan, so that you would not worry about our journey. We thought it best that Monica was on holiday in Peitaiho for the unpleasantries of the first three months. But she was not sick at all but behaved quite normally and is in excellent health. We are thrilled at the prospect and at present everything in the garden is lovely and growing well. It does not show yet of course.

170

Monica says she will carry on her work until near the end. So, another of life's adventures lies before us and we are very thrilled.[60]

Monica had her first tour of the hospital where she would soon start working in obstetrics and gynaecology, with Dr Gordon King and another, older English woman, Dr Gell, who never married. Monica also worked in the outpatient sections. She was impressed by the high standard of the hospital, which had largely been achieved because it was a university teaching hospital. So far, she had had no antenatal care herself, so she also had a first examination with Dr King, for reassurance that all was well. Before either of them could start work, Monica and Stanley had to be checked for tuberculosis. Each had x-rays and a 'fluoro-scope, where you actually watch the screen and see all of the organs working'. I am sure the radiation exposure is greater than anything we would allow for a pregnant woman today, but my father seems okay seventy years later.

And now comes another very good piece of news. I am feeling very proud of my husband, as yesterday he was appointed Hospital Superintendent! Any fears of him not having enough work to do are quite dismissed! This is a big job, as all of the hospital business, records, appointment etc. have to pass through his hands. He will dictate his letters and have two secretaries waiting on him. Last but not least, he will be the one who has to conduct tours every time our Japanese 'friends' conduct their inspections. It will be a new kind of task, but a grand experience.[61]

This was a considerable honour, as he was far younger than most of the staff, many of whom had already been there for some years. But with his skills, manner and reputation, no one questioned it. There was a large party to celebrate their arrival and Stanley's appointment as the new head of the hospital.

And so they began their work in earnest with the Japanese always looking over their shoulder. The campus was a haven for them, but they still had to go through one of the city gates to get to the hospital. Every time they did so they would be stopped and searched. Sometimes the Japanese would simply close the gate, refusing passage, and they could not get to the hospital for their work. But in their situation, there was little they could do but obey. As Monica told me many years later:

The only thing to do with the enemy was to be nice to them.

Every time we passed we had to sign on a piece of paper with our name, age, sex, nationality. Every day. Every time. Some of it was purely nuisance value. They would make us take everything out of our cases and handbags and then make you put it all back, just to show us who was in charge.

Once or twice the Americans got a bit annoyed about this and just walked straight through. They had their passes taken from them, and then had to walk about two miles around to the next city gate.

We just had to obey them, and we did. We toed the line, because if people did anything wrong they were shot.[62]

Living with the Japanese in Tsinan

After the invasion, the Japanese army had advanced in three columns: one went west to Datong in the Shanxi; the second moved south towards Paoting and a third had come south to Tsinan (Jinan), where Monica and Stanley were posted. The Japanese Army did not stop at inflicting damage on the fighting troops. They wreaked havoc among civilians with the extermination of countless helpless people, and destroyed cities and villages through indiscriminate bombing.

Cheeloo, as the Shantung Christian University was called informally, was renowned for its medical education program. It was established in 1909 as the result of the consolidation of earlier medical and theological colleges of the American Presbyterian, English Baptist, Anglican, and Canadian Presbyterian mission agencies. When a new hospital building was completed in 1936, the old hospital buildings were utilised by the School of Medicine, where Stanley had been based. As indicated by Monica and Stanley, in 1938 the new campus was on the south side of the city wall, separated by the Japanese-guarded wall from the buildings of the School of Medicine and residential quarters.

As I write this today, I am looking at a very different China. My hotel window overlooks a vast congested city of high-rise buildings and crowded streets. I am sure that it would be as unfamiliar to Stanley and Monica as it is to me. I have come to Jinan in hope of walking the streets where Stanley and Monica spent their days, and seeing the place where my father was born. There is so little left of the original city that I am not too optimistic. It is 2008, and Ms Zhou Hui and her staff from the International Office of the Qilu (Cheeloo) Hospital of Shandong University have come to greet my husband, Craig, and me and take us to meet the current superintendent of the hospital. I am anxious to see what remains of the old campus. They escorted us to the hospital boardroom, where we were joined by the current superindendent and president of the hospital, Professor Zhou Ri-Guang. It was a beautiful wood-panelled room in the original buildings where Stanley would have conducted many of his meetings. We were received with great enthusiasm and ceremony. I was presented with a plaque and, with the aid of an interpreter, Professor Zhou Ri-Guang told me that my visit was very auspicious and that I was very honourable indeed. But he then added that Craig, as my husband, was far more honourable – which I think they both enjoyed. I am not sure if I saw a twinkle in his eye as he said it.

We were then taken on an extensive tour of Qilu Hospital and the Shandong University campus, which are still co-located. I recognised the original hospital buildings from the old photographs I had seen. It was pleasing to see the old building where my father was born still standing and still recognisable among the many modern renovations. They also showed me an album of old photographs that had recently been donated to the hospital by Dr Mary McKim (daughter of Dr E. B. Struthers, President 1942–1946) and Mrs Margaret Wightman (daughter of Dr Godfrey Gale, president in 1942). To see the faces of so many of the people that I had come to know through Monica and Stanley's letters was wonderful. It was quite eerie to find myself standing in the corridor outside Stanley's corner office from where he had run the hospital. It is now occupied by the blood bank. I knew that he had walked these halls and stood where I was some seventy years before, but in such a different world from mine. It was very moving. I felt that I was in a parallel reality, and layered beneath it I could still feel them going about their daily business on the very same spot, unaware of my presence.

Later we walked through the beautiful grounds, now a residual sanctuary from the vast modern city outside. They were almost exactly as Monica and Stanley had described them, and I saw the row of houses where they had lived, although some had been pulled down and replaced by modern buildings. The remaining few were all run into disrepair with their gardens overgrown, now occupied by many students or families. They were a far cry from the bright and cheery bungalows that Monica had described, but I could still see traces of happier days beneath their tired facades and makeshift renovations. Of course, the neighbouring fields were built over long ago, and the old view of the nearby mountains was obscured by many rows of high-rise buildings. It was very sad in one way, but in another I was glad to see that there were still echoes of the past remaining.

In the 1930s, the university medical school was already of the highest quality and international standards:

> The medical school was quite well known in those days. To be there
> was equal to anything. And they were nearly all European lecturers and

professors. It was very good training. Six years' training, with three years' practising in the country. Before I arrived, Stanley had been appointed as a professor there. But by the time we got back there it was closed. Taken by the Japanese. Of course the whole thing changed when the Japanese took over.

As the Japanese needed the best medical care for their soldiers they let the missionaries stay. For the next three years Monica worked there as a doctor as she had always planned, and Stanley was as the medical superintendent. The Japanese supported the hospital generously to ensure good care of their soldiers. Where he could, Stanley secretly tried to divert some of these funds to treat the local Chinese, whose suffering was often far greater, and frequently at the hands of the Japanese. On many occasions they found themselves having to hide Chinese patients from Japanese soldiers.

The whole situation was very different from when Stanley had left there to meet me nearly two years earlier. We knew it was very dangerous because the Japanese knew that we were on the side of the Chinese. They were ready to shoot us if they had the chance. It was terrifying.

It sounds rather surreal, as though it might have been happening in a movie with the reassuring knowledge that all the protagonists will be safe in the end. Of course we know that they were, but at the time the situation was fragile. The expatriates had a tenuous relationship with the Japanese, who could be brutal to their enemies. The Japanese atrocities committed on Chinese soldiers and civilians, including women and children, are well documented. It was most important for the Westerners to maintain a civil relationship so they could do their work, and so they could survive.

> Things were very different once the Japanese were in control, but they needed us because they wanted treatment. When the Japanese were sick or wounded we gave them the nicest beds in the ward. It was a beautiful big teaching hospital, and the Japanese paid us extremely well for treatment. Meanwhile, we treated the Chinese with the money the Japanese had given us.
>
> But you never knew whose side people were on. Some of the nurses started wearing very smart clothes, with much better shoes. And we knew that they couldn't possibly afford them. We soon discovered that they were being paid by the Japanese to spy on us. So we had to be very careful the whole time we were there. We really had to watch ourselves. Very often a Chinese man would shoot at the Japanese, and unfortunately they would both end up in our hospital. So Stanley would have to put one at one end of the hospital and the other at the opposite end. No sooner had he done that, the Japanese would then turn up to take the Chinese away for questioning, or worse. So we sent them to the wrong ward. That gave us time to move the man and hide him.

We know that many millions of Chinese were murdered, raped and tortured. This happened in Tsinan, just as it did in many other regions as the Japanese penetrated further into the south. It was easier to kill than to take prisoners. Women were commonly raped before they were killed. These daily occurrences were well documented by other missionaries.

I have been speaking to Chinese families from the Shandong (then Shantung) province who were living in the Tsinan area at the time. Generations later there is still so much resentment towards the Japanese. There is great sadness that while the genocide and atrocities that took place during this period were on a scale far larger than anything taking place in Europe, these events have been largely overlooked by history. Particularly in North China, almost every family today has stories of tragedy and loss. I had lunch one afternoon in Tsinan with a woman whose father, Mr Yuan, had only survived the onslaught by some miracle. He told her of many of the terrible things he had seen: how he watched Japanese on horseback chasing down his friends and neighbours, Chinese civilians, as they tried to flee, herding them like animals then beheading them without even dismounting, leaving the bodies behind as they chased down the next group. They wiped out whole villages and he was one of the lucky few in his village to escape.

Another man, Mr Li, whose grandson I also spoke to, was stabbed in the stomach by a Japanese soldier with a bayonet, and left to die like so many others. Somehow he lived, and would show his grandchildren the scars to remind them of a pain that always ran much deeper than the flesh. The current generations are saddened to see their survivors now dying in their old age with still no acknowledgment from the Japanese, who they feel would prefer to rewrite their history than heal this relationship. In Japan I found that this was a much more difficult topic to discuss. The younger people will speak of the 'incident' and do so with a sense of deep regret. The memories are a source of great pain for their surviving elders, and this is something not discussed out of respect for these elders. The young generations would prefer to look to the future, hoping that time will heal these wounds.

愛

The Japanese looted the few valuables the Chinese possessed. Chinese peasants would bury their precious possessions in the hope that they might still be there when they retuned from hiding. Like so many, when Mr Yuan escaped, he hid in the hills for weeks at a time, close to starvation. Sadly, when he returned there was nothing left. Their village was burned to nothing and there were only holes in the ground where their possessions had been once buried. They literally had nothing.

Monica never spoke of the atrocities she must have both witnessed and heard of during this time. This may partly have been because she blocked out these memories for many years to follow, with no wish to relive them or bring them back to life. As with many people in these situations, she became adept at building walls around difficult memories to preserve her reality. Monica said that for a time, even if she tried, she could simply not recall what happened. Her memory of these things just seemed to be blank. From a woman with an infallible memory for detail, this implied that deeply disturbing things were there to be forgotten. It was not until much later in her life that the integrity of these barriers seemed to falter. After a time, she said that some of the forgotten memories had started to creep back in and she clearly found them extremely distressing. But still she did not speak of it. In a moment of quiet confidence shortly before she died, she said to my husband Craig that she had written all these memories down and then burned them. She did this to destroy them and break their spell over her. Once she had done this she said she never needed to think of them again. She never did speak of them. We will never know.

With the war raging around them, for the sake of her new family Monica managed to somehow shelter – at least for a time – from a reality that was dreadful for so many. She tried hard to maintain her respect for both the Japanese and the Chinese, although her personal allegiances clearly lay with the latter. When she wrote to her family during this period, she always used a positive spin to avoid worrying her:

> China is always in such an unsettled state that the only thing to do is to carry on in a normal way. And so living in a very abnormal environment we are probably managing to live much more normal lives than you are.[63]

Fortunately, because Monica and Stanley were important for the provision of medical care to their soldiers, their personal treatment by the Japanese seems to have been fairly good. There was also some safety in numbers working with the many other international doctors.

> the Japanese were generally good to us, because they needed treatment. And treat them we did. We saw some pretty horrible things. A lot of people were shot. We had to be friendly enough to the Japanese to get away with things, yet not so friendly that you became an enemy to the Chinese.[64]

It was a fine line. Showing deference and respect to the Japanese was the only way to survive. But they could only hope this did not alienate the Chinese.

On the whole, if you were nice to the Japanese, they would be nice back. It was very important to be polite. I don't think a lot of the outsiders realised how important politeness is to the Eastern races. We knew that you should always bow to them. Always. They would bow back. It was important to acknowledge them.

At this stage, the Japanese were not at war with the Allies, and the British were still bystanders to the Chinese–Japanese conflict. As Monica recently recalled:

We were still free. Completely free really. But our Chinese servants weren't free. They were under Japanese control. If they went out on the streets, they could be stopped by the Japanese at any time and asked to sweep the streets, instead of doing our shopping!

The Japanese could clearly be a major inconvenience on shopping day. I always enjoyed Monica's sense of humour, and I do not think that in this comment she was in any way belittling the Chinese struggle. The plight of the Chinese touched her and Stanley deeply, and it was easier for her to recall an interrupted shopping errand than a more murderous end to events.

At the time, Monica was frightened by the Japanese and all they had done, and did not have many kind words to say. But nearly seventy years later, her views of the Japanese invaders had mellowed somewhat, despite the brutal acts she must have remembered. The Japanese had been trained as warriors from early childhood to believe in their racial superiority and unquestioningly follow their emperor and commanders. Many were very young and had no grasp of the political situation.

Many of them were still not much more than children. It is important to remember that they had come to China without their wives or families. They probably came without fully understanding what they were doing, as so often seems to happen in war. They may even have been told that they were needed, such as to help China against the Communists and help with other problems. Then they arrive and discover what they are the enemy.

This is a surprisingly sympathetic view of an army that killed, raped, destroyed and set cities on fire. In later life she chose to see them as individuals rather than a collective evil. Most Chinese people of a similar age are not so understanding.

No matter how we see it, terror had invaded China. But Monica and Stanley remained in Tsinan to continue their work, and Monica prepared to have her first baby, my father David.

Cheeloo Hospital

Within a week of their arrival, Stanley and Monica had begun their work in earnest and were glad to be immersed in the daily life of the hospital. In the outpatient section alone they were seeing 5,000 patients per month. This was astounding for such a relatively small staff.

On Monday there was a big welcome at the hospital and the official opening of the new nursing and technical school. Stanley and I were introduced and welcomed and we got up and bowed in reply. It was a big meeting and was held in the outpatients' room.

Since then, we have been very busy at the hospital. I have been doing ward rounds and outpatients every day and Stanley has been delivered into the mysteries of hospital organisation. It has been a heavy week for us. We have to make a three mile journey by rickshaw to get to the hospital and the roads are very rough. We have not even had time to get home for our midday meals, so we had it at the homes of Dr Shields or Dr Ingle who live by the hospital. They are both surgeons and need to live inside the city gate, close to the hospital, for emergencies. I will have to move to stay with them close to when my baby is due so that we can get to the hospital in the night if we have to!

I work 'full-time' when the city gate is open and 'no-time' when it is closed!

How long this freedom will last we do not know, but we just
take what comes and are grateful if the Mighty only gives us a few
crumbs. We at last have had the opportunity to work and it has made
all the difference to us both. Having nothing to do is more depressing
and demoralising. Now in spite of everything we are happy as we can
be. We have not got as much time to be worrying about the political
situation all day, and that is mighty good as such thoughts are enough
to send anyone crazy these days![65]

Monica found that she was gradually able to understand her patients more and more. There was no social security or free health care, but everything had to be paid for somehow. In order to rationalise its cost and cover its budgets, the hospital divided its wards into first-, second- and third-class areas and charged patients accordingly. Third class only cost 7 pence a day. It was an open ward and patients only received basic cereal to eat. The other classes received a bit of meat and more variety in their food. In second class there were two beds, and first class was a private room that cost 10 shillings a day. In very poor and needy cases, money could be drawn from the Samaritan fund, for which they had regular collections. They had several full-time social-services people on the hospital staff who would work out how much each patient could afford and how to help with the costs.

The patients we get in our department are also varied but a large
proportion of the outpatients are young prostitutes of about sixteen
or seventeen years old. They come in for a twice-weekly application of
medicine for gonorrhoea, so we get to know them quite well. They are
very clean, pretty, intelligent girls whom it is a pleasure to deal with.

184

We then see the same class of girls when they are older, about twenty years, because of sterility. By that time they are married, but we think that as prostitutes they must have used some method to prevent conception, which also causes arrest in sexual development as these girls seem to have quite infantile organs. My Chinese is not good enough yet to ask them what they use.[66]

In response to her father's questions about all this, in subsequent letters Monica explained that the prostitutes did not come on their own as isolated cases, but that they were part of a licensed prostitute home, and that they were sent by the Prostitute Control Bureau, although Monica did not fully understand what that was, or what exactly it was controlling. The girls were sold to this society when they were very tiny. Many came from South China. They were apparently well looked after, well dressed and had plenty of freedom. They were educated in the arts of singing, dancing, conversation and hostessing, so that by the age of sixteen they were singularly attractive not only in appearance but also in accomplishment. They would go out at night to regular homes and often see the same man. It was quite common for them to eventually marry the man that they had been with regularly, and they would seem quite happy about it. The hospital mission staff sometimes found it difficult to know their responsibility. But although they could not encourage this organisation, they could also not let the girls suffer from infection.

The only saving grace is to see how happy and well treated the girls are. Yes, there is a lot of venereal disease in China. But I don't think this is much different from England, only here it is not kept secret!

Stanley was also settling into his new role. Although it was not what he had planned, he took the opportunity enthusiastically and was grateful to be in a position to help so many people. As he became busier, he had less time to contribute to the letters home. Monica continued to write most of their letters, with footnotes from Stanley at the end:

> I am getting used to my new position as Superintendent of the hospital. It is going to be quite a bit of work and plenty of responsibility. Later on I also hope to do some research as well. In my rush to get home yesterday to see my sweet wife I forgot my pen, so I am having to make do with Monica's.

But it was impossible not to worry about news from Europe, vague and unclear as it was. They had not had any newspapers in Tsinan for over a month and the only news came through on the wireless, but few people had one of those. They relied on their friends the Stanleys and the Lairs, who had radio sets that could pick up signals without too much interference. They would sometimes visit in the evenings for a meal, and then listen to the midday news from London, which was eight hours behind.

> These days are still anxious for us, and are likely to be until we hear news of the European war situation. If England fights we rather wonder what will happen to us. We may be enlisted of course, or we may be left where we are. All we can do is hope that war will not break out in Europe, and that we shall have a more peaceful time in the years to come.

As the weeks passed, Monica found herself alone more often in the evenings as Stanley became occupied by committee meetings and official duties that would bring him home quite late. But as Monica said, 'In China, one quickly learns the art of patience and waiting'. She gradually got involved with more of the activities on the campus and, among other things, became games mistress at the Foreign School and secretary of the Literary Society.

Stanley quickly learned that he had to be on the correct side of the city wall before the nearest gate closed at 6pm. Otherwise he had to make a slow and tedious three-mile detour by rickshaw to the next gate, which then closed by 9pm. If he missed that, or found an uncooperative guard, it meant a night at the hospital. He would have to spend a lot of time persuading the guard to open the gate and move the barbed-wire entanglements to let him pass. He described some of the kinder guards as 'the decent strangers'. They initially used Chinese to converse, but over the years Stanley also learned Japanese, and could speak to the guards in their native tongue. The kind ones would usually let him pass eventually, and they would bow deeply to each other in mutual respect at parting. Later, he bought Gordon King's bicycle when Gordon left, which saved on rickshaw fares. It was a quicker, but rather bumpy ride! They now realised that the soldiers must have made special allowances in permitting them through at midnight on the night of their first arrival.

When he was home in the evenings they would spend their time in the study together, with Stanley working on hospital business and Monica knitting or sewing.

Stanley is getting even busier, but he looks happier and he will soon have the full responsibility when Gordon King leaves here in November to be appointed Professor of Obstetrics and Gynaecology at Hong Kong

University. The British Mission Society are now refusing to let wives and children return to the field. The result is the loss of many of the best missionaries in China. The first thing Gordon did when he heard was to cable his wife and three children in England to set sail.

This will also mean that I am 'second' in the department of Obstetrics and Gynaecology here, as only Dr Gell and I are qualified to do it. I am getting the run of things very quickly.

They heard from other mission friends whose wives were on furlough or in safe zones, all trying to join their husbands in the field before they could be ordered home.

As her girth increased, Monica was concerned that she did not have a liberty bodice. I have never seen one, but I am told that this is a vest that laces down the front.

I somehow or other have landed in China without a single garment resembling a liberty bodice or a corselette, so I have nothing but roll-ons or suspender belts to keep my stockings up. The latter garment is a bit uncomfortable to wear as their efficiency depends on them being tight around the waist. Today I started the eighteenth week. In a few weeks I will have to discard them and I've nothing to take their place. I cut up one of Stanley's white overalls the other day and I am making myself a kind of liberty bodice. It will be serviceable enough but looks anything but beautiful. I wonder if you could send out a pattern book of maternity wear?[67]

She added a request for some magazines that might help in her motherhood, including *Mother and Home*, *Housekeeping*, *Woman and Home*, *Woman and Beauty* and *Parents and Strand*, knowing that they might take some months to arrive.

They entertained quite a lot, and went to a few lavish dinner parties, but one of Monica's favourite things was to have waffle breakfasts with Nunnie (Miss Nunn) from upstairs. They generally ate very well.

Food is much better than in England. We can get meat and fish the same, but the abundance of vegetables and fruit makes all the difference. The cost of vegetables is next to nothing. And everything always seems in season. Egg are 75 for a shilling so we eat as many as we like. Cereals are plentiful but have gone up in price, so the poorest people are suffering.

Coal is gradually coming down in price and we hope that by winter time we will be alright. There is very little wood in China so we can't use that instead, although we may have to cut down two of our own trees for fuel.[68]

Europe had reached crisis, and they became more concerned for the repercussions, but still nothing was clear. They were growing used to seeing and dealing with the Japanese, but this fine balance might slip again depending on Japan's allegiances in Europe.

These last few days we have been even more worried about the conditions in Europe and the possibility of war. We wonder if Japan will remain neutral and concentrate on winning the battle with China, or whether she will fight Britain. If she is wise she will remain neutral, and so achieve by peaceful means what might be difficult by war. One wonders much of the future, and we pray that Europe will be able to settle this issue without wastage of life. But we have had a wonderful

189

year of marriage and hope that we will be allowed to continue useful work and useful lives.[49]

By mid–October 1938 they had received a letter from Stanley's brother Malcolm with more details on what he knew of the European problems.

> It was a great relief to hear war is over for the time being. We are all proud of Chamberlain, who we thought was a poor fool before. But it is still clear that the nations of Europe still face a terrible crisis. I am no longer a pacifist. I am willing to fight for a just cause. But that might not solve the problems in Europe.
>
> Out here we see the effects of these old methods of solving problems. Whichever side wins the victors may be no better off than the conquered. It will take a generation to build up what is lost on both sides. And many generations to heal the hatred that has been born on both sides.[69]

How true that turned out to be. China and Japan have rebuilt themselves, and the hatred may have mellowed to deep resentment, but it is still there, however hidden it may be, in hearts of the older generations.

The cold weather would soon be starting and it would cost £1 per week to keep the house warm. But they had stocked up on most supplies and looked set for the winter. Christmas cards had to be sent in October if there was any hope of them arriving on time. Stanley spent his spare time preparing the house for winter, mending windows and frames. Even the parquet floors would shrink with extremes of temperature in winter.

Monica's pregnancy progressed, and life was much easier than it ever would have been had they been in England. Having said that, Mrs Ma, who was only thirty years old, was pregnant once again. She went into labour on 21 October. The whole thing was all over in forty-five minutes, and with hardly a sound, she gave birth to her fourth baby boy. Mrs Ma remained in the hospital for two weeks after the birth of her baby, although there did not seem to be any complications. The Ma family were Christians but they still observed Chinese customs, so Mrs Ma and her baby had to remain indoors for a month. During that time a mother was not permitted to cook or draw water, and all males, except the father, were prohibited from seeing the baby. Females could visit as they pleased, but even the brothers were not permitted to enter. On the twelfth day neighbours and friends brought gifts for the baby and received food in return.

> We also discovered yesterday that Ma and Lai Hsi are spirit brothers. Before they were Christian they worked together and became such great friends that they went to the Spirit of Ma's ancestors and Lai Hsi was made Ma's brother and Ma's mother became Lai Hsi's mother, and so on. Now although they are Christian they still believe in the strength of this bond. In fact it works so well that Stanley is thinking of putting 'Only Spirit brothers need apply' on the notices of employment! The Chinese have so many fine customs and we are only too glad for them to keep them.[70]

When the time came to celebrate the servants' new baby, Mr Ma asked for permission to have a party for his friends in their quarters. He asked if it was all right to make a bit of noise and keep the fires burning longer than usual to cook their food. The

Mas were so grateful that in return they offered to make a free meal. For lunch the next day Monica and Stanley were treated to a Chinese feast and loved it.

Monica's body was also rapidly expanding. She developed anaemia, for which she was prescribed 'massive doses of Bland's pills [an iron supplement] for a week'. The baby was kicking, and all seemed well as she continued to work.

They were also very pleased to get a letter from Monica's grandmother (Allen's mother) in Australia telling Monica she was very proud of their mission work in China. Frances was now eighty-seven and still walking to church every Sunday. Monica had not seen her Grandma Job since she left Australia as a little girl. She had always hoped she might see her again before she died, but that did not seem likely now.

Marriage of Mr Stanley L. Prescott and Dr Monica Job, 15 September 1937, English Methodist Church, Hong Kong.

ABOVE Monica (on her father's knee) with her sister (Hope) seated and parents Allen and Ethel Job, New Zealand, c. 1917.

BELOW LEFT Monica (left) and sister Hope outside their home in Manchester, c. 1928.
BELOW RIGHT Monica (on far right) with friends at Sunday School, 1926.

LEFT Stanley (on the floor) with his brothers John (seated), Malcolm and parents Jack and Jessie Prescott, 1918.

BELOW LEFT Prescott's Pharmacy by Royal Appointment, John 'Jack' Prescott on left, c. 1935.

BELOW RIGHT Stanley Lewis Prescott (right) and John Lamplugh Prescott, c. 1918.

LEFT Stanley at Lancashire College, University of Manchester, 1935.

RIGHT Monica graduating from medicine, University of Manchester, 1937.

ABOVE Monica with the Prescott family in 1936 before Stanley's departure for China.
l-r: John, Jessie, Stanley, Monica, Malcolm and Jack Prescott.

BELOW Monica and best friend Muriel Bennett celebrate graduation from medicine, 1937.
l-r: Monica's parents Allen and Ethel Job, Mr Bennett, Monica, Mrs Bennett, Muriel and
her friend Frank.

ABOVE Professor Stanley Prescott (indicated) seated next to (l-r) Dr Moss, Dr Gordon King and Professor Dingle with Chinese medical staff of Cheeloo University Hospital, Tsinan, China, 1936.

BELOW Monica, Hong Kong, 1937. The letter containing this photo arrived in England damaged and with a note indicating that the plane carrying it by airmail went down into the sea.

ABOVE Monica (under umbrella) at Peitaiho Beach, China, summer of 1938.

BELOW Monica (rear seat) with friends at Peitaiho Beach, China, 1938.

ABOVE Cheeloo University Campus, Tsinan, China, c. 1920 (postcard).

BELOW LEFT Medical School gates, Cheeloo University, Tsinan, China.
BELOW RIGHT Monica and Stanley, 1937.

ABOVE Cheeloo University campus gates, Tsinan, China, under Japanese occupation, 1939.

BELOW Wesley Bungalow, where Monica and Stanley lived on the Cheeloo University campus, Tsinan, China.

ABOVE LEFT Japanese soldiers at city gates, Tsinan, North China, 1939.
ABOVE RIGHT Stanley on the bike he bought from Dr Gordon King, 1939.

BELOW LEFT Stanley with Japanese soldiers inspecting Cheeloo University Hospital, 1938.
BELOW RIGHT TOP Camel train brings supplies, near Buddhist temple, North China.
BELOW RIGHT BOTTOM Christmas on the wards of Cheeloo Hospital.

ABOVE LEFT Stanley at Cheeloo University Hospital, Tsinan, China, some time in 1937–1942.
ABOVE RIGHT Cheeloo University students in the lab.

BELOW LEFT TOP Nurses off duty.
BELOW LEFT BOTTOM Operating theatre, Cheeloo Hospital.
BELOW RIGHT Children's section, Cheeloo Hospital.

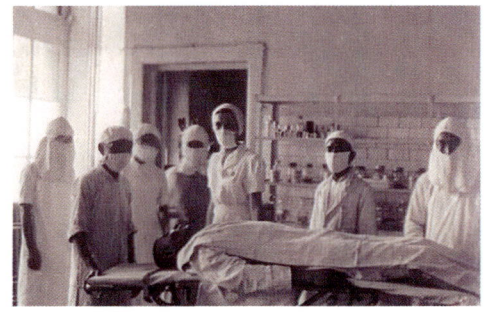

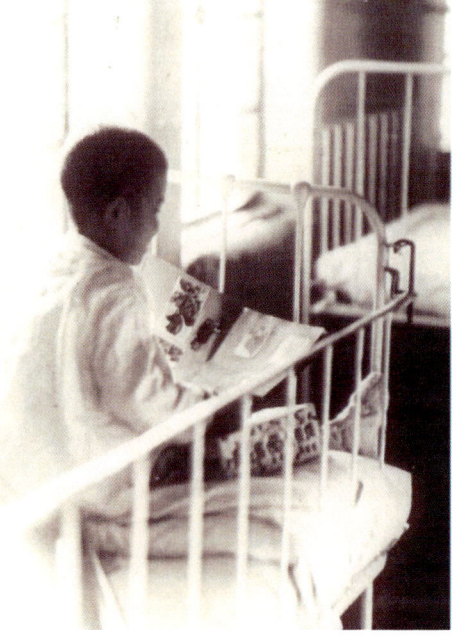

ABOVE LEFT Stanley as proud father of David, 1939.
ABOVE RIGHT David Prescott with some members of the Ma family, Tsinan, China, 1940.

BELOW LEFT Shih Ying (eldest daughter of Mr Ma) holding David, Tsinan, China, 1940.
BELOW RIGHT Stanley and Wang Ping (his Chinese language teacher) at Dr Smilies's house at Peitaiho Beach, China, 1938.

ABOVE LEFT Stanley with David, Wesley Bungalow, Tsinan, 1940.
ABOVE RIGHT Some members of the Ma family, Wesley Bungalow, Tsinan, c. 1940.

BELOW Winter 1940 outside Wesley Bungalow, Cheeloo campus, Tsinan.

一九四一年夏歡送普院長瑞桉回國紀念

ABOVE Professor Stanley Prescott (indicated), superintendent of Cheeloo University Hospital, with his staff, 1941.

BELOW Squadron leader Stanley Prescott (indicated) with Wilf Simmons to his left (later Foundation Professor of Physiology at UWA), Royal Australian Air Force, Flying Personnel Research Unit, 1946.

ABOVE The Lodge (Master's residence) where the family lived at Ormond College, Melbourne.

BELOW Monica and Stanley with their four children in Melbourne, c. 1952.
l–r: David, Monica, Margaret (front), Nigel, Stanley and Helen.

ABOVE Academic procession through Victoria Square, Perth, at the opening of the Medical school of UWA, 1956.

BELOW Premier Albert Hawke speaks at the opening of the medical school.

ABOVE Vice-Chancellor Stanley Prescott, Pro-Chancellor T. L. Robertson and Joseph Griffith, administrator at Royal Perth Hospital. The school is open and students are awaited.

BELOW LEFT Her Majesty The Queen with Chancellor E. W. Gillett (foreground), Vice-Chancellor Stanley Prescott and His Royal Highness The Duke of Edinburgh (rear). Royal visit to Perth, 1954.

BELOW RIGHT Vice-Chancellor Stanley Prescott with His Royal Highness The Duke of Edinburgh at UWA on the royal visit to Perth, 1954.

ABOVE LEFT The Prescotts at home, c. 1961.
l-r: Nigel, Helen, Stanley, Monica, David and Margaret.
ABOVE RIGHT David Prescott, c. 1962.

BELOW LEFT Monica and Stanley (right) with son David Prescott and his new wife, Jan, 1963.
BELOW RIGHT Sir Stanley Prescott at Buckingham Palace to receive his knighthood, with mother, Jessie Prescott (left), and Lady Monica (right), 1965.

ABOVE Prescotts relax at home in Thomas Street, Nedlands.
l–r: Monica, Jan, Margaret (behind), Susan (foreground), Helen (behind) and Stanley, c. 1965.

BELOW LEFT TOP The Prescotts and the Kings return to Hong Kong, c. 1962.
l–r: Stanley Prescott, Mary King, Monica Prescott, Gordon King.
BELOW LEFT BOTTOM Stanley (retired) with eldest grandchild, Susan, c. 1974.
BELOW RIGHT Monica nursing her first grandchild, Susan Prescott (b. 1964), with Jan
Prescott (seated) and Helen Prescott.

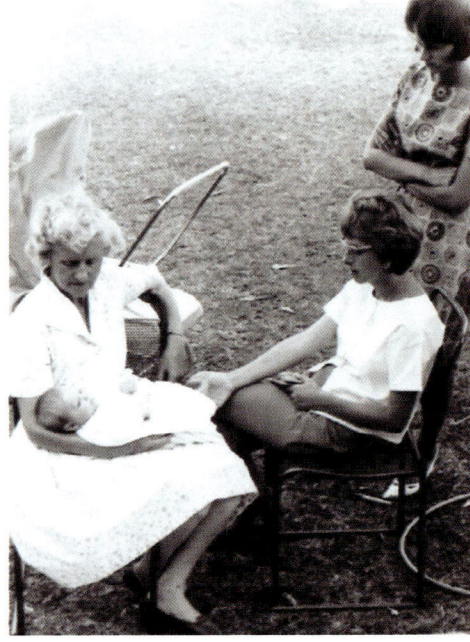

Portrait of Sir Stanley Prescott (hangs in the Vice-Chancellery at The University of Western Australia).

LEFT '*In mansuetudine sapientiae:* gentleness is the hallmark of wisdom'. A very apt description of Stanley on the family coat of arms.

BELOW Sir Robert Menzies, former prime minister, receives an honorary doctorate at UWA. Behind him seated are Chancellor Sir Alexander Reid (left) and Vice-Chancellor Sir Stanley Prescott (right), 1964.

RIGHT Monica at her granddaughter Susan's PhD graduation, with Jan and David Prescott, 2000.

BELOW Marriage of Susan Prescott and Craig Nunn, 2003. l–r, front: David and Jan Prescott, Craig Nunn, Elliott Nunn (aged seven), Susan Prescott and Monica Prescott; behind: Val and Nigel Prescott, Stephen and Emma Prescott.

LEFT Monica with eldest grandson Stephen Prescott (David's son).

BELOW Monica's extended family, 1999, at the wedding of her granddaughter Diana Prescott to Glenn Kelley. l–r: Margaret Peace (nee Prescott), Jasper Silver (behind), Helen Silver (nee Prescott), Paul Silver, Susan Prescott, Aaron Silver (behind with friend), Monica Prescott, Valerie Prescott, Glenn Kelley (groom), Diana Kelley (nee Prescott, bride), Nigel Prescott, Stephen Prescott (behind), Elizabeth Prescott-Price, Anthony Price, David Prescott (behind), Jan Prescott, Raymond Sebo, Christine Sebo, David Sebo and Suzanne Sebo.

Lady Prescott, aged 90, in 2003. Photograph taken at St Catherine's College.

Monica's first winter in North China

The autumn colours had come by November and the winter flowers began to open as the cool air crept in. They got a better view of the mountains as the leaves fell. Monica found it invigorating and very beautiful. The patients at the leper hospital grew flowers to sell, so she went to visit and to buy their lovely chrysanthemums. At Wesley Bungalow, they busied themselves preparing the house before the bitter cold was upon them.

Yesterday we put our stoves up for winter, but we have not lit them yet. I am not sure you understand what sort of stoves we have out here. They are made of porcelain and they can be placed anywhere in a room and from there a six inch pipe is connected across the room to a hole in the chimney, so the chimney is still free for a fire as well if we want one. We have several, so we can put the heat on wherever we like. We are also taking the mosquito netting down and putting up the double windows.

I do wish everyone could come and enjoy the goodwill and happiness that this bright sunshine and the cool nip in the air instils into everyone here. It is impossible to be dull or lazy. Everybody is positively aglow, and Christmas will be here before we know it.

Winter set in quickly and Chinese people everywhere started wearing their beautiful padded quilted jackets.

If the stages of life are comparable to the seasons of the year, I shall greatly enjoy the winter of old age.[71]

And so she did! Always with the same enthusiasm and wonder.

Within a week it has turned to winter and of all of the seasons, I think it is giving me the greatest thrill. I have just come back from a half-hour's brisk walk around the campus and felt as I walked that there was nothing more to be desired of life. Perhaps my only wish is that everyone else could have the same experience. It is just grand. The sky is ablaze with sunshine, the air cold and dry, your breath turning to steam as the leaves fall faster than snow.

The Chinese servants, wives and children were all out playing in the sunshine, their persons being almost invisible in a wrapping of padded garments. Shih Ying (Ma's eldest daughter) and her two younger brothers were playing in the field opposite our house. The little ones are so covered with padding that they have to hold their arms straight out. The men servants are all out with Chinese brooms, sweeping leaves into sacks to be used as winter fuel. They have all woken up from the sleep of hot summer. And let out their energy as cheery greetings to all who pass by.

I have come back with pink cheeks and burning hands into a room flooded with sunlight and gay with flowers and completely enjoying the new scene. The acacia trees are cut down for fuel and now straight in front of this room, only a few a miles away rise the mountains of Shantung. They are big, black and austere making a lovely silhouette against the blue sky. Half way up the mountains is a Chinese Temple which we can see quite clearly. Beyond our garden is a field of winter wheat still green and the houses of the experimental farmer people with their huge sacks of hay are also in sight.

As you can imagine, there are only sprawling city buildings visible from that spot now. But I was pleased to see that the rest of campus is still quite preserved, much as Monica had described it.

Monica was enjoying the winter routine. At 6.30 in the morning she would wake to hear Lai Hsi stoking the fires and making a terrible racket. But she would enjoy lying in bed waiting for the house to warm. Stanley would rise at about 7.15 when the sun was just climbing above the hills. After he had showered, Monica would join him at 7.30 for a 'mighty breakfast'. She was certainly eating well and gaining plenty of weight.

We bought seven tons of coal this week, thinking it was wise to get it while the going was good. It was a big layout (of $210 or £14). But it will last the winter. We also bought 200 pounds of potatoes but that was only 8 shillings! We still have to order butter from Tientsin.

While I am writing this Lsi Hsi is plugging the windows with cotton wool so that the cold January winds will not get in.[72]

There was a sad farewell for Gordon King as he left in early November, but they were happy to know that he would be reunited with this wife and children, who were travelling to meet him in Hong Kong. Their paths would later cross many times, but in 1938 no one was ever sure when they might meet again.

Stanley was busier than ever after Gordon King's departure. Gordon left before he had time to prepare the annual report for.

the previous year, so this fell to Stanley, who was often working late and would give Monica 'piles of statistics' to help with on her evenings alone.

> Stanley is still up to his eyes on the hospital report. We have spent every night this week delving into the statistics. He is out at a committee meeting again now, so I am alone again.
>
> He is doing his job so efficiently that he has received praise from all sides. The Chinese staff look upon him as an infant prodigy. Age means a lot to the Chinese and they think that if Stanley, who is so young, has been appointed to this big task he must be very unique.[73]

Monica was also busy in the hospital. She said they seemed to be having a 'run of cancers' in the gynaecology clinic, which was odd. There were also a lot of inpatients, and the numbers were growing. By early December it was the busiest they had ever known. Stanley was doing what he could to increase the capacity of the hospital in general and the efficiency of all its services.

> We have had to open another ward at the hospital, but today that is already full again. So once more I am hard at work trying to arrange more accommodation. Things are at last getting back to normal as far as the hospital is concerned. But it all means more work for the already hard worked Superintendent. I have to settle disputes between staff and between departments.
>
> The full burden of responsibility falls on my shoulders these days. My job is most varied. I have to deal with the entire personnel of the hospital, professional, non-professional, Chinese and foreign; sooth their troubles and help them work together; decide their salaries and wages;

196

interview applicants for jobs; and sack those that need it; encourage when necessary and be cross when necessary. I have to supervise all admissions to hospital wards and the discharge of patients; see that all medical records are kept properly and that all the statistics are in order. Quite a responsibility for my young shoulders. The advantage of the job is that I do the thinking and get someone else to do the work for me. And it is interesting. Everyone is cooperating with me and the impression I get from various comments it that I am making a real success of it.

My knowledge of pharmacy, pharmacology and something of medicine are all necessary and Chinese is a first essential. If I had not been good at the language I could not have done it.

Several members of staff have passed on very complimentary remarks about my job so far.

The strange thing is that people old enough to be my father come to me for help and advice, Chinese and foreigners alike.[74]

Stanley restructured a number of departments and developed a centralised and coordinated departmental system. He was chairman of many hospital committees and was responsible for purchasing all supplies. He had to oversee all medical staff, the School of Nursing, surgical services, accounting, business management, pharmacy, laboratory services, social services, laundry, radiology, building works, kitchen and other support staff. He was still not even thirty. I love his sense of humour about his authority:

Between committee meetings I am supreme dictator and have final jurisdiction over all hospital matters!

197

As time passed they developed an easier working relationship with the Japanese, who had a vested interest in keeping the hospital functioning.

> We are getting no interference at the moment. Perhaps the Japanese have at last realised that as far as our work goes we are absolutely neutral, and as foreigners we cannot and do not wish to take sides. While we are living here the History of Asia is being made and the Far East is changing before our eyes. The future may be shaped and we are still waiting to see what it will be. Who can tell?

They were all looking forward to Christmas, but one of their friends, Mrs Newton, the Reverend Newton's wife, had some bad news. She had become unwell soon after she married and had been confined to bed for three months for suspected tuberculosis. Her x-rays came back positive again and she was confined for another three months. This meant she had been in bed for virtually the whole time she had been married, and had been advised against travel home until her health had improved. Monica was careful not to visit.

After Gordon King left they also spent more time with another, older Canadian couple, Reverend and Mrs Ross, who had been there since 1903 and had no intention of ever leaving China. Reverend Ross had served as an interpreter during the Great War. They were part of the United Church of Canada.

> In their mission they have to work until they have done forty years or until they reach the age of seventy. So by that time of course they have become so much a part of China that they have no desire to return.

There was an outbreak of influenza just before Christmas, which heavily depleted the medical staff and placed an even greater strain on the hospital. It also exaggerated some emerging divisions among the mission staff. One of the general physicians was unhappy because he had to cover more work than usual. They had known him in Twickenham in England many years ago, and Monica felt that he had changed and become embittered since they first knew him. To make matters worse he was also invalided much of the time. He had a gastric ulcer and generally had to rest every afternoon.

The stress of living under the Japanese was splitting the foreign community into two, as Monica described:

> Our situation has divided people. Firstly, those who feel their life's work has been wrecked and who can only speak of the days that were. Secondly, those that forget the past and start from scratch with what we have and hope for the best. Dr Mosse is the leader of the former group. He has become like an old man and happiness and hope have left him. Dr Shields is a bit like that too. They are almost rude to the invaders saying that they represent what is wrong and therefore cannot be friends. Most of the others are in the second group, as are we, and try to show friendship and respect. Although we despise what they represent we still respect the individual. Yes, some of them have behaved terribly, but that is the fault of war. Their leaders need throttling, but many of the others need pity.[75]

Monica and Mrs Ingle found a German shop that sold Christmas decorations. They were very expensive, but celebrating Christmas now seemed even more important than in peace time. They even found a box of blue and gold Christmas crackers.

Monica got four small Christmas trees, and went to the Chinese shops to get presents for all the servants and their children. The shops were in the centre of Tsinan, all surrounding the natural hot springs. The water was steaming in the cold winter air. In modern-day Jinan, there is a large civic garden with monuments and statues on this site. There are no traces of the city wall, which was torn down long ago by the Communists. But still, in the congestion of the large choking city, there is sanctuary in these beautiful Chinese gardens. The local people come and sit by the water and collect it in large bottles for its healing properties.

The Christmas plum puddings were ready. The goose was prepared. The floors polished. The tree in place. Everything was ready for their Christmas guests. When they woke on Wednesday 21 December to a blanket of snow on the ground, it all seemed complete. On Friday there was a big party for all the hospital staff and their children, Chinese and foreign.

Saturday, Christmas Eve, was the most exciting day of all. It was a general holiday and a day for giving and receiving gifts. We, being new arrivals expected nothing but got the surprise of our lives. From breakfast time onwards our boys did practically nothing but bring gifts into us and we sat with amazed faces receiving them. There were plants from hospital employees, Chinese cakes, Chinese pictures, toffees made by people on campus, boxes of fudge and chocolate, fancy biscuits, little lavender bags made by some of the small children, boxes of dates and balls of wool. The gifts were almost countless and the end of our rooms looked like a flower garden. We now have eighteen lovely pot plants in the house. The pots all covered with all colours of crinkle paper. Christmas cards also poured in and filled every available space overflowing into the bedroom as well. It was an unforgettable day!

In the evening we wrapped up the presents for Lai Hsi, Mr and Mrs Ma and all of their children ready for Christmas morning. We also had extra money for them.

We had been asleep for several hours that night when in our dreams we heard the distant voices singing the First Noel and it was with unspeakable joy that our dreams turned into reality as we woke to hear the sweet voices of the Chinese girl theological students. It was just midnight, so as they sang, Christmas Day began. And I fell asleep again to the sound of Silent Night.[76]

They celebrated Christmas morning with their Chinese family, exchanging gifts and having a wonderful breakfast together. The Chinese went off later for their own celebrations, and Monica and Stanley had a full table of guests for lunch, including Dr and Mrs Ingle, Dr and Mrs Shields and Dr Gell among others.

Later, there were also several parties for hundreds of the poorer people connected with the churches of Tsinan, with a hot meal for everybody. There were over 400 children at one of these. They shared in the meal and the fellowship and sang Christmas carols. Mr Newton preached on the Christmas spirit and Monica and Stanley enjoyed a walk around the campus before a quiet evening together.

In England, Stanley's parents heard his brother John Prescott broadcast on the BBC. Monica and Stanley were still hoping that he might be one of the empire broadcasters, and that they might yet hear his voice all the way away in China! It seemed like that could be a miracle.

Although it was the holidays, the hospital staff were still on duty, including Stanley, for anything that needed to be attended to. The holidays of Christmas and New Year's Day were generally worked as Sundays, with attendance at the hospital in the mornings and the aim of being home for lunch.

Monica also continued to work, helping Dr Gell who was run off her feet. But as her pregnancy progressed she found that she was increasingly tired at the end of each afternoon. She was working every day, and often by herself in the outpatient section if Dr Gell was called to a delivery. It was becoming more and more exhausting. They normally also had a Chinese doctor helping, but she was away.

Stanley had some problems of his own. The community of fifty or so foreign families was small, and this put him in a difficult position sometimes when problems arose and he needed to point out shortcomings or make changes. While most of his staff worked well and competently as individuals, concepts of teamwork and integration were lacking.

Stanley is rapidly earning a name for himself and somehow has the exceptional gift of being able to tell people off who are older than him without exciting a storm. He is a real Jack-of-all-trades these days and apart from Superintendent he is also the general advisor on all pharmaceutical problems. He needs a lot of patience because most of the doctors are old and set, and while well-meaning they are as stubborn as mules. They all work well separately but have no idea of the workings of a hospital. One of the American woman doctors will spend the whole day on one case. She puts endless effort into it and writes reams and reams of notes, but in a hospital with hundreds of patients all waiting, it just doesn't work. Dr Greene the radiologist is nothing less than a genius, although at thirty-four he is as slow as a man of seventy, and if you ask him about a case, he keeps you talking for a least an hour. As I mentioned Dr Mosse had an ulcer, and Dr Gault has heart trouble. Dr Scott has tuberculosis in the hip and is quite lame. Dr Ingle and Dr Wolfe are almost deaf. The matron, Miss Wilson is almost sixty and can only walk very slowly. They are all fine people, with great personalities and excellent qualifications, but if an urgent call is made some of them cannot get there quickly. Dr Gell and Dr Ingle are Trojans, but both have far too much to do.[77]

Stanley had just recruited another young doctor who would be joining them soon. Apart from Monica, Dr Godfrey Gale would be the only other staff member younger than Stanley. Dr Gale had also come from England with the LMS (London Mission Society). They had met him some months earlier at the Peking Language School when he was still mastering the language. Although there were stories of others wanting to come out to help in the mission hospitals, their various organisations made it difficult for them:

Yesterday I had a letter from Nancy and David Francis. They have been moved from Karim Nagar and she has come up against a group of colleagues who won't let her enter their hospital. Nancy has done medical work in India for three years and she says it is awful to have to stand by. Women missionaries can be very cruel at times. She and her husband will have to go touring by themselves and do medical work on their own in the villages.[78]

Meanwhile, there was also the possibility that the LMS would move Stanley again. Now that he was settled and really starting to make ground, this seemed ridiculous. Monica was very reluctant. The principal of Yenching University had heard of Stanley's success already and was trying to persuade the LMS to move him to Yenching to set up a physiology department at the medical school. There were over 900 Chinese students enrolled there. They also wanted Monica there as the medical supervisor of all the women students and wives. Monica and Stanley were very flattered to be in demand, but were really hoping that this did not eventuate. They had no desire to leave Tsinan, but it was really up to the LMS. Like the Canadian couple, the Rosses, Monica and Stanley saw themselves spending the rest of their lives there, with the occasional furlough to visit family and friends in England.

We are even already dreading our holiday in the summer because it means leaving Tsinan again.

With Monica now more heavily pregnant, there was another good reason for them to stay where they were. She was finding it more tiring at work and started working part-time. On 19 January, Dr Gell palpated the baby in a breech position and 'turned' the baby successfully. Everything else appeared well. She was putting on weight nicely. This may have been partly the Christmas cakes as well. Ma had seen how much they enjoyed the cake at Christmas so he had continued to make them ever since!

She was still fit, running up the stairs two at a time, and hopping and skipping along the road; something she continued to do into her nineties. She was also busy making plans for how she might manage motherhood.

Yesterday I lined the baby basket with pink silk. If all goes well I'm not having an anaesthetic. I shall be in hospital for about ten days, during which time the cord will be off and the baby vaccinated. We do that on day four here. When I come home, Mrs Ma will help a bit. She will help with washing the nappies and I will do all of the ironing. Then when I am full of beans again she will be on duty for the baby in the afternoon while I resume work at the hospital.[56]

Busy as usual, all Stanley had to say at the end of Monica's letter was:

We are still here. I am doing all the work and Monica gets all the kicks!

In those times there was a belief that a strict feeding pattern in the first few days of life was important in setting the routine for the baby thereafter. They would use strict four-hourly feeds during the day and no feeds at night, even if the baby cried. They made an exception to this if the baby was of low birth weight. The attitude was 'a few days' discipline early on saves many days of trouble later on'. Certainly a different approach than most parents today would take. And I wonder if it was the reality or just the intention even back then!

For the summer, Monica planned to also take the Mas' eldest daughter, Shih Ying, with them to the beach. Shih Ying had never been on a train before and she was very excited to see the sea for the very first time. They were going to lose Lai Hsi soon. Dr Smilie would soon be returning from furlough and Lai Hsi would return to look after his house. They would be sad to see him leave, but Monica admitted that she was more fond of Ma Ru.

205

I don't know what we would do without Ma. He is just wonderful.[79]

It was still snowing heavily at night with glorious sunny days. Monica loved it. They continued entertaining, sometimes with quite large parties, such as the twenty people on Stanley's hospital committee. They also treasured their quiet evenings together. In her letters home Monica spoke of her love and appreciation of Stanley, of his patience, generosity and work around the house to help her.

He even holds the wool for me as I wind it!

Fortunately the cold did not last and it ended up being the warmest winter in years. With the horrendous poverty in the villages and less fuel than usual, things could have been more terrible.

They decided to test the Japanese by sending around advertisements that preliminary university courses would be starting in March to prepare for the main academic year.

It is an experiment and we don't know how it will be received by 'those who are mightier than ourselves', but we can only try and see. This is too good a place to keep closed.

The Japanese tolerated this but made sure that the plan did not proceed. Instead, they took an even greater interest in the running of the hospital and asked for regular inspections. Stanley found himself as tour guide on these occasions, conversing with the Japanese soldiers in a mixture of Chinese, Japanese and English.

The hospital was working to capacity. In January they had seen 6,039 outpatients, 500 more than before the war. Monica was no longer working but still attended some of the hospital education activities such as the regular 'Journal club', which she mentioned on 15 February was about 'the Streptocide drugs'.

> Stanley delivered his lecture to the Journal club on Friday and seemed to take the world by storm. He has had people coming in to congratulate him ever since. He really made a great impression. He is now getting his lecture ready for the Rotary Club where he is going to speak on 'Adaptability – The Essence of Life'. He really is clever.

In his 1939 report to the North China chairman, the president of the university, Dr Lair, praised Stanley saying:

> I am very happy indeed to send an informal statement from the station to your Mission as to the work of Mr Stanley Prescott. While I am not a medical man and cannot speak from a professional standpoint, I do want to express my hearty personal appreciation for the work which Mr Prescott has been doing since he took over the Superintendency of the University Hospital. He did so on short notice and with the benefit of only a very brief association with Dr King. Yet, in spite of the fact that this is a type of work for which he has not been trained, he has undertaken it with enthusiasm, with a vision of the possibilities, and with the attention to detail which none of his predecessors have been able to give. At the moment the hospital is the one department (of the University) that is functioning in an approximately normal manner and the position of hospital Superintendent is of the greatest importance.[80]

With less than a month to go before the baby was due, Monica prepared to leave her home. She had to spend the weeks before the delivery with friends inside the city wall to avoid being stranded outside the gates if she went into labour during the hours of curfew. During this time she arranged for the other half of their luggage, which was still stored in Tsientsin, to be finally brought home. She wrote as many letters home as possible, knowing that she would be soon otherwise occupied. Before the delivery a number of x-rays were taken of the baby, to determine the size. Alarmingly to us now, they took as many as possible so that the new radiologist could get experience. Stanley called it 'the pre-publication photograph'!

Having a baby in occupied China

Monica went into labour at 3am on 16 March 1939. After thirty-six hours she was 'nearing a state of collapse' and Stanley was also beside himself with worry. When there was no sign of progress Dr Gell called Dr Ingle to administer an anaesthetic while she delivered the baby by forceps. And so my father, David Lamplugh Prescott, was born.

> He came into the world at 4.52pm on March 17 and with wide-open eyes had a good look at everyone about him. He was a joy to behold with lovely features and big dark blue eyes, fine fair hair and a long straight strong body. He was put in a room at the end of the corridor and for the first two days lived happily on water. In between times he slept like a log. And now it is the fifth day, and anything more near perfection you could not have. He comes to me and Daddy, who nearly always comes to see him feed, at 6am, 10am, 2pm, 6pm and 10pm. He eats well for about half an hour then the nurse takes him away again and there is complete silence until about five minutes before the next feed is due. The nurses say he is so good that they haven't enough to do.
>
> Each day we look at him he just grows dearer to us. Soon we won't be able to describe him at all.[81]

The Chinese were very impressed that Monica delivered a son, proving herself worthy of such a husband.

We have risen greatly in the estimation of all!

Stanley was also rather pleased to have started another generation of Prescotts, especially the Lamplugh-Prescotts. Monica stayed in the hospital for almost two weeks before she made her way home to Wesley Bungalow. The staff showered them with gifts as they were leaving.

Today at 3pm Monica left the hospital and we came home. The nurses at the hospital presented him with a nice Chinese suit. The clerks and higher workers gave us a copper urn. The coolies presented us with a silver shield engraved with Chinese letters. These have a double meaning of a blessing to the family and that we are a blessing to the hospital. It is also engraved with the full names of seventy coolies. As you can see the advent of wee David has been such a big thing in all of our lives.

Dr Lair, the head of the University brought us home in his car so all was easy going. Wee David cried when he reached home because the car journey gave him 'hiccoughs', but he soon settled down. Our cook had the house looking all clean and bright. We had tea and then at 6pm I assisted Monica while she fed him, then we changed his napkin. He objected to this but is quite good, except for being sick all over his father's best suit and urinating all over the eiderdown. But he is a good little man and a real scientist having solved the problem of a dry climate most effectively. He is a barometer that is permanently set on 'wet and windy'!

Now we are back in our lovely home. David is sleeping, Monica is resting and I am thinking over the past, realising how richly we have been blessed.

Monica makes the most wonderful mother and it is a real joy to see them together, and to know that we three belong to each other.[82]

The doctors and academic staff at the hospital also gave them a framed embossed plaque that said in red Chinese characters 'Heaven's greatest gift, a son', which I believe David still has now. Their Chinese family, the Mas, also loved him, and he was often cared for by their eldest daughter, Shih Ying, who was around twelve years old when he was born. The Chinese called him *Da Wei*, meaning 'great protector'. David was baptised on Easter Sunday 1939 by Dr C. A. Stanley, using a pewter communion cup that Dr Stanley's own father had brought to China in 1882. There was standing room only.

With uncertain news from Europe, they had much else to occupy their minds. David brought them much joy, and Stanley's work increased further as he opened a new nursing home. There were over 120 seriously ill inpatients to look after and 400 outpatients to be seen each day. There was an outbreak of whooping cough and they had David vaccinated as quickly as possible with weekly injections over three successive weeks. Then they gave him cholera and typhoid vaccinations. With deaths among other mission children from dysentery, and no vaccinations for this, Monica remained very frightened for David's safety. He fortunately remained surprisingly healthy, despite the fact that several of the Ma children contracted whooping cough. The family was convinced that this was at least in part because he enjoyed eating several oranges a day from the age of two months.

Within only a month of David's birth Monica returned to work in the hospital every afternoon. Shih Ying would look after David at these times. Although Monica found that her own experience had enriched her 'obstetric' Chinese, the language and cultural differences made her work tiring.

211

We get a lot of women from the countryside and they cannot be understood at all. And none of the Chinese nurses or helpers can get anything out of them either. Some of them have never been outside of their homes and only know the terms of their household tasks. They have a very limited vocabulary and can't express themselves. They don't even seem to know the names of the parts of their bodies. They don't know how long a week is, or a month, or a year. They live from day to day. Getting a medical history from them is impossible because they don't know how to describe it or how long it has been that way. They only talk in terms of the present moment. They express that there is something wrong as *Fan Ch'i* which means that the air inside them is upside down. I feel like a veterinary surgeon. You can imagine how desperate we get in these cases. It is the most tiring job I have ever known.[83]

Many of the Chinese would bring another person as spokesperson because they did not feel that they could speak for themselves. However, even when a diagnosis was made and treatment decided, major obstacles remained. No matter how simple the instructions seemed, there was often little likelihood that they would be followed.

Even asking them to take one pill a day can be impossible. They will often take the whole lot when they get home. If we say take it each day at bedtime, they might take it each time they go to sleep which may be more than four times each day.

The hospital was so busy that they had to set up extra beds for patients in the laundry areas. Monica continued to work every day, and also began helping out in the medical department as well as her usual obstetrics and gynaecology ward rounds and outpatients. They saved as much money as they could and sent it back to Britain, knowing that at any moment the Chinese currency could become worthless. All the money that Stanley saved when he was lecturing the previous year was placed in different benefits, shares and stocks in England.

> By doing this we hope to be able to educate our children properly. Or how would mother like to come out as our governess? You really must come out here sometime when Dad retires and see the miracles of nature that can only occur in a land like this. It will only take two weeks via Siberia and Dad's services would be greatly appreciated.
>
> The school here is run in an American style which we do not approve of. They are brought up on the basis of non-interference and just do as they please. They have no respect for their elders at all. Their behaviour is dreadful. Not a trace of shyness. They answer all of the preacher's rhetorical questions and send everyone hot and cold all over.
>
> We are almost deliriously happy with our work and our life here. I have not missed a day of work since I started back.

Stanley was also extremely busy, and now only rarely added a footnote to Monica's letters.

> I am glad that Monica thinks that I am the model father, but as you have learnt I am not a model letter-writer! I have so much to do each day that I don't feel like writing letters. Stacks of work awaits me, it seems to be getting more and more. We have reached another record with 8,700 outpatients for the month of May. That is the highest ever. The hot weather makes most people quick tempered and I have my fair share of situations to sort out.[84]

All of the 'small' squabbles were in some ways a welcome distraction from the real unrest that had been going on around them. The Sino-Japanese situation was developing into even more of a stalemate, with neither side appearing to gain any ground. The strain was constant, but Monica and Stanley were careful not to voice much of their fears and frustrations in their letters. They had no wish to attract any further attention from the occupiers or to add to the concerns of their families in England.

The occupying forces maintained a tight grip on local infrastructure and made their authority known at all times. But fortunately, at that stage at least, they continued to tolerate foreign aid workers. Monica and Stanley both got to know the individual Japanese guards on their gate quite well, and a fragile harmony gradually developed.

> Once I had David the Japanese soldiers never made me get out of my rickshaw. They let me go straight past, which was kind of them.[85]

But none of this helped their larger scale efforts to try to reopen the medical school. The Japanese regime remained fundamentally opposed to any activities that might empower or enrich their Chinese captives. Ironically, the refusal ultimately came from the Chinese president of the university bowing to Japanese pressure.

> It seems tragic that our work should be restricted not by those who conquer but by our friends who think that they are being loyal. They forget that this part of the world is still inhabited by their own people if not owned by them.
> I do hope that we are allowed to stay on here. I will never, never want to leave Tsinan, even for a furlough. I am passionately fond of it;

214

the people, the work, the view, and everything! If we had to leave, I feel
as though I would be sad for the rest of my life. I never dreamed that
any place on earth could be so dear to me.[86]

This was an unhappy premonition, but one that did not eventuate for many months. Although Monica did later find a happy
life beyond, the China that she knew then always remained
firmly in the core of her heart.

Although deeply disappointed that plans for the medical
school remained in limbo, they were at least grateful that the
Japanese continued to allow them to have supplies for the hospital and to continue to treat the ill and the dying, Chinese
and Japanese alike. They had to be careful that their efforts to
lobby for the medical school did not draw unwelcome hostility
to other aspects of their work to the further detriment of the
Chinese. And so their hospital work continued. With the swel-
tering summer heat upon them, summer rosters were set for
July and August, and Monica was looking forward to another
summer at Peitaiho Beach. Shih Ying was looking forward to
seeing the sea for the first time.

We know that they had a wonderful and relaxing time
at the seaside, and that Shih Ying could hardly believe her
eyes when she first saw the ocean. Monica's responsibilities
with David meant that she was less involved with teaching and
medical support for the holiday community. There is a gap in
the correspondence during this period. They may have written
less, but it is more likely that the letters were lost, as war was
escalating in Europe.

News of war in Europe

They returned to Tsinan in September 1939 to hear the news from Europe: they were now at war.

> The news came last Sunday and was a terrible shock. More than we can believe. We listen to the wireless every night at 9.15 so that we can hear the 1.15 London news. It is difficult to know how this will affect us here. As long as our 'friends' here remain neutral, we hope that we will be alright. As far as we know at present we are not required to return to England, although we feel that it is our duty to do what we can.[87]

They had not received letters from home and were increasingly worried about their families and friends. But they had plenty of other problems to deal with. Local food supplies were now under threat and famine seemed inevitable in many areas. A hot summer with little rain meant crops had done badly. Then the meagre harvest was ruined by floods. Prices were rapidly rising, often to more than four times the prices of the previous year, and everything was becoming scarce. Planning supplies for the winter months was crucial for everyone, but the problems were magnified for the hospital, and Stanley faced many new challenges to ensure that Cheeloo would be adequately supplied without cost to the patients.

A pleasant distraction from this was the September wedding of their old helper Lai Hsi. He had asked Ma to find him a wife. He did not seem to care what she looked like, but his main requirement was that she must be a good cook.

> The bride had to bow before the ancestors of Lai Hsi and make her vows to them. The first night of a Chinese bride is not too happy. The men friends of the groom turn up at the home from 8–11pm and tease the bride and she has to do whatever they say. This goes on sometimes until she cries. Stanley asked Ma if he thought that this was really a good idea. The reply was 'yes, it does them good. It makes them obedient'. Part of the joke is to steal the bride's slippers. The Chinese hate to have their feet uncovered.

The wedding feast was more modest than it might have been in more abundant times, but was much enjoyed by all.

Their thoughts were never far from Europe and they kept tuned in for any news. They borrowed a ten-valve wireless and Mr Frank, a 'wireless man', came to show them how to use it. It seemed to be able to tune in to the BBC without problems. Knowing that they 'might hear the same voices at the same time' seemed miraculous and helped them feel connected to their families, as they had not received letters in months.

Their qualifications and credentials were being checked by the British in case they might be of use in the war effort. With alliances forming between many countries, they had no way of anticipating Japan's next move. While Japan remained neutral they continued to hope they were safe.

It seems horrible to believe that all our dreams of unending peace have come to nought, and that we should see so much harm and suffering. Yet we agree wholeheartedly with the prime minister that Hitlerism must go.

We here have seen something of conquerors and of war. Perhaps in the past I have had views which were almost pacifist. But I am anything but a pacifist now. The horrors of war are real, but in this case the necessity is just as real. In the face of the present day crisis, peace is not justice, and not to fight seems pure selfishness. England has done what she must. May it end soon, but not until justice and righteousness are restored.[88]

It was not until November that they received the first letter from their families, delayed several months, confirming that all were safe. It had been a long wait. And they found most of the news depressing. On one of the lighter notes, Monica's mother had enclosed the piece of paper that had contained her sugar rations, and it was so small Monica that thought it was a toffee paper.

They arranged as many distractions as possible. Country dancing became a regular event on Wednesday nights.

I love it! It is great exercise. Godfrey Gale always goes and then stays here for the night because the gate is closed. The most important day of the year was last Thursday. It was 'American Thanks Giving Day'. They make more fuss over it than they do Christmas. There was great rejoicing and a dinner for everyone on campus at which the engagement was announced between Dr Stanley's son and one of the Canadian girls. The Canadian girls are very popular.[89]

Monica was pleased to see a romance between their dear friends Dr Godfrey Gale and Betty Thompson, one of the Canadian nurses. She thought they would make a wonderful couple. Betty was the best friend of Florence Liddell, wife of Olympian Eric Liddell, and they had trained together as nurses. Everyone seemed interconnected in the missionary world.

David's first Christmas was another wonderful distraction from the worries of war. They celebrated with both their Chinese family and their many friends at the hospital. In her letters Monica catalogued the lengthy list of homemade toys that everyone showered on David, ranging from stuffed rabbits to wooden engines. A favourite was a padded winter coat from Mrs Ma.

All of these festivities were dampened when one of their senior nurses, Miss Brodie, had a stroke on Boxing Day, losing her speech and all movement on the right side of her body. She was admitted to the ward under the close care of all her colleagues. Being so far from home and family magnified her tragedy. Christmas was also overshadowed by the imminent visit from the mission chiefs. They were coming to assess Stanley's performance and provide operational directives. This involved a detailed inspection of the hospital and all of its activities, interviews and discussion with staff, and liaison with Japanese headquarters to assess relationships. Although this was stressful the result was favourable. Stanley had already completed the first half of his seven-year term with the LMS, and they seemed more than satisfied with his progress. He would have to wait another three-and-a-half years before he could take furlough, but that did not seem to worry Monica or Stanley.

If the other half goes as quickly it won't seem long. We get homesick to see you all sometimes, but we will be even more homesick for China after a whole year of furlough in England.

And just to sing Stanley's praises: He now knows so much Chinese there is no Chinese in Tsinan who knows enough to teach him any more. He has really done wonders and now sits and reads novels in Chinese with ease.[90]

Then there was some very happy news. Dr Godfrey Gale and Miss Elizabeth (Betty) Thompson announced their engagement.

Godfrey is going to buy the ring next week when he goes up to Tientsin to their meeting. We are all thrilled and very delighted as they are both so nice. Stanley and I are going to give them a party to celebrate the engagement next week. I think they hope to be married fairly soon.[91]

They adored the young surgeon and his fiancee. Like Monica, both Betty and Godfrey had been born into missionary families. Godfrey's parents (Kendall and Margaret Gale) went as missionaries to Madagascar, where they lived for years and where Godfrey was born. Betty was actually born in China (in Honan, now Henan, province) into the Canadian missionary family of Andrew and Margaret Thomson. She trained as a nurse in Canada until she returned to China through the United Church of Canada. Godfrey was later to become Stanley's successor as superintendent.

It was a bitterly cold winter. Temperatures dropped to thirty degrees below freezing. Ice covered the windows and the ground was frozen solid to at least a foot below the surface. For her birthday on 4 February Stanley gave Monica a squirrel-fur coat. Although she thought it was beautiful and extravagant, it was most greatly appreciated for its warmth. It was a mercy that the hospital had just enough coal. But by the end of February coal supplies were running very low and Stanley had to undertake some very careful planning. A more severe coal shortage, like the year before, would have been disastrous in the much colder conditions. They did what they could but many of the poor still perished, particularly the frail and the elderly.

Ma's mother was among the dying that winter. As her son, Ma was responsible for buying her coffin and making arrangements for her funeral. It was traditional to make these preparations before death. He made the journey to see her one more time. She only lived fifteen miles away but he insisted on walking all the way there and all the way back in the freezing cold, grateful to have seen her before her passing.

Monica and Stanley also had to say farewell to friends and valued colleagues. Miss Brodie had made some significant recovery from her stroke, and was able to walk almost normally. However, she could still not speak, and plans had to be made to repatriate her to Canada. They were also very sad that that their dear friends Dr and Mrs Ingle would be returning to work in England. Other colleagues, currently on furlough, had also decided not to return in the face of global uncertainties. Monica and Stanley still had no plans to leave.

Despite the hardships and difficulties they were still enjoying the experience and loved the directness of the Chinese people. They also continued to take great pleasure in watching their son grow, and in experiencing the wonders of the world through his eyes. By his first birthday David was beginning to develop a sound Chinese vocabulary. This was partly due to the time he spent with his adored 'big sister', Shih Ying.

David's first year

Monica gives a wonderful account of their daily life with David around the time of his first birthday. She wrote this description on 19 March 1940:

Just one year old. Will you come and spend the day with us and be introduced to David? You must come early because as soon as the light peeps through the shutters, sounds can be heard from the little boy in the nursery who believes in rising early. Mummy jumps up and brings him into the big bedroom and there the three of us say good morning to each other and David chatters away in his own language telling us of all the experiences in his short life. But soon a knock is heard at the door and Shih Ying takes him, dresses him and plays with him having given him his first two biscuits. Mummy and Daddy go to sleep again but are aware of the patter of little feet running up and down the hall and a loud voice shouting 'Dad, dad, dad'.

At 8.30 comes breakfast, and how we love it. David sits in an improvised high chair and Mummy feeds him. First of all there is porridge covered with sugar and milk with an extra blob of brown sugar in the middle to make it look nice. David has a spoon that he dips into his porridge and while he is trying to find his mouth Mummy puts several spoonfuls in with another spoon. David's spoon finally reaches his mouth, but alas the porridge that was on it has fallen off en route. Under the porridge is a picture of little Bo Peep with her sheep and as soon as we see her we sing the nursery rhyme together. Then comes a piece of buttered toast, a boiled egg and two spoons. David cleverly puts the little fingers of toast into the egg and pretty soon only the shell is left. He then takes the spoon and the shell and pretends to eat it all over again. The codliver oil is taken without any trouble and David is allowed to put the stopper back on as a reward. An eggy mouth and eggy hands are washed in vanishing water as David always pulls the plug out of the basin as soon as he reaches it.[92]

Shih Ying would look after David on weekdays when Monica was working. But on weekends Monica would play with David until his late-morning nap. The family would be reunited for lunch most days, if Stanley was not too busy.

Meat, potatoes, vegetables and gravy come first and then rice pudding or custard, but we always hurry through this meal as Daddy is home and that makes all the difference. So we get up and run to Daddy, sit on his knee and investigate all those mysterious pockets that men own. Pencils, pens and papers are all discovered and not until all the pockets have given up their secrets does he beg for a walk.

The garden is full of wonderful things for a little boy. David goes through the hedges, grovels in the earth, pokes into everything with sticks, plays with the plant pots and shoots at birds and rabbits. He never walks on a path but makes for the centre of flower beds or fields of wheat and if there is a hole to go into, all the better. He sits on his haunches to examine anything unusual and then moves on a few steps to study the next object. He chatters all the time and shouts 'Gee, gee, gee' which is Chinese for chicken, and runs towards the farm where he knows they are kept. No child passes without being shouted to and he goes on shouting until he gets a reply. Daddy meanwhile follows the little boy, and carries him over difficult places.

If Monica was home she would take David for walks or for a rickshaw ride to visit friends. If she was working or at Chinese lessons, Shih Ying would take him to play in the garden with his Chinese friends.

Then at 5pm David has his supper which consists of prunes and custard and bread and butter. And then he suddenly wakes up again and he is the happiest little boy in the whole wide world. He runs around the house playing hide and seek behind the easy chairs, covers his head with newspaper or a piece of cloth and sees how far he can run without falling into anything and tries to stand on his head. If a visitor comes he immediately tries to bring them into his games and laughs so loud and oft that soon the most downcast person is laughing too.

At 6pm his bath is ready and it is the perfect end to a perfect day. He loves the water and plays lots of games in it and laughs at his secret jokes. We often wonder what he is laughing at. When he is out of the bath we play 'this little piggy went to market' and David always provides the little squeak at the end. After the bath he has hugs for everyone and goes into his sleeping bag looking the cleanest, happiest and loveliest boy in the world. He sinks into dreamland without a murmur. He forgets everything but others do not forget him. Even the quiet of the evenings stresses his absence and makes us look forward to the dawn of another day.

Working life continued in the background. To cope with the demands of increasing patient numbers they needed to expand wards and build new areas for the hospital kitchens. With limited resources Stanley found himself as both architect and engineer.

The food shortage was getting worse and food prices were soaring further beyond the reach of the poor. Even Monica and Stanley had to plead for bonus payments from the Mission Society to pay for their own food.

> China is in famine again. Still there is no rain. It spotted once or twice but no more. Prices are so high that even we cannot buy. We have spent more than half our month's salary on food. Our milk and butter bill was more than $70. A year ago it was only $14. Flour is rationed and we have to queue up for one bag every three weeks. Lipton's Yellow Label tea has gone up from $3.20/lb to more than $25/lb so we have given up drinking tea altogether!
>
> We have had to double Ma's wages and even so we have to give him nearly as much again because they haven't enough to live on. The Japanese are refusing to let the Chinese plant new crops this year and they are taking the cotton harvest for export to Japan. We don't know what the Chinese are going to live on.[93]

News of the war in Europe was still worrying and in April (1940) they were dismayed to hear than Germany had reached Norway. They felt helpless and did what little they could for the war effort in Europe. Hundreds of balls of wool arrived and all the British missionaries began knitting blankets for their soldiers. It seemed such a small and feeble contribution but at least it was something.

> The news these days from Europe is so terrible that we make no comments.[94]

A copy of Hope's novel was a welcome arrival. During her time as a teacher and missionary in China, Monica's sister Hope wrote her first book, called *Five Cloud Valley*, the romantic story of a young woman missionary and her adventures in China before the war. Monica enjoyed reading it and, although it was set in a different area of China, she found much that was familiar. Over the months that followed, the book gradually made its way around most of the missionary staff in Tsinan, and was said to be well liked by all. But it was only a momentary distraction from the troubles of war.

> We have certainly had our anxieties this week, but they must be nothing
> compared to yours. The 'situation' is getting so bad that we wonder if
> you will be alright when this letter reaches you. Things are moving so
> fast in the wrong direction and at present we see no hope. The whole
> campus is affected and the families that are separated are positively sick.
> But we must believe that 'Where there is life there is hope' and continue
> to have faith.
>
> We can only hope that Japan does not join in the war.[95]

Direct conflict with the Japanese was a looming possibility. There was growing anti-British propaganda appearing on the streets in China, and a realistic concern that if Japan did not remain neutral Monica and Stanley would be deported, imprisoned or worse.

> The news gets worse as the days go by and now we have almost lost
> hope. We will have to accept what happens and those that are left
> will have to make the best of a bad job. The Americans are just as
> anxious. This is really disturbing their peace of mind. If Japan decides

to take advantage of our weakness they might try and get rid of us. We might flee to Australia or Canada. Stanley favours Canada as he is sure that Japan will have designs on Australia. Perhaps we will meet you in Canada. We all feel so helpless out here.[96]

Everyone was still anxiously awaiting the fate of France in the European war. In May 1940 the German attack on the Allies (the *blitzkreig* or 'lightning war') saw Belgium and the Netherlands surrender and the British forced to evacuate through Dunkirk by early June. Stanley's brother Malcolm, by then an army chaplain, was among them. France sued for peace, signing an armistice with Germany on 27 June, leaving continental Europe under Nazi rule.

The horrors in Europe were becoming more palpable every day. A number of their friends and colleagues who were separated from wives and children in Canada or England received cables urgently calling them back home. Despite the looming difficulties, most of the remaining missionaries still planned to travel to Peitaiho Beach for their usual summer holiday. In retrospect, this may seem odd, but they had no clear indication of Japanese intentions and it seemed likely that the existing, albeit precarious, balance would persist for sometime yet. Monica and Stanley had planned to leave for Peitaiho Beach with many of the others in late June. But in view of the growing unrest and potential for political difficulties, it was decided that Stanley would have to stay behind in Tsinan to oversee the skeleton staff at the hospital. Monica went on without him, taking David, Ma and Shih Ying, hoping that Stanley might join them in late August if all went well.

Although she never forgot it was a false paradise, Monica

was grateful to live by the seaside for a few months watching David playing in the water, making sandcastles with Shih Ying discovering crabs and starfish. Monica had never seen him so happy. There were no letters from anyone and she was actually relieved to be temporarily sheltered from the news of war. They found an old glass aquarium and Ma went down to the rocks to find some inhabitants. He came back with an octopus, some crabs and some fish. Every day he would replace half the tank with fresh seawater and seaweed. David loved it. He was now chatting in Chinese with a growing vocabulary of at least fifty Chinese words.

There were still hundreds of missionaries at Peitaiho Beach, although far fewer than the year before. Monica missed Stanley terribly and was overjoyed when he paid them a surprise visit in early August. He made several flying visits before they all returned to Tsinan together on 27 August.

Everyone was looking forward to the wedding of Dr. Godfrey Gale and Betty Thompson in September. Stanley was thrilled to have been asked to be Godfrey's best man. Some of the wedding photographs were included in an album donated to the Cheeloo archive in 2007 by Godfrey and Betty's daughter Margaret Wightman, when she returned to visit the place of her birth. On my own pilgrimage there in 2008, I saw among them a photograph of Stanley in his borrowed morning suit. It was an unexpected delight to see his smiling, tanned face looking up at me from the pages, his young features so familiar, like seeing both my father and my brother, out of place and out of time.

Becoming the enemy

Monica and her little family returned to their fragile routines and listened hopelessly to the BBC every evening, filled with sadness at the distant tragedies that were occurring in Europe.

Then it happened.

In September 1940 Japan entered the war, signing a treaty with Germany and Italy. The implications for the hospital and the missionaries were not immediately apparent, but it was clear that war was now on their doorstep again. Although they were desperate for any reliable news from the outside world, listening to the radio was now extremely dangerous, and they had to do this carefully and in secret, for fear of what the Japanese would do if they were discovered.

There was another surge of anti–British sentiment. As leaders in the community Monica and Stanley were at the centre of this hostility, and things became even more precarious. While anti-British propaganda was likely driven by the Japanese, the Chinese also started to turn on them. For some Chinese this was clearly only to appease their invaders. For others this was driven by a burst of frustrated nationalistic pride. They saw the British and Japanese as both invaders alike, but the missionaries were a much easier target. Chinese fear of the Japanese was far outweighed by any appreciation for the missionary efforts to provide health care. The first overt sign of ill intentions towards the hospital came when the Japanese would no longer cooperate over essential supplies.

> The need for medical care is greater than ever, but we will now have great difficulty in getting enough coal from the Japanese to keep the place running.[97]

The hospital was full to overcrowded and staple food supplies, such as flour, were also being blocked. Without food and coal, Stanley could see no way of sustaining the system through the winter.

> Things are very uncertain here and tension is in the air. There is talk of the American women and children leaving China. But no one quite knows what will happen.[98]

Within days it became clearer that they would not be allowed to continue their work. They also had to face the likelihood that they would be imprisoned in Japanese concentration camps. There, even if they survived the Japanese, they would still face starvation and disease. This still seemed unthinkable. But as British subjects, they were now the enemy and they already had some experience of the Japanese at war.

> Now that Japan has joined the Axis we cannot pretend that we are friends any longer.
>
> Things are getting so hot out here that Stanley thinks that David and I should leave. The American evacuation from this part of the world has precipitated this matter. All of the Americans with children on this

campus will be leaving as soon as the boats arrive to take them, and many men are going too. The Canadians are also going.

Although there is no immediate risk Stanley does not want me to wait until it is too late. We don't want David to spend his early years in a concentration camp.

The immediate future of this place is nil. We don't think that the hospital will be able to stay open. The Japanese won't give us coal unless we register with the new regime and the Chinese are no longer supportive. So we are just waiting for the doors to shut.[99]

It was devastating to see the Chinese close ranks against them. Until then, the Chinese had always treated them as friends. But now their photographs appeared on the streets with notices warning the people that they were the enemy and not to be trusted. Even just before her death, Monica found it hard to talk about this. The Japanese were frightening, but to have their Chinese friends turn on them was heartbreaking. So many years later she was still extremely distressed to remember the hostility and the graffiti that appeared on walls and banners saying 'Prescotts Out'. They were no longer welcome in the land they had come to love.

Living for three years in enemy occupied territory has been a mighty big strain and we are all nervously worn out. Now it is terrible living in a place where every time we go out on the street we see 'Down with the British' attached to the most gruesome looking posters. We even have our names printed in the papers with comments on our evil attitude.

We love this place and we love the Chinese. But this sort of life is not good at all.

They remained at the mercy of the British mission chairman, and they urgently lodged a request for Monica and David to join the North American evacuation, but as yet there had been no directive from the British Government to evacuate its citizens. So they had to wait. Again. Their only source of income was the missionary stipend. What little savings they had were secured in England and, without the support of the mission, they could barely afford passage out of China. But, for David's sake, Monica would resign and leave anyway.

If the worst comes to worst and the mission will not consider our plans I will get work somewhere as a doctor and send the money back to Stanley for travelling and until he can find a job.

Although Stanley still favoured Canada over Australia, Monica's family connections made Australia a more logical choice. He still felt certain that Japan would try to invade Australia, but nowhere seemed safe from the war any more. Monica wrote to her Australian grandmother, Frances, in Parkes to explain their situation. She also wrote to her father hoping that she might get any names and addresses of other Australian or New Zealand friends and relatives. She was still not quite sure where she might end up.

While they continued their work in the hospital, it became increasingly difficult. They knew that increasing numbers of their Chinese co-workers were being threatened or bribed to spy on them. Many were doing so in fear of their lives. Monica and Stanley knew that their letters were being read. And some of their mail was lost. They had to be very careful what they said and what they wrote. For the sake of the many patients still in their care, Stanley wanted to continue the service as long as he possibly could. In November, even as it got cold, they continued their work.

> None of us is sure what is happening out here. We hope that the fever of war will not spread but it is difficult to know what the future may entail. The whole of the Shantung plain is crying out for adequate medical attention. The hospital is full of patients, and some are still waiting for treatment. We are now terribly short of coal, and I am unable to start the heating yet even though it is getting colder each day. We are still hoping to find enough coal before the real cold starts. If not we shall be forced to close, but with so many patients we still hate to do that. We are still divided into two groups, the optimists and the pessimists, which hotly debate the chances and the hopes of the future of this big institution. Unless we can find coal, I am now a pessimist.[100]

Stanley had enjoyed being medical superintendent and took some comfort in the fact that he had done a good job. But it was not what he had come out to do. His higher goal had been to teach the Chinese so that they no longer relied on foreign doctors for medical care. His greatest regret was that the medical school had not been allowed to open and that when the missionary doctors were forced to leave, there would not be enough trained Chinese doctors left to do the work. This was frustrating and heartbreaking. They still hoped that some day they might be able to return to help in the rebuilding of China. Stanley still firmly believed that while health care provision was important in the short term, research and education should be the long term goal. He longed to return to academic research and teaching, but was afraid that if this was delayed too many more years he might get very rusty. Before long he suspected he would be called up to enlist, and possibly be sent to India or Africa.

While Stanley was preoccupied with keeping the hospital afloat as long as possible, Monica was preoccupied with planning her escape. Because of the chaos in the region, each time she was promised passage it was cancelled or delayed. Many of their friends had gone and the foreign population was dwindling every day.

> I can't say that I am sorry to leave under these circumstances. Most people here fear that things are coming to a head and that war is inevitable. It is now just a small minority who are optimistic. In any case, we feel that I should try to get out while the going is good. What Stanley will be left to face we don't know. But he much prefers to do it alone.
>
> Getting out of a place like this is not easy. I still don't know how I will get to Hong Kong in time to get a boat to Australia. The railway between here and Tientsin has been blown up three times in the last few weeks.

Monica was finally booked on a ship called the MV *Neptuna*, which was to sail from Hong Kong before Christmas 1940. She planned to take as much as possible with her to Australia, and focused her energies on organising everything. Then, a letter arrived to say that the MV *Neptuna* had been delayed and would not be sailing until 15 January 1941. This was a mixed blessing. Monica was anxious to make it to safer ground with David, but she was ambivalent about leaving her home and did not want to part from Stanley. This way at least they would be together for

Christmas. There was nothing they could do but wait and hope. With enemy ships in the region, they wondered how many more times the ship might be delayed or if it would make it to Hong Kong at all.

> Although we are thrilled at another month together we can only hope that by that time it is not too late.
>
> Our poor hospital is still without coal and we have been informed by our rulers that it will remain so until we register under the new order. That is of course impossible. Stanley is wearing a waistcoat with two pullovers today. The patients are cold and the nurses are half frozen. It will be impossible to go on when the real cold weather begins.[101]

The Japanese closed the city gate permanently so that everyone had to travel by rickshaw the long way around. It took Ma a whole day to go to the shops 100 yards away. Monica and Stanley were also worried about what would happen to the Ma family when Stanley ultimately had to leave. Monica had returned from Peitaiho to discover that Mrs Ma was seven months pregnant again, and now she was expecting her seventh baby any time soon. Monica and Stanley were anxious about how this large and growing family would survive without their support in the worsening famine. On the day of Mrs Ma's labour she felt a twinge at 9.15am and walked to the hospital; the Japanese kindly made an exception and let her through. She had the baby and was back on the ward sleeping by 10am. David was reportedly 'tickled pink' with his new 'brother'.

Although she knew that they would not reach their destination in time, Monica distracted herself painting Christmas cards.

I do hope that something of the spirit of Christmas will penetrate the clouds of war.

And that was the last letter that Monica ever sent from China.

Separated again

It was heartbreaking to leave. Monica knew that in all likelihood they would never see their Chinese family again. The Ma
family had become part of their lives and shared their home.
This feeling was clearly mutual. For the little girl who looked
after David this was probably the most devastating. We don't
know if any of this family survived. Many decades later, Monica
recalled:

> On our last night there Shih Ying went up to put David to bed but she
> didn't come down. After about an hour we were still wondering what
> had happened, so we went up stairs to see. She had put him to bed
> for the last time, and she had gone to sleep beside him on the floor.
> She didn't want to leave him. She had looked after him for so long and
> she could not bear to see him go. It was enough to make you cry. It
> really was.
>
> When we left the next day they presented David with a little
> padded Chinese coat to keep him warm on the journey down. He kept
> that tiny jacket all his life. Oh yes, there were many tears when we left.[102]

Although David has no memories of this time, he had a strong
bond with his Chinese family and already had some Chinese
vocabulary. Perhaps this may account for the familiarity he felt

for the language when he studied it at university some forty years later. Around that time, in 1980, he reflected on this in some of his own writings:

> My mother and I were in the stream of foreigners leaving China. The Japanese occupation was tightening its grip on China. But those early months among the Chinese people at my most impressionable age may account for my continuing love of people different from myself.[103]

The first challenge was to get Monica and David to Hong Kong in time to reach the MV *Neptuna*. They took the train from Tsinan to the port of Tientsin, and from there they made a difficult journey in a cargo boat, which had to sail in 'black out' through the China Sea to avoid German raiders.

> We all travelled together by train to Tientsin where I was to get the boat. Stanley saw us off and then returned to carry on with his job until he might get a chance to escape.
>
> We just lived one day at a time and hoped that we weren't going to be shot at by some passing ship. I had to sleep with David on a single bunk, with a man above me and another man on the floor. Everyone was escaping from China. More people got on the ship at Shanghai and by the time we eventually arrived in Hong Kong the boat was badly overloaded.[104]

Although it was lovely to see Hong Kong again, Monica's main priority was finding a way out. Everyone was scrambling to get onto any passing Allied ship. Although Monica was booked on the MV *Neptuna*, it had already been diverted once, and she just had to pray that it arrived this time.

I liked Hong Kong, because we had been married there. I felt quite at home there. We just had to wait then, for *any* ship that would take me *anywhere!* It was just a matter of waiting. Everyone was waiting. Many husbands had to stay behind so that women and children could get out first.

Monica had to report to the police every day and just wait. And hope. While she was waiting, the only news she had was of ships being sunk in the South China Sea.

Monica remained terrified for Stanley's safety. There was no way of knowing whether they would see each other again. In the months that followed she would hear that many of the missionaries who remained were imprisoned or killed, including those she knew and had worked with, but she never regretted taking David to safety.

Stanley's last words from China

As the superintendent of the hospital, Stanley felt he could not leave until he knew its fate. That was still not an absolute certainty. The idea that their work might have been in vain was almost too difficult to bear. To find solace he had to focus on the good that had been done.

> It has been hard and full of set-backs and disappointments. But one has only to realise the number of mothers who would have died in childbirth, the men, women and children cured, the number who have also learned something of the Christian message and those who have gone back to their homes with no hope of recovery and yet happy in the knowledge that they may have found something greater. When we remember these things we realise that our work has been worthwhile.[105]

They had achieved so much. When Stanley had arrived there were only about fifty inpatients and 3,000 outpatients per month. Since then they had returned the service to full operation and then exceeded pre-war conditions with around 150 inpatients and up to 9,000 outpatients. This compared to the highest pre-war monthly outpatients census of only 7,000. The hospital served not only Tsinan and the surrounding countryside but also as a consultation service and referral centre for other smaller hospitals in the region. And now it was possible the Japanese might march in and shut them down completely.

In the meantime there were still patients and staff to look after. After seeing Monica and David off in Tientsin, Stanley returned to his post. A number of the other doctors had stayed behind, including Dr Godfrey Gale and his new wife Betty.

I didn't write last week, or the week before. I am sorry to have missed, but I was helping Monica pack and seeing them off on the boat. I am back hard at work and feeling a little lonely. But with things as they are and with relatives in Australia we felt for the sake of David and each other's peace of mind that it would be best for her to go to her Grandmother's. We were really rather hoping that there might be hard evidence of a little sister for David, but perhaps that is a good thing.

We have had three years of the happiest married life possible and David is a real joy. But it would have been selfish to have kept David here in the face of what might happen. Also I am more mobile alone. I don't know what restrictions apply, but it would be good if you can send £100 of my money to Monica.

Don't fret for me but know that your grandchild has gone to where there is good food and no hard cold winter. And in this world of strife and unrest – separation by space counts so little compared to the unity that one feels in the spirit of love and memories.

I am back at work now in Tsinan and we are all busy. My home is still here and I live in the memories of real happiness and love. David is a grand lad and he must have a good chance. Which he will get down South.

241

He received some news from Monica, and was sure they had made the right decision for her to leave.

> I had a letter from Shanghai, and so far she seems to have had a safe journey. Then I had a telegram that she had arrived from Hong Kong. She was glad to be off the boat and David was behaving like a little lamb.
>
> A few boats have been sunk by German Raiders in the Pacific, but she said whatever the risk she felt it was well worth it. I shall naturally be in anguish until I hear that they have landed safely in Australia, but risks are unavoidable these days. God keep them safe.[106]

Somehow, Stanley managed to keep the hospital going. He does not give a clear account of how he managed to secure the supplies to do this. But in his only remaining letter from China, Cheeloo Hospital seemed to be functioning, if not normally, then at least in a very close approximation. In fact, they seemed as busy as ever. In addition to their usual burden of disease they seemed to be dealing with an outbreak of worms!

> One of the big problems at present is worms – round worms and hook worms. We have had young children with intestinal obstruction, and on operation we find masses of worms coiled up in a compact mass. It is a real problem. Now most people have worms and the eggs are excreted in the faeces, which are put on the land for manure. The eggs get into the food so fresh people get infected and so the tale goes on.

Not very glamorous, but a sign that things were at least 'normal' enough to be writing home about intestinal parasites. Stanley was also preoccupied with trying to improvise treatments. Foreign drugs were now unaffordable and the Japanese were as obstructive as possible. They were experimenting with local products and traditional medicines. Employing his pharmaceutical skills, Stanley had some success with dried pig's stomach for treating a case of pernicious anaemia, and a preparation of a dried thyroid extract for thyroxine replacement.

In his final words from China:

I have settled down to a new life. I have kept the old staff on (Ma and his family), but I am living simply in only 2 rooms. It is sometimes a little lonely, but not as lonely as before marriage. We have had happy years, rich with memories that keep me conscious of the splendid spiritual unity that has been ours. It has been the rich process of married life that has enabled us to part more easily. Now we are parted by danger but the love that is ours and the joys and hardship that we have known still bind us firmly together. Sacrifice it is, and must be, but it and all of the risks involved are worth it if only for the sake of wee David who is the perfect expression of our love.

Perhaps, if the worst comes to worst, David can carry on what his father failed to do. I already believe that David has been a better missionary than his father. He has won a place in the hearts of these people. He and his mother are a great force for good in the hearts of our helpers and across the campus. I tried to do my bit, but David succeeded without trying.

Missionaries are interned

Stanley stayed on for many more months, keeping Cheeloo operational. There is no further correspondence from him, although we know that his friend Dr Godfrey Gale succeeded him as the next superintendent of Cheeloo. Stanley tried to leave just before the Japanese soldiers finally marched into the hospital.

Shortly before my own visit to Cheeloo (Qilu) in 2008, Godfrey Gale's daughter Margaret Wightman had also visited with a Canadian group tracing their missionary history. So I was able to contact her to find out what had happened to her parents. The Gales were still there when the Japanese finally captured all of the remaining missionaries and interned them in concentration camps. Margaret was born in Tsinan in 1941 and spent most of her preschool years as a prisoner of war until the family was finally released in 1945. Both of her parents survived internment to eventually settle in Canada. But Godfrey developed tuberculosis as a result of his incarceration and it took many years for him to recover. He went on to become the chief of medical staff at West Park Hospital in Toronto.

A number of their friends were not so lucky, including Olympic medallist Eric Liddell. His wife Florence was pregnant with their third child (Maureen) when the war broke out and she was evacuated with their other two daughters to Canada. Florence always remained the dearest friend to Betty Gale, and Margaret always knew her as Auntie Flo. Like Stanley and so many others, Eric Liddell stayed behind hoping to follow and be reunited once the conflict had settled. He was also among those captured. Sadly, Florence never saw him again, and Maureen never met her father. He died of a brain tumour in one of the camps.

If David and Monica had stayed, there is no doubt that my father would also have spent his early childhood in a concentration camp, with likely malnutrition and disease or worse. We are all very thankful that Monica escaped when she did.

The uncertain voyage south

Meanwhile in Hong Kong, the MV *Neptuna* finally came to their rescue. It was one of the merchant vessels in the Burns Philp Shipping Company that had been mobilised for the war effort. With extensive familiarity of the region, the fleet was ideally placed to assist in the evacuation of civilian families throughout the Asia-Pacific. This was generally limited to women and children, and although no official figures exist, many thousands were taken to safety.[107] Despite crowded and difficult conditions, Monica was very thankful to be among them.

Monica began her new journey early in 1941, as the Japanese were amassing their forces for the horrific Asia-Pacific campaign, the worst of which was yet to come. This was in the months leading up to the Pearl Harbor attack on 7 December 1941, and the simultaneous invasion of British Malaya, Hong Kong and Thailand on the other side of the date line on 8 December. The battle with the British for Hong Kong was to last until Christmas Day 1941, when it finally fell to the Japanese Empire. Malaya fell not long after, on 31 January 1942, with more than 50,000 prisoners of war captured by the advancing Japanese forces. After that, the Japanese moved quickly south to invade Singapore. That battle lasted from 8 to 15 February 1942 and resulted in the largest British-led military surrender in history, with the Japanese taking a further 80,000 prisoners. Then came the campaign against Australia, as Stanley had predicted. Darwin was bombed on 19 February 1942 by well over 200 Japanese aircraft. The magnitude of the shelling and the bombing far exceeded the assault on Pearl Harbor, with at least 250 deaths that day. That was only the first of around 100 Japanese raids on Australia that continued through 1942 and 1943. Part of the reason the Australian campaign is far less well known than the Pearl Harbor bombing is government policy to downplay damage in an attempt to reduce the psychological impact on the Australian people.

It was in the prelude to all this that Monica entered the region.

With so many ships already sunk under enemy fire, the voyage was an uncertain one. The MV *Neptuna* had been fitted with modest defense weapons and extra life rafts, but sadly she too was to suffer at the hands of the Japanese bombers. For now, though the MV *Neptuna* was a welcome refuge:

Finally the *Neptuna* came in. It was so over crowded. Definitely just one class at that point! All the dining rooms had been converted to sleeping places and many people had to sleep on the floor. At every port we called at even more people got on. A few people wanted to look around or stay on a while, but we were warned not to get off. It was a strange journey. We were not allowed to know where we were going. We had no idea. It was very hard. There was not much food. We were told this was the last ship that might ever get out, or least the last one that was likely to give safe passage.[108]

The MV *Neptuna* had been bound for Hong Kong in late 1940 when Japan escalated hostilities in the region. She was diverted to many ports to assist in the evacuation ahead of the Japanese southward advance and became heavily overcrowded, far in excess of what her safety certificates allowed.

I am writing this from the first bit of American territory that I have set foot on. We left Hong Kong in winter time, and here were are in the Philippines three days later sweating under a tropical sun. The first day we left in a storm and I was sick twice, and looking after David was nothing less than a nightmare. However, it is amazing what one has to survive. The next day it was a millpond.

It is a lovely boat. The decks are wide and the sides are closed in so David can't fall overboard. He is very happy, but is having to learn that all the toys are not his.

As I write this the boat is doing cartwheels, but I've got quite used to the sea again. I'm glad that I had David to keep me up when the sea was rough in those first days.

A week has gone since we saw any land and we have never been able to elicit where we were. Dad wouldn't be able to write a diary on this kind of journey. All he would be able to do was describe the conditions of the sea but as one does not even know which sea it is or if we are north or south of the equator that would not be much use. Our whole course is a secret even to our ports of call.

We are a very happy community and all the adults are kept busy with their children. It helps to keep our minds occupied, which is a good thing as we aren't able to spend our days worrying about the raiders that are in these seas.

David loves the men on board and does not even bother to look at the women, I think he is missing his Daddy. Needless to say I miss him too. I do so hope that he will be able to get out of China soon.[109]

Their voyage was interrupted or diverted on several occasions to avoid German raiders operating in the region. Monica recalled the terror she and the other passengers felt every day of their voyage. Dawn, in the half-light, was the most frightening time of day, when they had been told that the enemy submarines were most likely to attack. Although they were all glad to be fleeing the north, their fears were still far from over. The ship was ordered into Madang while off the northern coast of Dutch New Guinea, to shelter from raiders suspected in the vicinity.

Drop, drop, drop. The perspiration trickled down my back and around my chin. Such is life here in Papua New Guinea, but it was a great experience. On Saturday at 6am our boat sailed alongside a tropical shore. Coconut palms and green grass for miles and miles passed before our eyes. At last the boat stopped at the port of Madang.

David and I together with his ball were the first to get off the boat and we had a happy time running over the grass and dodging the coconut palms lest a coconut fall on our heads. The grass was greener than anything I had seen for three years. Nestling among the trees are a dozen houses, all built on steel supports to avoid the white ants.[110]

From Madang, the MV *Neptuna* sailed on to Rabaul. Before leaving China Monica had received some Australian Methodist magazines from her aunt Ethel (Allen's sister, still in Parkes).

From this she determined the names and locations of the missionaries in New Guinea. As soon as they landed in Rabaul she took a taxi to the mission headquarters, where Mr Macarther, chairman of the district, welcomed them to his home. Mrs Macarther and Malcolm aged six were there to greet them. David settled himself down with great glee to play with Malcolm's toys, while they all had afternoon tea. Monica formed a very quick bond with the Macarther family and liked them immensely. It was a quiet and relaxing time for them all. And it seemed like a paradise. But violence and tragedy were close at hand for the Macarthers and so many of the other missionaries and civilians of Papua New Guinea. It is another blessing that Monica and David left when they did, and were not tempted to stay longer with her new missionary friends.

During their stay, Mr Macarther took Monica to visit the various churches and schools run by the mission. Monica was fascinated by her first encounter with the indigenous peoples, wearing only scant pieces of cloth between their legs. This was quite a change from the modesty of China.

We stopped at the natives' hospital and one of the doctors showed me around. I got one of the greatest shocks of my life. The natives sleep on trestle boards. They have no bedding what so ever and it is no wonder that the majority of them refuse to lie in bed at all. They were treated roughly, there are no qualified nurses and there was practically no care. It was a pathetic sight.

The next day at noon David and I went to one of the Mission out-stations, called Vunairima. It was over an hour's journey and we passed the remains of many houses that had collapsed during the earthquake three weeks previous to our visit. Nothing I can write would do justice to the hospital there. There is one Australian nurse there and she has a few native boys that she has trained to help her. There is no doctor. The general atmosphere was so different from that we had visited the previous day. The two wards were spotlessly clean. The patients and the helpers and the children all adored the nurse. There were over 170 babies born in the hospital last year and there are medical and surgical cases as well. The mothers had their babies with them and all seemed happy. The nurse, Miss Beale deserves the highest praise. Not only is the work good but so is the whole atmosphere. I shall never forget the hospitality of the Macarthers. They are lovely people and were more than good to us.

Later, after her departure, Monica was devastated to learn that the Macarther family was among the hundreds of missionaries massacred by the Japanese during the invasion of New Guinea in 1942. Many were shot or bayoneted with their hands tied. Although the Japanese also took some prisoners in New Guinea, few survived the war. This was another terrible blow that touched Monica personally, and another reason to be grateful that her own journey had not come to a similar end. And also a reminder of their likely fate had they not escaped China when they did. Even in the face of this terror, for the rest of her life Monica never held any resentment for the Japanese as individuals. She was upset by and quick to condemn any racial hatred.

Once the naval authorities believed the threat had lessened, the MV *Neptuna* resumed her interrupted voyage. Safe, for now at least, they continued, and 'with enemy aircraft audible above the monsoonal cloud she remained undetected'.[111] The onward journey took them on another diversion to Townsville, where a number of passengers had to disembark to comply with safety regulations. Finally, the heroic crew of eighteen Australian officers, four cadets, and 125 Chinese[112] delivered the remainder of their precious cargo to Sydney, and Monica found herself back in Australia after almost twenty years, safe at last.

The story of the MV *Neptuna* and many of her crew did not end well either. In 1942, her final voyage was to supply defence stores and equipment for the armed forces in Darwin. Her new cargo virtually made her an ammunition supply ship, and a likely target for the Japanese. She was bombed by Japanese fighter planes and sank in Darwin Harbour on 19 February 1942. It is reported that forty-five of her crew were killed, including ten of her Australian crew and many Chinese.

Australia

Where dreams are made

Safe in Australia

Separated from Stanley once more, not knowing if he was safe or when she might see him again, terrified that she might not: this was another very difficult time. But it was made a little easier by the company of her much-loved son David, and the prospect of returning to her Australian family. After 'two months on the high seas' Monica was also desperate for firm ground. In their final week at sea, the MV *Neptuna* ran into a southerly storm and almost every one aboard was dreadfully sick, Monica among them. It seemed to last for days. And so, when Sydney Heads finally came into view, the relief and jubilation were incredible.

Approaching Sydney Harbour, Monica's childhood memories were rekindled by familiar sounds of birds and cicadas, the almost forgotten smell of eucalypts and the hot February sun. She was reminded of the words of Amy, Grandma Frances' sister, when she too returned from her missionary travels in Africa and beyond, the century before, of her joy in the glory of the bright sunshine, songbirds, flowers, and even the sounds of cicadas.

So many families of that era had been separated by such long times and distances, and many died before they could be reunited. Monica had not seen her grandmother Frances Job since she was a child, and she had thought she might never get the opportunity. Frances was now almost ninety, and still lived in Parkes with her unmarried daughter Ethel, once trained as a nurse. Knowing that her father Allen may never get the chance to return, Monica felt very fortunate that she might find a new home with them. As she recalled in 2006:

> Arriving in Sydney was especially lovely for me, because my father's people were still in Australia, over the Blue Mountains. But I arrived at the port with hardly a penny to my name, not even enough to catch a train to Parkes. We were refugees. I was so fortunate that I could contact the Mission Society for help. They granted me my passage and were also able to get a message through to Parkes to let them know I was coming.
>
> When I arrived it was into the open arms of Grandma Job. She was standing at the gate ready to take us into her arms. It was simply unbelievable and absolutely wonderful. She was so sweet. And almost ninety. Quite funny really to think of that now I am ninety-three myself! Oh yes, and Dad's sister, Auntie Ethel was there then too. I recall she spent her days making wreaths for funerals. We were most fascinated by this.
>
> Life in Australia was different again. In China we had all the 'mod cons' or thought we had back then, but in Parkes they had nothing. Although, there was a choice of going outside to find your way to the dunny in the dark, or using the pot under the bed and leaving it for someone to clean up in the morning! Again, I didn't know what to do! It was a bit embarrassing.[1]

Monica could hardly wait to send her father Allen news of his family and of her safe arrival. Allen was almost sixty by then and had not seen his mother Frances for decades. On 27 February 1941 Monica wrote from her new home, 'Halcyon', in Ward Street, Parkes.

Auntie Ethel was on the platform to meet us and we took a taxi to Halcyon, where Grandma was at the gate waiting for us to arrive.

I am more than amazed by Grandma's ability. She can do almost anything. She washes the dishes, sweeps the rooms, makes her own bed, does the slops every morning and carries the bucket down to the lavatory, which is right at the end of the garden. Of course she is not quick but at eighty-nine she is a wonder. She talks most intelligently and reads without difficulty. Her eyesight is as good as mine. Hope's novel *Five Cloud Valley* is on the mantle piece here and Grandma was reading it again last night. Give my love to Hope. We are always thinking of you all and yesterday Grandma said 'I've been thinking of Allen all day'. She is so proud of you. So is the whole of Parkes.

What I think is the most wonderful is Grandma's ability to adapt herself to modern life. She is always willing to sample new foods, she likes the wireless, goes to the pictures and she just loves motor cars. And does she eat!? She can beat me.

On Saturday night Auntie Ethel took me and David (in a push chair) to the shops. It was a terrific thrill for us as in North China we were not allowed in the streets in the evening. I love the life here...I could not be in a better spot, and everyone has been lovely to me.[2]

But now that Monica was more settled, she also had more time to worry about Stanley. She was not sure if he was still in North China, or if he had evacuated with other missionaries to West China, where the unrest was not as bad.

It is a very miserable life without him and I know that he will be missing us just as much. But so many others have to suffer separation these days. Poor Stanley.

257

I know how he longs to be with us. But I don't see how he can get out even if he wants to. Boats are all booked up. But I do know that it must be a great relief for him to know that we are here. And since arriving, I know that this was a very wise move. The situation there seems to be getting hotter every day and our journey was hard enough.

We are all listening to the wireless as I write this. Oh it is good to be in a free country again.

David was adapting to life in Australia, although he apparently still reverted to speaking Chinese in such emergencies as wanting to go the toilet. He always felt fortunate to have the opportunity to meet his great-grandmother, although he barely remembers any of this now. He put on weight and was clearly thriving in his new environment.

It was not long before Monica noted the beginning of Frances' decline. One of the striking things to me is that as she describes her own grandmother in both behaviour and appearance, I am very much reminded of Monica herself as she was in the months before she died.

Grandma amazes me more every day. She is so active – but she is forgetting things so easily. She keeps saying the same thing. Nearly all day she tells me how afraid she was of snakes. She can tell some really good stories of the old days. And she is still proud to see how nice she looks. She always looks neat. Her hair is never out of place and she always wears pretty dresses. And Auntie tells me lots of interesting things about Dad. She says you used to help her do the washing up. It seems unbelievable. And Grandma tells us of all the mischievous things you used to do.[3]

> She is very proud of you. She has photos of you all over the house
> and looks at them every day.

Monica also began to focus on doing what she could to secure Stanley a job in readiness for his arrival, partly to avert worry that he may not arrive at all.

> I've written to all sorts of people in the hope of getting a job for Stanley.
> I could get one quite easily. I've been offered the General Practice at
> Tottenham where Aunt Amy is, and the government will guarantee
> £1,000 yearly. But I am more interested in Stanley coming here at
> present. I do hope I can get something for him.
>
> David and I are really being educated in Australia. It is a completely
> new world. I shouldn't think there is another country like it. I hope that
> David can have a few years in the country. He is so happy with the
> horses, sheep and hens. It would be a great shame if he lived too long
> in a city.

Once it had begun, my great-great-grandmother Frances' decline progressed quickly, and I am again reminded of my own grandmother Monica. If the same fate were to befall me, I can only hope to have lived a life as rich as theirs.

> Poor Grandma, I feel sorry for her. She is physically wonderful and
> fortunately she was able to take delight in David. But I fear that we
> arrived only just in time. Her memory is just disappearing. And it's going
> quickly. Even these past few weeks it has got worse. And she is always
> worried. If Auntie goes to a meeting she looks at the clock every five
> minutes and worries herself into a head ache. From tea until bedtime
> she goes around and shuts all the windows and doors. As soon as she

has done them she sits down to get up half a minute later to do it again,
because she has already forgotten. But I think she is wonderful. She is
so strong. But I don't think that she is very happy any more. She can't
crochet any more and although she reads it makes her tired. I hope
she does not live very much longer because she is very aware of her
inabilities now and is always wishing she could do more.[4]

When Frances was a much younger woman with young children, her husband Tom was away for very long periods. She
would often be nervous at night-time, so perhaps in her ritual
surveillance of the windows and doors she was revisiting her
earlier life in the 1880s:

I spent some very lonely nights. The kangaroos and emus and kangaroo
rats would come right up to the house, and I being very nervous would
lock the house at dark and nothing would bring me out after that. In the
daytime I would burn up great trees and logs around the house to get a
clear look out.[5]

Monica felt for Frances much the same as I did later for Monica
when her mind started to go in the months before she died. I
did not want her to suffer long. Even in 2006 when Monica
and I made the recordings that we are sharing with you in these
pages, her short-term memory was starting to fail in much the
same way. But there was nothing wrong with her long-term
recall.

In the same letter Monica declares that she can't live without
Stanley. Her feelings for Stanley had grown so deep in the years
since they met.

I have had three letters from Stanley this week. I think he might be here this winter. I do hope so. Neither he nor I can live without each other.[6]

While she was hoping and waiting for Stanley to arrive, Monica also occupied herself giving public addresses to the Rotary Club and at other community gatherings. They enjoyed her addresses so much that they invited her to come again. Wonderful news also arrived from her best friend, Muriel, who had been writing almost every month since they finished studied medicine together. Muriel was expecting her own baby in October and this lifted Monica's spirits.

She also planned to move to a flat in Bogan Street:

It is half a house where the Pearces used to live. Two old ladies live on one side and on the other side I will have a breakfast room, scullery, bathroom, bedroom and front room. A dear old lady and friend of Grandma is going to use the front room and give me 5/- a week. It is unfurnished, but lots of people are sending me things so I'll practically have nothing to buy. I'll be paying 25/- a week for it. It is near here [Halcyon] and the shops.[7]

On 16 April 1941 she had more news of Stanley:

I was thrilled today to get an Air-Mail letter from Stanley written on the 24th March. It only took three weeks. I do hope that he will be able to obtain early furlough or something to come here. He is very well indeed and very busy. Wutingfu seems to have been evacuated and Dr and Mrs Pell are on their way here too. Aren't things a mess these days? I would so love to have a really good talk to you all.[8]

Around the same time Grandma Frances got shaky, very unwell and had to take to her bed. Dr Henderson, the local general practitioner, was called. He 'prescribed bromides to soothe her down' and confined her to bed. Most curiously, sixty-six years later it was also a Dr Henderson who did much the same for Monica in 2007. On 21 April, Grandma Frances was still in bed and Monica received letters from both London and China.

These are anxious days for us. I had a very quick letter from Stanley. He is applying for early furlough. I hope he gets it. Otherwise he will resign and that means looking for work here. I don't care any way, as long as he gets here safely. Stanley says the Mission has granted me a rental allowance. I don't know how much it is, so I will have to go carefully for a while. I have bought the sweetest little wireless set imaginable. It is the latest model. I must get the news and these days it would be awful without a radio.

Grandma is still in bed. She is no trouble at all. She is as happy as the day is long. And heaps of visitors call to see her. She says to let you know that she loves having us here and that David is the greatest great grandchild in the world. My new house is nearly ready and I'll be moving on Wednesday. It is really a good thing that I am here otherwise Auntie Ethel would never be able to go out at all. We can't leave Grandma alone now that she is in bed. I will still come up whenever Ethel wants to go out.

Monica moved to 67 Bogan Street but still visited Halcyon every day. David slept in her bedroom in the evenings after she listened to the 7pm news each night. She liked him sleeping there while she read and wrote.

262

The light does not bother David and he does not wake when I move, I like having him in the same room as it does not make me feel as lonely.

Monica clearly adored David. Everyone seemed charmed by him. He was always described as a beautiful-looking boy and later became a very handsome man. She described him as 'full of beans, but never naughty'. Monica was always full of praise for his progress in all her letters home. She took David on her daily visits to Frances:

Her eyes light up when she sees him and she says 'here is the little boy with the lovely eyes' and when David puts his hand under her bed clothes to hold her hand he says 'thank you'.

I am sure that she will never get out of bed again. This morning she said she went down to the tool shed in the night to tidy it up and she asked Auntie to take the splinters out of her foot. Grandma is in no pain and she is very contented, but she looks a ghostly pale all the time. She thinks Auntie is a little girl and she does not like her being alone because of the Air Force men. It is a terrible strain. Auntie has to lie awake half the night because Grandma tries to get out of bed. I am so glad that I was here to help and I am so glad that David is able to give Grandma so much pleasure.

I had a letter from Stanley dated March 30. He says that the Cheeloo executive have recommended he goes to West China and that he has three months' leave in Australia first. This request has been sent to the Mission and Stanley is still waiting for a reply. If they refuse he will resign. Even if they agree I imagine the end will be the same because David and I can't go back to West China with him, and he will not return without us.[10]

The death of Grandma Frances

They cared for Grandma Frances for as long as possible at home. Monica's letters describe her as 'a wonderful patient who never asked for anything'. Frances used to laugh that she must have been terribly important to have both a nurse and a doctor at her personal call all day. But she was heavy and helpless and Auntie Ethel could not lift her alone. Not long before Grandma died she was transferred to the local hospital (Niola) because it became too difficult for them to care for her. She had always said that she wanted to go there if she 'became a burden'. The night before she went to hospital, she got out of bed and fell on the floor. After that night she thought she was in bed because of the fall.

Monica wrote to her parents the day of her grandmother's death, 18 May 1941:

> Grandma passed peacefully away at noon today, Sunday...She went
> downhill awfully quickly and more and more lived out of this world.
> It was as if she was half in heaven and half on earth.
>   I saw Grandma twice after she went to hospital. She has a little
> private room just opposite the matron's room. She loved the ambulance
> ride. She said that she had travelled in many things but never in an
> ambulance and she was thrilled with it all. She continued to slip rapidly

away in hospital. She said 'I will see you again, but this is goodbye'. Her mind by that time – or rather her spirit – was already in heaven. She used to lie quietly all day and only come back if someone came to talk to her.

The last time I saw her was on Tuesday. She had gone by then. Her eyes had closed and she looked so calm and peaceful. We touched her and spoke to her but she just smiled in her sleep. She woke one more time after that to ask Auntie Ethel to pray for her. But apart from that she was in another land.

The last five days have been dreadful, not for Grandma but for Auntie and the rest of us. Uncle Dick and Auntie Amy have been here all week just waiting. Grandma's soul has left her body but her heart kept beating. She couldn't even take a sip of water. I have never imagined such a state. It was terrible for anyone who saw her, but we were happy that Grandma knew nothing. This morning her pulse gradually weakened and while we were all up at Halcyon at 1.15pm the phone went to say the end had come.[11]

Frances was to be buried out among the gum trees beside her husband, teamster Tom Job, with whom she had fallen in love so long ago when she was just eighteen. Monica did not like attending funerals and she almost never went on to the cemetery after a funeral service. However, because Allen could not be there, she made a rare exception this time. His mother had meant so much to him, and Monica dearly wanted him to know how proud she had been of him, and that his life's works were still celebrated in his home town.

The last Sunday that Grandma was still up with us I stayed with her and she got out her Bible. In it she had every cutting you had ever sent her and she brought them one by one to show me. A few days before she went unconscious she said again 'I've been thinking of Allen all day'.

Monica was so glad that she had arrived in Australia in time to share Frances' final months.

I still see her at the gate standing out waiting for our taxi the day that we arrived in Parkes. She looked so thrilled. She was too happy to speak. Just three months after that she went.

I want you to know what tremendous pleasure that Grandma got from David. She always said of David that 'He is such a good little fellow, but he is the nearest thing I have seen to perpetual motion'. Auntie Mary thinks that Grandma only lived to see David and then she decided to go.

This letter can have a no more fitting ending than what David said this morning after Mrs Grayson called to say Grandma was dying. As we left David turned to me and said 'Grandma not dying, Grandma better now'.

After that Monica told me that she went back to Parkes and stayed a while longer, not knowing what to do. At that stage she had no idea where Stanley was, or even if he was all right. Looking after David, she was not really able to work. When I asked her about this shortly before she died, she said the government gave her an allowance of some kind, so she just stayed, waiting in Parkes.

Stanley's escape

China was already torn apart by the Japanese when Monica left, but the situation became worse as Stanley remained in the months that followed. The systematic extermination of Chinese continued, and they knew that soon any remaining Westerners would be captured.

We only have Monica's letters during this time. Any letters that Stanley wrote to Monica or his parents have not survived. And Monica only gave scant accounts of his story in her letters, probably because she was not fully aware of the details. I am sure he was limited in what he could say and did not want to worry her either.

The mission was slow to grant Stanley leave. Although many would have chosen to leave under these circumstances, Stanley's sense of honour, duty and purpose prevented him from deserting his responsibilities there. So, for many months he continued his work, helping the Chinese and trying to keep a low profile with the Japanese occupiers.

By the time Stanley was granted six months' leave, the opportunities to leave China were extremely limited. By then, most Allied ships had left the region and few civilian ships were willing to venture into occupied waters. Any remaining Westerners were being advised to flee into West China, where the Japanese were yet to have a stronghold and where the dangers were not thought to be so great. But Stanley now had only one objective: to be with Monica and David in Australia. He had to bide his time and wait for any chance, much as he had when he first fled to Hong Kong to meet Monica in 1937.

Knowing he would be unable to carry anything with him, Stanley packed all of his family's remaining belongings in a large brown trunk, which he entrusted to Ma Ru, who stayed with him at Wesley Bungalow right up until Stanley left. Ma promised he would guard the trunk and do everything possible to ensure that Stanley and Monica would be one day reunited with it. Between the looters and Japanese raiders, Stanley never expected to see these things again. The contents were of great sentimental value and included the gifts that Monica and Stanley had received from many of their Chinese friends. Ma faithfully kept his promise and years later, after the war was over, this trunk miraculously arrived with all its treasures. Among my favourites of these is a most beautiful set of four wrought-iron wall hangings that depict the four seasons. These have been hanging on the wall in my father David's home for many years now. Best of all, although they never saw him again, the arrival of the trunk gave Monica and Stanley hope that Ma and his family might have survived the war.

With no official means of transport left, Stanley had to resort to more desperate measures. His fluent Chinese and oriental ways were yet again invaluable for negotiating passage at a time when hostility and paranoia were rife. It is not clear what kind of vessel he escaped on, but as legend now has it, and as told by Monica over the years:

He had finally escaped, but there had been no passage for him, so he had to tie himself by a rope to the deck of a ship. It was the last ship to get out.[12]

And so Stanley made the same 1,300-mile journey he had made four years earlier when the Japanese had first invaded Shanghai. Monica believed that he travelled much of the way to Hong Kong tied to the deck in this way. He was fortunate that he left when he did. Others were not so lucky. Many who worked for the same mission were captured by the Japanese and imprisoned. At least one other British family that Monica and Stanley knew well were killed trying to escape.

At the end of May 1941, Monica received a cable to say that Stanley had arrived safely in Hong Kong and was trying to work out how to reach her in Australia:

> What excitement. Stanley is actually on the way here for a six month furlough. I had a cable from Kong Kong this week and I will be going to go up to Sydney to meet him. I have just written to the Corbetts to see if they know of some nice spot where we can have a second honeymoon. David is nearly as excited as I am and we have been buying ourselves some new clothes today. David is a real treat. He is so funny and attractive. Auntie Ethel says that David spoils you for an ordinary child. David is just 'it'. I think so too.[13]

Then there was another month of waiting. The anticipation was almost unbearable – excitement tinged with fear of uncertainty. It was excruciating, and at the same time unreal. By the end of June it was almost within reach:

It is lovely to think that this time next week I will be in Sydney waiting for Stanley. David and I are going up on the night train on Thursday. Thank goodness I have David to keep my mind occupied these days. It would have been dreadful if I were alone. I hope that by the time you get this you will have already had a cable of his safe arrival. I go to bed before nine each night to make the next day come more quickly. I'm terribly excited and I bet Stanley is too.[14]

There is no letter providing an immediate account of their reunion and it is unlikely that Monica would have shared any of the more intimate details with her parents anyway. She did tell me shortly before she died that their reunion brought them both incredible joy. Even if the world around them seemed to be descending into chaos, they found a deep sense of happiness, completeness and peace. She had been waiting so long that it took a while before she could believe it was real. Their 'second honeymoon' was also productive in other ways, and was it was not long before Monica wrote to her parents announcing her second pregnancy.

Starting over

Although the war was still raging in the north, life in Australia seemed idyllic in comparison. Many Australians lived in fear of a Japanese invasion, and with their first-hand knowledge of the Japanese, both Monica and Stanley knew what this could mean.

After their happy reunion in Sydney, the little family returned to Parkes, and as Monica said many years later:

> We began life all over again, without even a cup and saucer to our name, but it was WONDERFUL.[15]

The first month of Stanley's return was spent recovering from his journey and reconnecting with his young family. Monica was overjoyed. David was beside himself with excitement. Stanley spent many long hours playing with the son he once thought he might never see again. He met Monica's extended family for the first time, although he was sad to have missed meeting Frances.

> Stanley is enjoying life in Australia despite its drawbacks. It can be a frightfully uncivilised place can't it? These awful lavatories crawl with maggots and are only emptied once a week. No wonder there are flies everywhere![16]

David has been very happy with his Daddy home. He plays with
him all day. He is now sleeping peacefully. This week he learned nearly
all his nursery rhymes. He is very happy at Sunday school. Yesterday he
asked to see God and demanded that I took him in his pram to see Him.
He said that if God was so far away that we could not walk to see Him,
then we should go in his pram!

He looks far healthier here than he did in China. His cheeks are
roses. I wish he weren't quite so highly strung. He gets so excited and
won't sit still for a moment. Stanley can't believe how he can have
progressed so far in six months.

The most pressing issue was for Stanley to find work. He applied
to the Royal Australian Air Force (RAAF) and within a few
weeks had to travel to Melbourne for an interview.

It has been a bitterly cold day today and poor Stanley is travelling to
Melbourne all night. He would have to go on the coldest day of the year.
He has been here for exactly four weeks now and today is off for his
first interview. I hope he gets the job. It is a position with the RAAF.
It is a rather awful journey. He has to change trains four times. It is
terrible with him away. I've moved into the bedroom with David for
the evening as I don't like being all alone. I still dream of the day
when peace may come, and we will all be able to meet again in
a wonderful reunion.

The RAAF enlisted Stanley within a few weeks. He started as
a pilot officer but by the end of the war had become a squadron
leader. Before he started he had to do a six-week intensive
course in administration and law. He also had to learn to drill.
Monica always found the idea of this very amusing.

They had to make arrangements to move to Melbourne fairly quickly. In August Monica wrote to tell her parents the news from their new flat in South Yarra:

> We have had a rushed but thrilling month since I last wrote. We went to Cudal for a weekend and got back to a letter from the RAAF to say Stanley was to start in five days. So we rushed on with packing and arrived in Melbourne last Saturday to stay in the Victoria Palace Hotel.
>
> In the afternoon we started to look at Melbourne. I love it. I feel like I am back in England again and the good old Yarra reminds us constantly of the Thames. We found a very posh furnished flat here after a few days. Wall to wall carpets and an automatic hot water system. Its chief advantage is that it is directly opposite the Botanical Gardens. They are the most beautiful gardens I have seen in all the world. They beat the Hanging Gardens of Bombay and the renowned gardens of Penang. And to be within twenty seconds walk of them (just the width of the road) is perfection.
>
> On Friday Stanley started work at his station – the largest in Australia. Unfortunately he has to live there, but he will be able to come home on Saturday nights only. He is sleeping in a tin hut with twenty other men. Quite a new life, but I think he is enjoying it. The flat here is quite beyond our means but we will live in it for a few weeks until I can find something else. It looks like we will be stationed here for a while.[17]

In October 1941 during his early training Stanley became very unwell with pneumonia. He had to be taken by ambulance to hospital. Although he recovered uneventfully, this was ironically the same hospital where he was due to be appointed as administrator after his training. Meanwhile Monica and David were settling into a comfortable routine in Melbourne.

We all like Melbourne more and more. It is a most delightful city to live
in and we are all in the best of health. David and I have been out every
day, on train and tram and bus trips, trying to make the most of life
while Stanley is away.[18]

Despite their love of Melbourne, Monica and Stanley had every
intention of returning to China after the war. They still regarded
it as home and missed their Chinese friends and the way of life,
as Monica wrote to her parents:

I hope that you realise that after the war is over we definitely intend to
return to China. There is no doubt whatever in our minds about that.
We are still in the mission but have leave for the duration of the war.
Our campus life in China was ideal and we both miss it and long to be
with our old cook and little sister again. I love the Chinese and I long to
return but not under the present conditions. It is good to see Australia
again, and after living here I don't think that I can ever live in England
again. But after living in China I don't want to stay here any longer
than necessary.

But that was not to be. Stanley returned to China many years
later, but Monica never did. She remained in Australia for the
rest of her life, but made numerous and regular trips back to
England, especially in her later years.

Separated by war in the 1940s, it must have been very difficult not knowing when she might see her ageing parents again.

Although I can't see us meeting for years, no doubt the way will open
for us somehow.

274

It was only September, but Monica busied herself preparing Christmas hampers for her family in England, hoping they would make it in time. Money was tight initially, with Stanley earning £7 and 14 shillings a week. However, promotions soon came and his salary increased. The government also gave a child allowance, which was soon to increase with Monica's news:

> David is just two and a half years old today. How time flies. I think that next April a new little Prescott will be born. I am about nine weeks along the way with a second baby and I don't feel half as bad as I did three years ago.[19]

Now she was in Melbourne, she was initially not sure who to turn to for help and advice with her pregnancy. But she soon realised that she had a kindred spirit. As another coincidence would have it, Gordon King's wife, a doctor too, had also been evacuated from Hong Kong to Melbourne. At that stage Gordon King was still stranded in Hong Kong, or so they believed. He had been a great friend to them and it was especially lovely for Monica to finally make the connection with his wife after all these years. They had no indication of how, or if, Gordon would join them in Australia. Monica understood the separation that Mrs King must be feeling and was ever more grateful that her own time of waiting was over.

> I am going up to see Mrs Gordon King on Friday to see what clinic to attend as I don't know what there is in this part of the world. She is also a doctor and practises here now so she will know who to recommend. I will have to wear a tight abdominal belt after the fifth month as my tummy muscles are non-existent. Any future labour will have to be

terminated quickly with forceps. My muscles are incapable of doing the job themselves so it is no use waiting for them.

I wish that you were here and could enjoy our babies with us. I know that you would like David. He is intelligent, lovable and good looking. Although he is two-and-a-half his knowledge is equal to a child of five. He can already count and read some capital letters. His vocabulary is enough to write a novel. He is mechanically minded and screws, nuts, bolts, gate catches and cogwheels are his toys. We went to the zoo today and paid 4 pence to see the performing animals, including monkeys on bicycles. David laughed so loudly that everyone turned to see him. When we came home I asked him why he had laughed so much and he said 'Because I was so happy'.

David was only to enjoy the limelight for a few months more. His mother was the centre of his perfect universe. She had been the only constant thing in a world that was forever changing around them. He had sustained her in her loneliness and distracted her from her fears as they had crossed the hemispheres. But his world was soon to change.

A new community with old friends

By October 1941, Monica and David had moved to a house at 27 Gordon Street in Hampton, Melbourne. This was the house of Mrs Plummer, who, like so many others, opened her home to refugees as part of the war effort, and to make ends meet. Mrs Plummer had a very grand and beautiful home with sixteen rooms and a 'garden like a park' and Monica said that she had 'never lived in such a superior residence'. She was always grateful for how good Mrs Plummer was to them.

This was a fortunate move in other ways as well. Mrs Plummer was a 'keen Presbyterian' who took Monica and David to church every Sunday. A strong church community had always been familiar and important to Monica. She was already starting to feel at home in Melbourne, but she said that 'there is nothing like a Church for making new friends'. The most exciting coincidence of all was that this Brighton church was a strong supporter of a large number of Chinese missionaries, so it was there that she was reunited with many other mission evacuees who had escaped from North China before her.

> The people nearly fell over me when I said that I had come from China. Quite a number of our old friends from North China already attend the church. It made me so happy to see the family who lived next door to us in Peitaiho were in the seat in front of me.[20]

Monica was very contented there, although they all lived with the distant threat of the Japanese in the north.

> We are all very, very happy here, but the world would be happier still if the Japanese were getting nearer their own homes instead of ours.
> I suppose that if the cities here are evacuated David and I will be on the move again, but at the moment we are not in a very vulnerable area and I hope we can stay. I am so contented here. I love the house, the friends and the Church and I don't want to move again until the war is over.[21]

They continued to struggle financially as the price of food and other essentials continued to rise. Even so, Monica would still put small amounts of money aside to send back to her parents in England, always apologising that she could not send more. She remained well during her second pregnancy. Her Auntie Ethel came to stay in January 1942, to help her with David and to escape the summer heat in Parkes.

> Things are pretty good, but we have odd famines occasionally. At present we are potato-less. Dad's country of birth is a wonderful place but the politics are hateful and it is terrible how culture and education seem to be despised. The unions are choking the country. A bread deliverer gets £5/10 a week and a qualified nurse only £2. The standards are up-side down.
> I am as fit as a fiddle and Auntie Ethel can't get over my energy. Of course my activities are somewhat curtailed these days and are mostly in the form of sewing small garments and looking after David. I wish you could see David. The minister's wife says you only have to look at him to see what an outstanding child he is. He must take after you.

> What a life it is. I wonder where we shall meet again. I hope it
> won't be long before we find ourselves over in England again.

As ever, Monica's letters seem more addressed to her father Allen
than her mother.

> Things are much the same here but trenches are being dug all over the
> place. We are relying on an inner room in the event of bombing, but
> of course if anything much happens we will escape to the country.
> But I don't want to leave Melbourne one tiny bit. I just love it.[15]

In March they had good news from Hong Kong. Dr Gordon
King was finally on his way, along with some other mission
friends who had escaped from China. Although they were still
uncertain of whether they would make it to Australia, it was still
a great relief.

> I do hope that things don't get so bad that we have to evacuate. But
> we were thrilled this week to hear that Gordon King has escaped. His
> wife had a cable from him. We don't know if he will make it here or not.
> There are always a few bits of cheerful news to make up for the rest.
>   We have to keep calm and hope for the best. Auntie gets so het up
> most of the time, but Stanley and I have got so used to trouble in the
> last few years and know to expect anything.[22]

Stanley's war effort

According to Monica, 'Pilot Officer Prescott landed on his feet alright'. He enjoyed his work in the Air Force and found more excellent chances for promotion.

> Stanley is getting along well. He finishes his six months' probation at the end of February and will start looking for a promotion then. He is dreadfully tired at the end of his 13 hour shifts and sleeps most of the time he is home. As usual he is working harder than anyone else, and so he gets along a little further.
>
> You would be very proud if you knew what a responsible position he now holds. He seems very happy and contented. He feels that he is really doing something worthwhile.[23]

As he progressed, Stanley's work took him further away from his family for longer periods.

Then, when the military intelligence services realised Stanley's talent for oriental languages, he vanished by stealth and Monica had no idea where he was. All of her mail was forwarded by a central service to his secret location, where he worked as a translator and code breaker. His years dealing with the Japanese administration in China had taught him much. He had become so proficient at the language it is said that, in his dealings by telephone, they had thought he was Japanese. His fluent Japanese made him an invaluable asset to the American and Allied forces, intercepting and decoding Japanese radio transmissions. He soon became section head of the Intelligence Unit that served General MacArthur in the Asia-Pacific. There he met and supervised a young Zelman Cowen and they became firm lifelong friends. Later, as Governor-General of the Commonwealth of Australia, His Excellency Sir Zelman Cowen honoured Stanley in his speech at Government House in Perth on 3 October 1979, describing him as a 'remarkable man in mind, style and history'.

The following words are taken from the beginning of Sir Zelman's speech, and reflect on their shared wartime experiences and indicate the high regard Cowen had for Stanley.

Early in February 1978, when I had been in this office for a very short time, I received an official and a personal letter from the late Sir Stanley Prescott inviting me to be a guest at the 1979 Annual Meeting of the Royal Perth Hospital. Sir Stanley pointed to the fact that 1979 would be the 150th Anniversary year of the State of Western Australia; he also observed that this hospital would be in its 150th year of service to the community and would be contributing to various activities to mark this special occasion.

The personal note was rather differently addressed and signed, and it recalled 'old times' sake'. It is my normal practice to consider invitations somewhat closer to the event, but on this occasion I replied within days to say that I should be pleased to accept. I did so because the occasion is historic and because Sir Stanley, an old friend, was your Chairman at the time.

We cannot share 'old times' sake' because he is dead and I am deeply sorry that it is so. I first met him in 1942, when we were both members of a war-time staff that served General MacArthur in Brisbane, which was then the General Headquarters, South West Pacific Area. That joint services body bore the title of Combined Operations Intelligence Centre, and Stanley Prescott, an air force officer, was head of a section that I worked in as a very young junior naval officer. It was a very happy and simulating association: he was a remarkable man in mind, style and history.[24]

Later, from 1943 to 1945, as squadron leader, Stanley went on to command the No. 1 Flying Personnel Research Unit in Melbourne. Back to his old love: research. This was a physiological research unit focused on aviation medicine. He was involved in testing pilots for high–altitude flying. My second cousin Jeremy recalls that Stanley was very personally involved in his research:

Uncle Stanley told us that he had been 'centrifuged' at one point to assess the effects of G-forces, and ended up not being able to speak for some time![25]

It was there that he met Wilfred Simmonds, another physiologist and a great friend to Stanley. 'Wilf Simmonds was such a nice man' as Monica later recalled.

I think I still have a picture of them both together in their uniforms. Years later, Stanley appointed him as the foundation Professor of Physiology at The University of Western Australia when we moved there. They were great friends.[26]

In fact, Professor Simmonds was my lecturer in physiology when I studied medicine in 1983. That was rather special to all of us.

Another son is born

Nigel Ian Prescott was born at St Vincent's Maternity Hospital on 9 May 1942. The birth actually took place in buildings opposite the main hospital. There were no elevators and the local fire brigade was on call to carry patients up and down the stairs. Because of the ongoing war with the Japanese, Monica and Stanley revised their original plan to name him John Allen Prescott because of what his initials would spell, but Nigel remains bemused by their chosen alternative.

Monica and Stanley were delighted with their new arrival, and were determined to shower love equally between their wonderful boys. They had already made many firm friends and Monica was pleased to get many letters and cards of congratulation, including one from the head of one of Melbourne's largest newspapers, who wrote that 'if Nigel shows himself possessed of the attractiveness and mental alertness of his elder brother, you will have abundant reason to think yourselves blessed'. Although were no complications, Monica remained in hospital for a week, enjoying 'a little holiday' before the hard work began.

> But I long to go back home to David. Children are not allowed in here. I told him I was going away and he accepted it wonderfully. He is very

understanding. How I miss seeing our little bit of sunshine that has smiled at me every day over the last three years.[27]

Children were not permitted to visit, so Stanley was not able to bring David when he came to see Monica and Nigel each day on his way from work. Mrs Plummer looked after David during the day and Stanley took care of him every night. It was a wonderful treat for Stanley to have David to himself during this brief time. He loved it. And he arranged for David to make his first phone call.

It was a great thrill yesterday when I got a call through from David. He had never spoken on the phone before and I don't know if he heard what I said, but his little voice came over so clearly. He said 'Hello Mummy, how is Nigel Mummy? Are you coming home soon Mummy? Goodbye Mummy.' I don't think that anyone could have a treasure we prize more than David, and Nigel will get just as much love as David gets and gives. I am already looking forward to the next baby. They're heavenly little things aren't they? And they become lovelier every day.

Monica took such great pleasure in the simple things, including planning the short journey home from the hospital. She was so happy that Stanley had been granted a day's leave for their arrival.

We are going to take a taxi as a special treat when I come home with Nigel, as with all the petrol rationing we rarely step outside these days. The taxi will bring Mrs Plummer and David to collect us. It will cost 25/- but after all it isn't every day. Stanley is going to arrange to have the next day off work. It is all too thrilling for words. As you always used to say: 'Monica was born to be lucky'. I think I must have been.

There are not many letters over the following months as Monica devoted her energy to her new son. She described him as a very contented baby who was much more manageable than David. By the time Nigel was four months old, Monica's relationship with David was changing. Comparisons between the children appear in her letters and although she clearly loved David dearly, she began to show some frustrations towards him.

> Nigel is nothing less than perfect. He lies in his room all day and never cries to be picked up. He is much lazier than David. Rattles don't interest him and he is a more contented baby.
>
> David is the sensitive one. We are having a very hard time trying to turn him into a man. He is like a sensitive plant. His tears are always ready to fall, just as his smiles are. He cries terribly easily at the silliest little things. He longs to play with other children, but every time he does he cries. He just can't stand up for himself (still sucks his thumb too). But he is improving and will be alright.[28]

Nigel and David could not have been more different. And, it was not long before they were joined by their first sister, Helen, who was born in July 1944.

Return to campus life

The end of the war signified another new phase in their lives. Although they did not return to the campus of Cheeloo University as they had always planned, another opportunity soon presented itself. In 1946, Stanley was appointed master of Ormond College, University of Melbourne. Monica found herself in a large house with plenty of help for her children. This made it possible for her to work again at Queen Victoria Hospital during this period, mainly in the outpatient section. She continued working until mid–1947, when she had her fourth and final child, Margaret.

> Not long after the war, Stanley got the position as Master of Ormond College at the University of Melbourne. Well, that was a beautiful eighteen-roomed home. Very, very Lovely. It was a Presbyterian college of course. Stanley had all his meals in the college itself and we could have a meal sent down any time we liked.
>
> You could get plenty of help with the children in those days. The house was so large, we had room for a very nice girl who came from the country. She was happy to live in, and would look after the children while I went to work.
>
> We had a lovely time there in Melbourne. I went back there for a visit recently and there is a lovely portrait of Stanley in the Dining Hall,

done by Clifton Pugh. Quite an interesting one that. There is another
wonderful painting of Stanley that was done much later in Perth
and it now hangs in the Vice-Chancellery at The University of
Western Australia.[29]

Although she appreciated modern art, Monica was never sure that
the Clifton Pugh portrait quite captured who Stanley was. She
thought it made him look 'all spidery' with too much attention
drawn to his long fingers. I saw it myself on a visit to Ormond
College in 2003. I was attending a national meeting of my society when Professor Andrew Kemp, an old student of Ormond
College, kindly agreed to take me there to view the portrait. It
had just been taken down for repairs, or that is what they told
me. But they did get it out, so I did get to see it. And I had to
agree with Monica. It gave me no sense of the man I remember.
I much prefer the more traditional painting that hangs at UWA.
That one has somehow captured more of the gentle wisdom in
his eyes, and the quiet confidence of his manner.

In the Ormond College *Chronicle* from that period, Stanley
was once again noted for both his achievements and his drive
in bringing about much needed change, but also his diplomacy.
The situation into which he came was not an easy one, following significant administrative difficulties in the last years of
the war. He had been tasked with considerable expansion and
improvement of the college buildings 'a feat that he achieved
with ingenuity and success' according to the Ormond *Chronicle*.

Relations between Master and Students' Club must repeatedly assume
the form of dialectic struggles and such discussions were made lively and
fruitful by his fine wit and capacity for adaptation.

The General Committee were often surprised by his grasp of events within the College and found him ever ready to turn their suggestions to the best interests of Ormond. But his association with the students was not always through the official channels – from informal discussion came schemes, such as that for acquiring paintings for the Common Room walls.

He gave a strong lead to almost every aspect to College life and was a delightful and entertaining figure in the daily life of the College.[30]

While Stanley undertook these commitments and many others, including his membership of the Melbourne University Council, Monica played an important role behind the scenes. She enjoyed entertaining many academics and other visitors in their wonderful home at the Master's Lodge of Ormond College. After their more humble dwellings in China, she felt like she was living in a castle.

Mr Prescott was most ably assisted by wife, Dr Monica Prescott, and the Lodge was the scene of many functions over which they presided with dignity and charm.

The family enjoyed campus life for another six years. Before long David was at Geelong College.

With each passing year David came to feel that his parents' high expectations of his academic abilities were never realised. Although he was gifted mechanically and became a accomplished speaker in his later capacity as an Anglican priest, he was not suited to traditional education. Some years ago, in 1980, when he was forty-one, David reflected on this in some personal notes:

My brother was born in 1942. At first our personalities clashed, later his academic ability against my apparent failure widened the gap. If anything forced me to face the reality of day to day living, it was school. Perhaps I was too immature, too innocent, too busy in my own little world of exciting things, but I hated it, and continued to hate it for the next eleven years. In my early days I can still remember a special chart hung up in the dining room where we ate our meals. A chart with red stars on it. The red-stars showed the days when I went to school without a tantrum or, having appeared to go to school, was not later found hiding in the house.[31]

Nigel suffered a 'weak chest' from an early age and was diagnosed with asthma, which was still fairly uncommon in those days. He was not as athletic as David, and despite David's recollections, was apparently more prone to tantrums. Monica once told me that Nigel was jealous that David could 'do somersaults' and became obsessed with mastering the feat himself. Although this apparently took some time, his eventual achievement of this milestone also brought greater confidence and an end to his tantrums. At least that is how the story goes.

Perhaps as a result of the perceived rivalry, Nigel was always more determined and more ambitious. He was also more independent. According to another family legend, Nigel decided to enrol himself in a new school without consulting his parents. He apparently did not care much for the primary school they first took him to, so he found a more agreeable alternative. In those days the children walked themselves to school, and this went on for a whole school term before Monica and Stanley realised.

290

A reunion is planned

With a growing young family and Stanley's mounting university commitments, plans to return to England to visit their families became more difficult. It was decided instead that Allen and Ethel would pay a visit to Australia. In many ways it was perhaps more fitting for Allen to return 'from the land of his fathers' to the 'land of his birth' one more time. This was planned as a very special homecoming. Although his proud mother Frances was no longer there to meet him, there were many others who still remembered him. However, with all the plans set, tragedy struck in April 1947 before this reunion could take place.

One of the Empire's Finest and Most Brilliant Sons

The passing of Henry Allen Job recently at Dolphin Square, London left the British Empire poorer for the loss of one of its finer sons – one whose life was devoted to the uplift of humanity, and one who always lent a helping hand to those fighting evils, yet never pushed a weaker brother downhill.[32]

This news must have devastated Monica. She had not seen her dad since she had left for China almost ten years earlier. Now she would never see him again, and he would never see his grandchildren.

———————

His younger daughter Dr Monica Prescott, whose husband is now Master at Ormond College at the University of Melbourne, after many years in China, had been looking forward to greeting her parents at the end of the year and all arrangements had been made for them to sail. She had a home ready for them. But it was not to be. Her father died at his post, loved by many and respected by all, political friends and foes alike, for he had no personal foes.

———————

It was at least fortunate that Monica's sister Hope had returned briefly from Africa for a visit to England and saw her father only days before his sudden death. Their mother Ethel was alone now. With Hope returning to Africa, it was decided that Ethel would join Monica in Australia sooner than planned. According to Monica, it was disastrous. She had never been close to her mother and she could not handle her mother's grief. They both found it difficult and Monica was relieved when her mother chose to return to England about three months later. They probably both were.

> Mother came to stay for a while when we were there in Melbourne. Dad had just died, and she came more or less the next week. And it was just too soon. She hadn't really given herself time to adjust and get used to being a widow. She was so very unhappy and she had left her friends all behind.[33]

Stanley's parents, Jack and Jessie Prescott, made a far more successful trip to Australia in 1949, staying for around six months with Monica and Stanley in Melbourne. The wonderfully large house at Ormond College made this very comfortable for everyone. They may have stayed longer if Jack had not fallen ill. He died shortly after their return to England. It was not until 1956 that Monica and Stanley returned to England to see each of their mothers again, taking with them their daughters, Margaret and Helen.

In her remaining years in Melbourne, Monica got more involved in the local community and supported Stanley in his university activities. She joined the board of management of the Royal Women's Hospital, and later became the vice-president. She was also the board's representative on the council of Victorian Baby Health Centres. This was an immensely enjoyable and stimulating time for Monica. On the hospital board she worked alongside many other eminent members of the community. This included Mrs Pattie Menzies until her husband Robert again became Prime Minister of Australia in December 1949 and they moved to the Lodge. This early friendship was rekindled many years later when, after both of their husbands were knighted, Sir Stanley celebrated Sir Robert's career with an honorary doctorate from UWA. Curiously, their husbands also later died in the same year.

During this period Monica was often asked to talk of her life in China to both church and other community groups. Her audiences were always fascinated. With tender nostalgia she enjoyed showing the embroidered silks, padded coats and other treasured possession that Ma Ru had returned to them from China. At every gathering, her message was always one of service, and treating others with respect. She would say the Japanese guards were always kind to her and they were only doing what they were told to do, and she would be quite upset whenever she heard of any racial hatred.

By the time they came to leave Melbourne in 1953, both Monica and Stanley had become highly respected members of the community. But their work had only just begun.

Perth

In 1953, when he was just forty-three years old, Stanley was appointed as the first full-time Vice-Chancellor of The University of Western Australia (UWA). The family found a new home in Perth, and Monica and Stanley both fell in love with the campus, the community and the city. Already accustomed to academic life in Melbourne, they felt very much at home hosting the dinners, parties and events that came with his more official duties. This was a wonderful way for Monica to quickly make new friends.

An enormous highlight was the royal visit in 1954, only a year into Stanley's appointment. The preparations and the excitement went on for months. The recently crowned Queen was enormously popular. Aside from being the first tour of a reigning monarch, it was also the first royal tour to Australia for twenty years. Its scale was immense. And not only was the Queen visiting the campus, but UWA was hosting the royal ball, and Stanley had to oversee every detail and temper heady enthusiasm from every direction.

In the lead-up to celebrations, tragedy struck. The state of Western Australia was hit by an epidemic of polio, and there were grave concerns that royal events should be cancelled in the interest of public safety. According to statistics from the Poliomyelitis Committee of the National Health and Medical Research Council, 206 cases of polio were registered in Western Australia between September 1953 and March 1954. This was devastating in such a small community. Because the previous major outbreak of 1948 was believed to have been exacerbated by large public events such as the Royal Show, medical authorities were concerned to limit crowds to avoid even greater spread of disease. With the imminent arrival of the Queen, the royal schedule was urgently revised and a number of engagements were cancelled or transferred to outdoor venues. All food for the royal party was to be imported from the eastern states, the shaking of hands was forbidden, and the presentation of bouquets to the Queen strictly curtailed.[34]

In the face of public disappointment, Prime Minister Menzies, already a friend to Monica and Stanley from their days in Melbourne, announced in a press statement at the time:

> If there is the slightest risk of infection to Her Majesty or a risk of added danger to the people, and in particular the children, of Western Australia, and the medical authorities say there is, then it is unthinkable that any Government should not act immediately on medical advice. That is what I have done.[35]

Instead of the original plan for the Queen to stay at Government House in the city, she and her party were to stay aboard her yacht, the *Gothic*. This new arrangement actually afforded the public additional opportunities to see the royals as they travelled to and from the ship.

To everyone's relief, the university events went as planned and were a great success, as reported by the UWA *Gazette* at the time.

> Her Majesty the Queen and His Royal Highness the Duke of Edinburgh officially visited the University on Monday, 29th March. They were met on the south side of Winthrop Hall by the Minister for the North-West, the Hon. H. C. Strickland, M.L.C., who presented the Chancellor and Mrs Gillett and the Vice-Chancellor and Mrs Prescott.[36]

This was only the first of a series of occasions on which Monica met Queen Elizabeth. The royal ball was held on 30 March at UWA and the dance floor was built especially for the occasion on Whitfield Court by the reflection pond. It was, by all accounts, a beautiful and stately occasion, certainly one that Monica and Stanley spoke of for years to come.

The following year, the Salk vaccine against polio became available in Australia.

One of the main reasons for Stanley's appointment was to establish a new medical school, the one that I ultimately attended myself. As Monica recalled:

> Before that the medical students did the first three years of biological science in Perth, but then had to go elsewhere to finish their training. We knew all about this from our time in Melbourne, as many of the students from Perth stayed in residence at Ormond College while they

were doing their last three years of clinical training. So his job was really to start a full medical program in Perth.[37]

To begin with, Stanley played a pivotal role in community fundraising, and in establishing the Raine Foundation, which has since underpinned the success of medical research in the state of Western Australia. This brought out the very best in the local Perth community. A vast fortune was raised by the generous support of its citizens.

> It was a truly wonderful time, because so many people gave money towards it. Especially Ma Raine, who used to run a whole series of pubs and hotels in the city. So funds for the medical school and the Raine Foundation were really raised from people running pubs! Rather funny when you think about it. Everyone wanted a medical school. Money just rolled in because people didn't want to have to send their children interstate. It was such a great success.

On the death of her husband, Mary Raine, a successful hotelier and wealthy businesswoman, was faced with enormous death duties. Stanley wrote to her on behalf of the university, asking whether she had considered donating the fortune to medical science and research. According to Monica, 'Ma' Raine apparently jumped at the chance to make such a valuable contribution and 'to diddle the government' at the same time.

Monica also recalls the difficult phone calls Stanley received from a small minority in the community who were opposed to the medical school being established on the proceeds of 'pubs and drink'. He used to say 'I don't care where it *comes* from, as long as it is not going to be *spent* on drink!' We can only imagine what Monica's teetotal father, Allen Job, would have thought of all this. But most of the Western Australian community was solidly behind it, and it really was a wonderful time.

In those years they worked hard to prepare a new clinical school at Royal Perth Hospital, where Stanley served on the board for nearly twenty years. There are some lovely photographs in the Medicine Faculty office of Stanley leading the first procession through the square outside Royal Perth Hospital.

Stanley had an important hand in the selection of many of the founding professors of the new medical school.

> By then Gordon King had returned to live in England, when Stanley invited him to be our first professor of obstetrics and gynaecology. It was quite nice having it like that, with our old connections from China.

And so the Kings also made Perth their new home. Kindred spirits in every sense, Monica and Stanley were overjoyed to be able to share another episode of their lives. Shared history. Shared philosophies. And a shared love of the Chinese people. They all remained close friends for the rest of their lives.

> And we had many other wonderful professors to start the clinical school, including Professor Eric Saint, Professor Wilf Simmonds, who Stanley knew well from his Air Force days, and of course Professor Neville Stanley of Microbiology.

Monica and Stanley went down to Fremantle port to meet the ships as each of the new professors arrived with their families.

Notably, when the Professor of Microbiology, Neville Stanley, arrived, Monica vividly remembers his small daughter Fiona in her shiny red shoes.

He arrived with his now famous daughter Professor Fiona Stanley, who was Australian of the Year quite recently. I remember her as a little girl with red shoes and white socks, so very sweet. Her mother was quite extraordinary too. We thought she was a little eccentric, but perhaps that's why Fiona has achieved so much. Yes, I clearly remember when she arrived with her family by ship.

In the kind of symmetry that seems so typically to pervade this story, that same little girl Fiona became a major figure in my own life many years later. Although we went to the same school, St Hilda's Anglican School for girls, she was many years ahead of me and I did not meet her there. But I saw photographs of her as the head girl of that school, welcoming the Queen to Australia.

I did not meet Fiona Stanley until 1990, when I was still considering my career prospects after spending a post-internship year of reflection in Fiji. There I had met a paediatrician, Professor Ian Lewis, who had taken up a position as head of the Fiji School of Medicine after retiring as dean of medicine in Tasmania. He had spent time in Perth in the 1960s and recalled my grand-father Stanley well. By that time he had also met a young and enthusiastic Fiona Stanley, who was starting to establish her own career as a medical researcher. The first thing he told me to do when I got back to Australia was to seek her advice and encouragement. Although I did not realise it at the time, from that moment my own destiny was set. When Fiona looked at me with her intense gaze, anything seemed possible. Over the decades that have followed, she has become a great mentor and a special friend.

Although I returned to the ranks of the resident medical staff to finish my basic training in paediatrics, it made all the difference having someone like Fiona in the wings of my life. She was in the throes of establishing the Telethon Institute for Child Health Research (TICHR) and was always a source of inspiration and encouragement. As one of the first female professors at UWA she has also become one of the most successful. Within a few years I had passed my paediatric exams and discovered a unique opportunity to specialise in immunology and undertake a PhD at TICHR with Professor Patrick Holt. At that stage it was uncommon for medical graduates to undertake PhDs, but following my heart as I always do, I knew it was the right thing. Monica was very excited about this and was most pleased to hear of my contact with Fiona.

In 2003, when Fiona Stanley was honoured as Australian of the Year, a special celebration was arranged for her and all of the other UWA staff who appeared on the Australia Day honours list. This took place in the Prescott Room of the UWA Vice-Chancellery, and I was surprised to discover that I was invited. I was even more surprised when I discovered why.

As my first official invitation to the room named in commemoration of my grandfather, it was already an auspicious occasion. Initially under the impression that I had been simply invited as member of the academic staff, I soon realised that each of the honorands had been asked to invite only two or three special guests. I found myself in a room of who's who in Perth. I played along trusting that all would become clear.

Each of the new recipients of the Order of Australia or Companion of Australia made a speech acknowledging the role of each of their selected guests in their success. When it came to Fiona's turn, she firstly thanked Professor Lou Landau, the then Dean of Medicine, for his role in establishing the TICHR. The second guest she thanked was Dr Janet Holmes à Court, well-known businesswoman, benefactor and wife of the late Robert Holmes à Court, for her lifetime of friendship. Fiona went on to discuss the importance of an inspired future, then announced that her third guest 'was the future'. Her arm swept the room to where I stood. With no forewarning, I was overcome with both honour and surprise as she introduced me. It was a very good thing that all I had to do was smile in humble and gracious thanks as the eyes of the room turned curiously to see what in fact 'the future' looked like. This exemplifies the kind of generous leader Fiona is and I will always aspire to be. When I told Monica, she was too proud to speak.

It is so strange the way life works. The way a young girl, inspired by her unique father, dreamed of going as a doctor to China and set in motion such as series of interconnected events that brought a group of equally unique and inspiring people to Perth. I was still experiencing the ripples of this fifty years later.

Perhaps in one final twist of irony, the state government announced the planned closure of Royal Perth Hospital as part of the proposed restructuring of medical services around the same time. A new hospital was to be built in the southern suburbs of Perth to cater for the expanding population in that region. It was to be named the Fiona Stanley Hospital. While I was happy for the recognition for Fiona, the impending death of Royal Perth Hospital was cause for considerable sadness for many. It had been a historic landmark for the first generations of local medical graduates and had been the site of my own training. More deeply for me, I knew that Sir Stanley Prescott had devoted twenty years of his life to the development of that hospital. He could not have suspected, as he watched her disembark with her family in 1957, that his new university hospital might be later lost in the name of the little girl with red shoes. I feel I am being melodramatic. Let us instead say that the end of an era that began with Stanley will pave the way for an even better future, one that I am glad and proud to be part of.

Developing the UWA community

Stanley's progressive vision and stealthy efficiency played a much wider role in the development of UWA as a world–class university. Ever modest, he was not one to document all of his achievements, but at least some of these are summarised in the biography by G. C. Bolton:

> He took office as vice-chancellor of the University of Western Australia on 1 April 1953 and presided over a period of unprecedented growth in students, staff, budgets and building. New faculties of medicine, architecture, and economics and commerce were created, and work on the (A. J.) Reid Library was commenced. Determined that the new buildings should harmonize with the Spanish-mission idiom of the university's pre-war core, he persuaded the town-planner Gordon Stephenson in 1958 to act as consultant architect for a revised master-plan. The result was probably Australia's most unified and aesthetically satisfying campus.
>
> Tall, slim and prematurely grey-haired, Prescott looked the diplomat he was. He cultivated amicable relations with the university senate and an able, but combative, professorial board: 'Come, let's not get cross with one another', he would say. Maintaining strong ties with the business community and Rotary, he kept on good terms with leading

politicians of both major parties and chaired (1962–64) the Australian Vice-Chancellors' Committee. His own university escaped much of the student radicalism of the late 1960s and early 1970s.

Wider recognition came with Prescott's appointments to the Commission of Enquiry (1957) on the University of Malaya, as chairman (1959) of the Nanyang University Commission, Singapore, as a Commonwealth consultant (1960–71) on the Inter-University Council for Higher Education Overseas and as a member (1967) of Sir Lawrence Jackson's committee on tertiary education in Western Australia...

Prescott left the University of Western Australia thriving and well nourished. His leadership was perhaps underestimated because of his preference for operating through a quiet diplomacy at times verging on mandarin subtlety. It was easy to believe the story that he once concluded a testimonial: 'You will be fortunate indeed if you get Dr...to work for you'.[38]

During the period that Stanley was at the helm, student numbers increased from 1,741 in 1953 to 7,500 in 1970. During the same period full-time teaching staff also rose, from 115 to 429. In addition to the Medicine Faculty, new faculties of Economics and Commerce, Music and Architecture were also established. The recurrent expenditure increased from $1 million to $8 million per year. Commenting on this period of expansion at the time of Stanley's retirement, the Chancellor the Honourable Sir Lawrence Jackson said:

It is a tribute to his wisdom, capacity and forethought that this growth has not been at the expense of high standards of teaching and research and that the University has maintained its high standing in the

community and the academic world. Moreover, the physical expansion
of the campus has been achieved without the loss of its beauty, and the
many fine buildings erected during his administration will long remain
as memorials to his outstanding service. He has secured himself a
distinguished place in the annals of our University.[39]

Over that same period Monica was also active on the board of St
Catherine's College. Among many other things, she oversaw the
building of a new wing and lobbied to have washbasins put into
all the students rooms, perhaps only a small luxury to us now,
but I can assure you that it made a vast difference to generations
of girls since, including myself. When I became a resident in St
Catherine's in 1982, it took me another three years to secure a
room in the sought-after Prescott Wing, which was named after
Monica as much as Stanley.

As in Melbourne, the Perth community was drawn to
Monica's stories of their life in China under Japanese occupation. She again took the opportunity to share these experiences
together with her message of love, service and respect for other
cultures.

For the first years of Stanley's tenure, the family lived in
Tuart House on the river in Matilda Bay, opposite the university.
The view from the two-storey house was magnificent. David
and Nigel made the most of their waterfront home, sailing boats
in the bay. During these early years, David also sailed with Jon
Sanders, who later became world famous for his solo round-the-
world sailing feats.

Monica presided over the Tuart Club for the wives and
families of university academics. Fiona Stanley told me this after
Monica's death and I don't have many details. By all accounts,

she helped provide support in many forms for newly arriving academics and their families.

They later moved to the house in Thomas Street, Nedlands, that I recall visiting as a child. It was a beautiful three-level house in a leafy street. I most remember the cellar and the wonderful sunroom, where I enjoyed playing with farm animals on the carpet while Stanley was reading. And the dining room with leadlight windows.

Monica and Stanley had arrived from Ormond College in Melbourne as practising Presbyterians. However, not long after their move to Perth, they and their children were all confirmed as members of the Anglican Church. St George's Cathedral in the city centre became their place of regular worship and their spiritual home. They attended every Sunday and Monica also went regularly to the Wednesday service.

Their faith was not just a matter of attending services. They both read widely to develop their understanding of Christianity, with Stanley taking a theological approach and Monica a more spiritual one. Stanley also became part of the cathedral chapter.

In his capacity as Vice-Chancellor, much of both Stanley and Monica's social life naturally centred around the academic community, and the frequent need to entertain visiting academics. While they enjoyed this, their involvement with the cathedral opened up a new group of long-lasting friendships with people Monica felt more relaxed with. In particular, they formed close friendships with Robert Moline, then Archbishop of Perth, and his wife. And, for the rest of her life, Monica treasured her close friendship with Merle Davis, wife of Russell Davis, the cathedral precentor, who later entered a Catholic religious order as Sister Michaela.

Monica became a member of the Mothers' Union and for many years was responsible for the washing, ironing and maintenance of the church linen. Helen remembers the many hours her mother devoted to this task every week, with the greatest of care. The linen was in such a poor state when she started, and Monica lovingly restored and cared for all altar cloths and other linen used during the communion services. She loved rediscovering her embroidery skills and also found enormous satisfaction in making new cassocks, albs and other associated cathedral vestments. Her work was exceptional.

There are so many things she did in her community without recognition of any kind, nor any wish for it. As her daughter Helen recalls:

> With Mother, so much of her giving was behind the scenes. There were so many other hidden undertakings not publically known that were a symbol of her faith in action.[40]

Monica also developed a strong connection with the Society of the Sacred Mission (SSM), an Anglican religious order established in 1893, partly through Father Lawrence Eyres, whom she had met through the university. She maintained her connections with SSM for the rest of her life.

It pleased her greatly when her elder son decided to follow the family tradition of service and spiritual devotion and enter the priesthood. She even made his cassock and surplice in preparation for his ordination.

Although he was the eldest of the four children, my father David was curiously the last to be confirmed in the Anglican Church. He eventually also joined the Student Christian

Movement, initially not because of any particular religious calling, but because it was popular at the time, and a good place to meet nice girls. And he did.

Sir Stanley OBE

In 1958 Stanley was awarded an OBE for his services to medical education. And when he was knighted Sir Stanley in 1965, Monica became Lady Prescott. Stanley's mother in England was so proud to see her son kneeling before the Queen. As Monica recalled:

> That was a very exciting time. It was very important and we had to dress in just the right clothes. We went to Moss Brothers in London so they could fit us out for the occasion. When Stanley said 'What do I want the gloves for?' they said, 'They are to leave with your top hat in the cloak room'. That's all. They were never actually worn.
>
> Stanley's mother Jessie came down from Peterborough, of course. His brothers wanted to come too, but no, there was only room for two guests. Jessie was so excited to see her son knighted. We sat in the gallery, which is where the relatives sit. Then one by one, they were called before the Queen. When they announced his name, Stanley walked in and faced the Queen, bowed and knelt down in front of her. After putting the sword on his shoulders, she announced 'Arise, Sir Stanley' and said a few quiet words to him. Then he rose. He had to walk two paces backwards before he moved off. You can't turn your back on the Queen, you know. His mother kept saying 'Oh, she talked to him

longer than anybody else!' She was so thrilled. She could not believe it, just so excited.

We have seen the Queen a few more times since. A Royal Garden Party, and we have been to Buckingham Palace as well for some other special functions. I recall that Stanley was identified to be one of the first in the queue to speak to her. I don't know what he'd done to deserve it that time!

It was very nice to have a chance to talk to the Queen. She is very chatty to talk to, very friendly. It was very easy, no problem at all. She came to Perth as well, and we have some photographs of that. I recall she came on the *Britannia* that time. We went and had dinner with her on the ship. There were about fifty or so of us. At about six o'clock we all stood on the deck with her. Her band was down below and they played to her. Then she turned to say goodnight to them. I think she does that every night when she's on board.

We used to go back to England almost every year. We went to another Royal Garden Party the last time we returned to England together in 1978. It was always a very lovely time. We met people from all nations there. It was a very big party, and we had another chance to speak with the Queen.[41]

Monica proudly kept a number of newspaper clippings acknowledging Sir Stanley's achievements.

W.A. Man Knighted In Queen's Honours

One of the 14 West Australians listed in the Queen's Birthday honours has been knighted. Stanley Lewis Prescott, vice-chancellor of the W.A. University for the past 12 years, becomes a Knight Bachelor in the State list. He is the 11th West Australian to be knighted in 12 State honours lists since the government took office in 1959. Sir Stanley

Prescott O.B.E. has been Vice-Chancellor of the W.A. University since 1953. Born in England, he graduated in science and was later appointed to the staff there. In 1936 he became a Professor of Physiology at North China's Cheeloo University and enlisted in the R.A.A.F. at the outbreak of the World War, attaining the rank of squadron-leader. In his term here, university buildings have doubled and many modern buildings have been erected.[42]

Sir Stanley Visits Mother In City

Sir Stanley Prescott, who received his knighthood in the Queen's Birthday Honour's list this year, is in Peterborough for a holiday at his mother's home, 93 Park Road. Sir Stanley, who is Vice-Chancellor of the University of Western Australia at Perth, received his knighthood for services to education. He has been Vice-Chancellor at the university for 12 years. He was educated at Tetbury Grammar School and later at the University of Manchester and is a Master of Science. As Professor of Physiology, the study of the functions of the body, he moved to China in 1935 and married his wife Monica in Hong Kong. He moved to Australia just before Pearl Harbor. Sir Stanley and Lady Prescott have four children, two girls and two boys. The boys are David Lamplugh, who is named after a great grandfather, who was once Mayor of Peterborough, and Nigel. The girls are Helen and Margaret.

Next week, Sir Stanley goes to Buckingham Palace to receive the accolade. Sir Stanley's father, Mr John Prescott died 15 years ago, but his mother Mrs Jessie Mary Prescott lives at 93 Park Rd. The Prescotts are on a two-months working holiday in Britain. Before they go back to Australia Sir Stanley will attend various conferences and visit some Universities in Britain.[43]

There are other clippings, but I think you get the idea. However I will also share parts of the following family profile published in 1966 by a Perth newspaper, the *Daily News*, because is more from Monica's perspective:

Today Is Always Better Than Yesterday

Young Dr Monica Prescott, refugee from Japanese-occupied China, arrived in wartime Sydney in 1941, alone except for the baby in her arms. She had to leave her husband and did not know when, or if, she would see him again.

She had lost the only home she had since her marriage as well as what went with it, except for her clothes and linen. All she knew of Australia was that she had a 90-year-old grandmother over the Blue Mountains – and that was where she went. So she felt she was lucky. Luckier still when her husband was allowed to come about six months later.

They have been living happily ever after since, because, as Lady Prescott told me: 'Today is always better than yesterday, and each year better than the year before'. Although she practised medicine in China, and part-time during the earlier years in Australia, Lady Prescott is now fully occupied as the wife of the Vice-Chancellor of WA's rapidly growing University – and being a mother. 'I found that as the children grew older they needed me more.

The family includes The Rev. David Prescott (27) who lives in Kalgoorlie with his wife, formerly senior games mistress at John Curtin High School, and their daughter Susan (2). The China-born baby David left School before he took Junior (exams), tried both farming and banking before making, at 21, a surprise decision to study for the priesthood in which he found his natural vocation.

Nigel (24) who, like his wife, has an arts degree, is an administrative assistant on the University staff concerned with music, ballet, and drama. He works for three months a year on the Festival of Perth. Helen (22) completed a psychology degree last year and is now administrative assistant to the Medical Director at Princess Margaret Hospital. Margaret (19) who is doing an arts degree shares her brother's enthusiasm for the theatre.

Family feeling is strong in the Prescott's family. When they wanted to put down roots in this state, they gave up the former Vice-Chancellor's house (now the Department of Music) next to St George's College and bought a big, pleasant English-looking home in Thomas-St Nedlands, where they live on three levels. Lunch-time is a family time at the Prescotts and as many of them as possible assemble at that meal. 'I run the house myself with no help at all now' Lady Prescott said. 'I manage very well, and I insist on a tidy house – except for one room for continuous activities. We have the sewing machine in there. Margaret makes her own clothes. I do all the gardening except cutting the lawn and the edges. It gives me the right amount of exercise. I am not a knowledgeable gardener but I like the physical work. I like the roses best. I know what to do with them.'

The Prescotts enjoy each other's company, partly because of shared interests and partly because of earlier separations.

'I have not had much time for hobbies' said Lady Prescott, 'if I have one it is my church. Not so much church work as observances. I would never miss Sunday or mid-week communion. Our religion means a great deal to us.'

Sir Stanley and Lady Prescott love to get away for a weekend together now and then, and just after one of these, on the day that I called round at any rate, the Vice-Chancellor was washing his own car.[44]

Given the family history, Monica was pleased with my father David's final choice of career. In the beginning, it was probably more with a sense of great relief that she saw him apply himself to theology. Having left school without even his Junior Certificate, and after a series of very uncertain jobs, he knew they never expected him to get the basic qualifications to enter Wollaston Theological College. To prove them wrong David attended Leederville Technical College. He also became more active in the Student Christian Movement (SCM). That was how he met my mother.

Janice Hackfath was a young teacher from Cottesloe, the beachside Perth suburb. She was also a keen sportswoman, surf-lifesaver and part-time dancing instructor. Her friends had talked her into travelling to Melbourne for a Christian youth conference. The train journey across the Nullarbor took many days, and she could not help but notice the very handsome young man travelling with a much younger girl. David had

314

been sent along to chaperone his younger sister Helen while she attended the same youth meeting.

It was not until after they reached Melbourne that he first noticed Jan, at a tram stop on the busy corner of Bourke and Elizabeth streets. She was crossing the road with one of her girlfriends, and the moment has stuck in his mind ever since. Something very special happened to him, and it was not just the vision of her wonderful ankles.

Not long after that, as part of the conference activities, Jan had to play the part of a drunk in a play and needed a pair of man's trousers. Taking the perfect opportunity to talk to David, she bravely asked him if she could borrow his trousers. He was only too delighted. 'So that', my mother tells me, 'is how I got into your father's pants'. Although Jan was noted not to return to the girls' dormitory that night, things were rather more innocent in those days and remained so for some time. To Helen's delight, David's appointed role of chaperone was somewhat abandoned, and she had plenty of time to spend at the pool with other boys, while he became otherwise distracted.

On the long train ride back to Perth, David and Jan enjoyed each other's company, but perhaps Monica heard of these goings-on, because they soon discovered a monk, Dunstan McKee from the Society of the Sacred Mission (SSM), sitting opposite them for the most of the journey home. The chaperone had quickly become the chaperoned.

To this very day, I have never seen two people so connected or in love.

Monica watched as the romance blossomed. Jan always told me that 'I just knew the moment I saw him that he was the one'. David and Jan have always been devoted to each other and I have never heard a cross word between them. Even so, it was Monica who suggested to David that it was about time that he proposed.

He had been preparing for the priesthood when he met Jan, and became tormented in his theological studies. At a time when he was trying to be 'holy', he felt anything but. Although Anglican priests could marry, it was an era still dominated by guilt and piety. In his turmoil and confusion, he even considered becoming a celibate monk. But only for a moment. When it came to his true feelings there was really never any doubt. They were married on 24 August 1963. So, as with many of my forefathers, religion played a part in how my own parents met.

Although David initially appeared to be embarking on a traditional path, Monica became steadily more concerned in the 1970s. The first sign of trouble was when David and Jan became vegetarians, and would not partake of the Christmas duck after 1975. They allowed Stephen and me to eat as we pleased, at least when we went out, but had no meat in the house. I am not sure what Monica thought when they went to India to live in an ashram for a few months. Stephen and I had a great time; we were sent to live on a commune in Margaret River. When my parents came back, they started teaching meditation 'in a Christian context'. This later became very popular and David was much loved in the local community for his own quiet wisdom. Jan continued to teach, but also used to write relaxation and meditation music. All this was initially frowned upon by the Anglican Church which kept David safely tucked away in parishes like Kwinana where they didn't think it mattered or at least that is how it appeared. It seemed to take twenty years for them to realise that he had something important to offer, something that more people wanted. He might not have continued life as a traveller like his forefathers, but he certainly was a pioneer, but that is also another story.

Although Monica had a more traditional spiritual perspective, she learned to appreciate David's way of doing things. In the end, she often enjoyed telling me how 'enormously proud' she was of him, and how he had helped so many people. Of course he is my hero, but he has also touched the lives of so many and is greatly loved. I feel sure that Stanley's wish, that his son might one day continue the work he was unable to finish, has indeed come true.

Early retirement

When he was only fifty, Stanley suffered his first heart attack. Another followed a few years later. Their daughter Helen recalls this as the same day President Kennedy was assassinated. He eventually took early retirement in 1970 at the age of sixty. That same year, the university conferred on Stanley an honorary Doctorate of Law (LLD). Although I was only in my first year of primary school and had no understanding of his achievements, I was already very proud of him. After Stanley retired, Monica eventually returned to medical work for several years. She did research for the World Health Organization, surveying coronary heart disease at four major hospitals.

Monica and Stanley sold the family home in Thomas Street, Nedlands, and took a seventh-floor apartment in Esplanade Court on the South Perth foreshore. They had wonderful views across the Swan River to the city of Perth. I used to love sitting with Grandpa on the balcony looking through his binoculars. Each time I would pick out the Perth Concert Hall, because they had told me that Uncle Nigel was now the manager there.

It was a place I loved to be. Quiet. So many old and interesting things. I loved the embroidered Chinese pillows and the sound of the old Chinese clock. Stanley loved to tell me things I knew were important, such as how far away the sun and the moon were, and how we could tell the world was round. I could sit there for hours. I found knowledge and learning fascinating. I could feel his gentle wisdom.

Grandpa had so many fascinating treasures. Some of them were hard to believe. My favorite was a stalagmite. It was wrapped like a jewel in a soft cloth, so I knew it was precious. We carefully unwrapped it to see its millions of years with some key historical dates marked on the side in pencil. Quite close to the end, in its more recent history, the time of Jesus Christ was annotated. I loved to touch the history of that stalagmite. It filled me with wonder, and Grandpa did not let me feel small against its immense scale of time. I felt that I was 'born lucky', just like my grandma Monica.

Another thing I can remember is that Stanley liked a glass of sherry, and after a while he liked one quite often. I thought it smelled quite nice.

I met all sorts of people there too. One day I remember a man called Sir Charles Court, who they said was the Premier of our state. I remembered him because he had very large hands. He shook my hand like a grown up and told me that he could play a trumpet, just like me.

Monica and Stanley continued to enjoy their many friendships through the cathedral, and they both became even more involved in that community after Stanley's retirement.

They always remained close to Gordon and Mary King, and in 1962 they all travelled to see Hong Kong together again. A lovely photograph taken during this return visit is included with these pages. I love seeing Monica throwing her head back, looking relaxed with Stanley, Mary and Gordon King and their shared memories of Hong Kong from so many years before.

Although he had retired from the university, Sir Stanley continued to serve on the board of the Royal Perth Hospital, becoming deputy chairman (1973) and chairman (1976), and sat on the planning board (1971–1973) and senate (1973–1976) of Murdoch University.[45]

One of his final duties as chairman of Royal Perth Hospital was to recruit a new and brilliant Professor of Medicine, Lawrie Beilin, who was also to play a critical role in my future career. As a fourth-year medical student in 1985, I somehow found myself in Professor Beilin's office, metres from where Stanley had presided over the opening of the medical school. I can't really remember how I came to be sitting alone before his desk without my fellow students. I think he was reflecting fondly on how he appreciated my grandfather's belief in him. Perhaps he wanted to repay the favour in some way. In any case, he gave me an opportunity for which I will be forever grateful. I took it, without question. In my heart I knew it was the right thing to do. My fellow students did not understand the attraction of taking a year off from my medical training to undertake a year of research and write an honours thesis. Incomprehensible. Medicine was long enough as it was. But it was my first taste of academic life, and I don't regret it for a moment. Monica, as ever, was pleased and excited by my decision. Many years later, in 1999, when I was appointed as a tenured academic at UWA myself, one of my first and most fruitful collaborations was with Lawrie Beilin's group. Although we worked in very different fields by then, that very diversity paved the way for some quite novel research.

In his retirement, Stanley also pursued his great love of the Chinese language and continued writing a Chinese–English dictionary. The work he did on this was quite impressive. The following is taken from the preface of Stanley's book, written in the 1970s:

How did this book come to be written?

Late in 1941, not long before the Japanese attack on Pearl Harbor, I arrived in Australia from China where for some six years I had worked in Cheeloo University, Tsinan, Shantung, as Professor of Pharmacology and later, after Japanese Occupation, as Superintendent of the Cheeloo University Hospital. When I left China, having used the Chinese in my day-to-day activities, I was pretty conversant with Mandarin (Kuan Hua), speaking and writing it with ease. A change of scene and service in the Air Force, followed by the headship of a residential University College and then a University Vice-Chancellorship, all in Australia, gave little time for Chinese study. At the end of 1970 I retired from the Vice-Chancellorship of the University of Western Australia after nearly eighteen years in that position, and after twenty-nine years of not having spoken or thought in Chinese, much less written it. Part of 1972 I spent in England and while in London I happened to visit Collet's Chinese Bookshop, opposite the British Museum, and was surprised to find that I could still make myself understood in Mandarin. At that time the thought came to me that being no longer a University administrator, a physiologist or pharmacologist, I might, in retirement, still find intellectual excitement in pursuing again my second love – the Chinese language and its intriguing characters.

The decision was easily taken. But what did I find? In thirty years, Mandarin had developed some subtle changes and had become Pu Tong Hua, the so-called Modern Standard Chinese; the classical 'Wade-Giles' romanisation had now officially been replaced with 'Pin Yin', and there was a whole host of so-called 'simplified characters'. I was nearly frightened off. But the language still had its old spell, even if it were only nostalgia for the past – and so I decided, after thirty-one years, to relearn it.[46]

He even took the chance to visit China again in 1975. I am not sure that he rediscovered any of his old Chinese friends. I somehow doubt it, but you never know. It was clearly a very different China from the one he had known, but he was inspired by the experience. He was apparently 'welcomed as an outsider with authentic reminiscences of its pre-revolutionary past'.[47] He continued industriously with his dictionary. His beautiful and detailed work is on display and still has been much admired by Chinese visitors. In 1978, when this much-loved endeavour was almost complete, his efforts were sadly interrupted.

A final visit to England

Now we come to a more melancholy chapter in this story and I am relying on Monica to tell it for us, as she can do a much better job than I. Monica and Stanley had returned to England in 1978 to visit their daughter Margaret, who had been living there since her marriage to Englishman James Peace in 1973. They had now had two English grandchildren, Douglas and Jessica. Monica and Stanley even had plans to return to live in England for a while.

> It was while we were there that Stanley discovered he was not well. He found a lump in his neck and we knew it was lymphoma. He was in bed most of the time. The doctor said that we really should go back as soon as we could. We had only just found a beautiful house in the Cotswolds, and we had hoped to stay for rather a long while. But that was not to be.[48]

Monica was always glad that they had made a final trip to England together. She was so happy to see that Stanley was also recognised there for his achievements.

> He was invited by the Archbishop of Canterbury to afternoon tea in the Lambeth Palace. It all sounds rather wonderful, doesn't it? And it was

too. You hardly dared eat anything because you didn't want to spoil it. It was all such a thrill for me.

That was Stanley's last social engagement before his last fateful journey. I never saw him again. His deterioration was so quick, and perhaps my father David did not want me to see him as he became so quickly ravaged by his lymphoma.

It was a terrible journey home. I was quite frightened for him. Terrible. He was so sick, you could almost say that he died on the plane coming home. He got greyer and greyer and he couldn't get off when we arrived. It was very rapid indeed. The Royal Perth Hospital people actually met him at the plane ready to take him to hospital, but he wanted to go home. He said he had to have one night at home before he went straight to the hospital by ambulance.

Stanley knew he was dying, but he knew he had one final task – to write his last letter, a letter of love to Monica for sharing his life and for being his source of inspiration for so many years.

We only had that one night together in our lovely place by the river, looking across at the city. One night. And then he was gone. When we got home the only thing he wanted was to sit at his desk, that last night. I thought that was odd, but I agreed. And he sat at his desk writing for about half an hour. Then he had to go straight back to bed again.

It was not until later, after he had gone to the hospital, that I opened the desk and there was a letter written to me. A love letter. A beautiful letter, saying what a beautiful time we had spent together, and how much he loved me. It was so wonderful and so touching. That's what he did. He sat as his desk and wrote that. He was a very ardent

324

lover, was Stanley. He fell in love with me so many years before in medical school. He couldn't stop telling me that he loved me. He always did, for the whole of our life. Oh yes, it was all so rather wonderful.

Stanley's immune system was failing quickly and, as the lymphoma spread through his body, so did a disseminated varicella (chicken pox) infection. He must have been horribly ill and I am glad that was not my last memory of him.

He knew there was nothing that could be done. We both always said, 'If I am going to die, let me drink whisky and let me die'. The staff said whatever he'd like – let him have it. So he had some whisky by his bed so he could drink as much as he liked. I am glad it was so rapid. He was too. He knew he was going to die and he didn't want to be hanging around. Still, it was an awful shock to us.

In his last moments I don't know if he was conscious or not, but I thought it might be like when you are going under an anaesthetic and you can still hear, even though you can't respond. Well I thought: what would Stanley want to hear more than anything? So I held his hand and I said to him 'Stanley, I love you', because I knew that he would certainly die happy on that.

I was so glad I was able to go the Royal Perth with him that night, because I had just got back from seeing him when the phone call came to say that he had died. So I like to think that he might have heard me say 'Stanley, I love you', even though he could not respond. We had such a very good life together, an exciting life in so many ways when you think about it.

That is certainly true! As Monica told me this, I could not help reflecting on the earlier part of her story, when she had implied that she was not sure about her feelings at the time she first met Stanley and that she didn't have time to think. When I asked her more about this she said:

Yes, well he picked me out first. But I soon learned how wonderful he was. And what a wonderful life it was together. I loved Stanley so much, and I still miss him now. Funny really, because it was his friend, Tom Bromley, who first invited me out, so I thought it was Tom Bromley who liked me.

In the end it was Stanley who was her one true love. Although he had been gone for more than thirty years when she said those words, I could tell how deeply these memories still moved Monica. There was always such a bond between them.

Stanley died of his cancer on 14 July 1978 in Royal Perth Hospital where he had worked so hard for many years, and was cremated with Anglican rites. His memorial service was at St George's Cathedral in the heart of the city. I was only thirteen years old, but I remember Sir Charles Court was there and I remembered his hands. I was wearing a new matching bright-blue velvet skirt and waistcoat my mother had made. And my brown knee-high boots. I am not sure why I remember that particularly. There were many very prominent people there. Stanley had been an important personality in the cathedral, the city and the state. I remember how proud I was of my father David when he gave the eulogy and how touched everyone was by it. Although David was an Anglican priest, I think he gave more of a spiritual perspective than a religious one. And in family tradition it was positive and uplifting. I share it here because it gives us each pause for reflection on our own journeys. I am sure Stanley would have been pleased with it too:

I wish to welcome you with great love and great respect, and on behalf of my father Sir Stanley, my mother and my brother and sisters, I thank you for being here with us at this special time. Each one of us is here because in some way or other we have been affected by my father. It may have been by a direct relationship or an indirect one, or it may be because we are representing an organisation that wants to express its gratitude for the work he has done.

I do not believe that this is the time to dwell too much on the past. Let us build upon the good that he has done, and bring it to bear good fruit. Then will his earthly life be blessed and his purposes achieved.

Clouds have silver linings and even today there is good news for us. The good news is that life continues through the gate we call death. The journey is not finished – it continues. This is exciting news for it opens up an understanding of life. My father has done many exciting things in his life, and of all that he has experienced, this continuing journey must surely be the most exciting of all. When a dying prior of an English community was asked how he felt, he answered 'excited!'

The process of death is but a step along the way and as my father Stanley said as he was preparing to take that step, 'it is all so simple'.

At times like these, we are often confused because we do not know what to do or what to say, so I suggest three things which I think are necessary for us to do.

The first and most important is to give Stanley our help so that he can feel us behind him, encouraging him and giving him a sort of back up support. To do this we offer our love and affection to God, so that God may pass it on to him as it is needed. This is the sort of thing friends should always do for each other.

The second is to help those who are confused and find it hard to cope in times like these. So we ask God to give them our spiritual support so that they too may see death as a process of life and discover the real purpose behind it.

The third is to make use of yet another opportunity – that of realising and considering that soon we too will be making this same step, and to ask ourselves what preparation we are making. For this is a most exciting journey – through the gate of physical death into an abundant life that must surely be more than the fulfilment of our wildest dreams.

I want to end with a quotation from Father Andrew: 'because he is nearer to God, he is not farther from us; loving God more, he does not love us less'.[49]

I remember there was a ray of light coming through the cathedral windows, and I thought I could see Stanley smiling on.

The family all returned to Helen's house for refreshments after the funeral. David went on to the crematorium, but Grandma would not. She still did not like cemeteries. We all gathered in a protective ring around her, and had tea and cake. I have learned that there is nothing like a good cup of tea in a crisis.

In the days that followed, Monica was inundated with letters of sympathy. She was especially touched to see the tribute from Royal Perth Hospital:

News of the death on Friday, 14th July, of Sir Stanley Prescott brought with it a sense of profound regret, not only on the part of his colleagues on the Board of Management, but also among members of staff who knew him and worked with him, and in the community at large.

Sir Stanley's association with Royal Perth Hospital has spanned a period exceeding 22 years, during which time the Hospital has benefited greatly from his wisdom and energy. In particular, he played a leading role in the establishment of the University School of Medicine, which resulted in Royal Perth Hospital becoming the first teaching hospital in this State. His own commitment to higher education has helped to promote and maintain the close association between the University of Western Australia and Royal Perth Hospital, which has done so much to establish the high regard in which the teaching of medicine is held in Western Australia.

The Minister for Health, Mr. Ridge, has said that almost every doctor who had trained at the W.A. University Medical School would have cause to mourn Sir Stanley's death. 'His (Sir Stanley's) untiring efforts to integrate the practical and academic aspects of the training of doctors in Western Australia will be remembered forever', Mr. Ridge said. 'He also distinguished himself with outstanding service to the Royal Perth Hospital Board of Management.' Sir Stanley leaves a widow, two sons and two daughters. We offer to them our respects and our deepest sympathy.[50]

The same comments were echoed in *The West Australian* a few days later. In a more personal tribute, in *The Record*, Monsignor McMahon said of his long time friend:

During the 25 years of my friendship with Sir Stanley Prescott I could honestly say that for him also 'a merry heart goes all the way'. Within the long senate meetings and countless committee gatherings, never once did he become impatient with 'stirrers' who mean well but are a constant irritation. His understanding smile listened without comment. He greeted us with a cheerfulness that was infectious, which lightened our task, wearing a smile that starts from the heart. How much a difference that can make to life's joys and sorrows and tasks!

He launched my book *College: Campus: Cloisters* with a dinner in the exquisite Prescott Room inviting my closest University friends and presented a copy to each of them. He and Lady Prescott honoured my Golden Jubilee Mass in St Columba's South Perth in 1969, and I was hoping that he would be with me again in 1979.

So *au revoir* Stanley Lewis; we shall meet again, for the Preface of our Requiem Mass assures that: 'Life is not ended in death'. No it is enriched and elevated and consoles us that there will be no more tears of separation, when the joys that await us will be increased by our reunion.[51]

It was a time for memorials and keepsakes. As his eldest grandchild, and because I had the same initials, I received his cygnet ring with 'SLP' engraved in the gold. It was his engagement gift from Monica. David has also since given me Stanley's nineteenth-century microscope, and collection of slides, some of which have mounted specimens dated as early as 1874. Best of all, I have his magnificent coat of arms, which consists of two doves and a serpent. The doves signify 'gentleness' and the serpent 'wisdom'. By rights, the original should still be with his elder son David, after that my brother Stephen, and after that his new son James. But I am happy to be its temporary caretaker for now.

The university also honoured him. There was already the Prescott Room in the Vice-Chancellery, so in addition to this, a memorial slab was laid near the Physiology Building and Monica was invited to officially open the gardens there as Prescott Court. Monica said 'it was lovely of them to remember him in that way', and she always greatly appreciated it. She liked to remind me that he was one of the longest serving vice-chancellors.

Finally, there is now Prescott Avenue in the southern suburb of Murdoch, not far from Murdoch University, in acknowledgement of his contribution to its planning board (1971–1973) and senate (1973–1976).

Monica was glad to be kept busy in the weeks following his death.

> I kept every letter that came after he died, too, and I wrote and answered every one of them. I am so glad that I had to do that, because it kept me going. Otherwise I would have been lost. The thing that upsets you the most is the empty chair.[52]

The empty chair

There is a lot to do when someone dies. When things settle back to normal, that is the hardest and most lonely time.

> At home we always had two chairs opposite each other. I nearly wrote a poem called 'The empty chair', but I didn't want to think about it any more. For a fortnight the empty chair nearly sent me mad, it really did. We always sat there, either side of the fireplace.
>
> The empty chair; nothing could fill it. When you got home late in the evening there was nobody there, just the empty chair. It really would be a wonderful title of a book. We had always sat opposite each other. I couldn't stand it. So in the end I was so glad that I had so many letters to write: to the Governor-General, the Governor, the Archbishop of Perth and all sorts of people. I kept telling Stanley I was glad that he had given me so much work to do.
>
> It was that emptiness that was so hard. To come home, to open the door, and...nothing. Turning over in bed, and...nobody there.

I wanted to follow Monica's suggestion and name this story 'the empty chair' but that title is too desolate for the inspiring story of Monica's life. Thirty years had now passed, so I asked her if she still got that feeling after so long, now that she was ninety-three. She replied:

Oh yes, but that is why I am glad I am here [at the Sundowner retirement village] because I don't have the remembrance of him here, whereas I did at Esplanade Court. I stayed there for a while before I moved to Kings Park Road. It was very suitable there. It was very easy to get to anywhere from there. I was quite busy.

I always liked Monica's new apartment in Kings Park Road. It felt very cosy and she was there for many years. Nigel and Helen also owned units there. Many years later, after I moved out of St Catherine's residential college, I rented one of these units during my final year of medicine. That would have been in about 1988. It was lovely living just upstairs from Grandma, and I am sure my parents were glad to have her near me.

Travel is the best education

Three years after Stanley's death, as I finished high school at St Hilda's, Monica announced that she would like to honour her father's belief that 'travel is the best education' and take me to Europe for several months as her travelling companion. My parents, David and Jan, did not have the financial resources for distant travel, so this was an unbelievable opportunity at that time. We planned to go in December 1981 after my final exams, so that we could spend Christmas with my Auntie Margaret and her family. I spent months planning my visit to a long-imagined cold world. I had never seen snow. Although I was enjoying Year 12 under the watchful eye of headmistress Dr June Jones, I could hardly wait to get through my exams.

I really must mention an important aside at this point. It is another one of those early connections that have ripple effects through the years. The only way I could afford to be at the expensive private girl's school was because my father was clergy and because June Jones had recognised my worth and allowed me to enrol for my final year of school. I owe much to her kindness. I had just spent four unhappy years at Kwinana Senior High School, a 'rough as guts' state school where I was persecuted for achieving. It took me quite a few years to recover from the paranoia induced by being the target of ridicule and chewing-gum missiles.

By comparison, St Hilda's was a paradise I could hardly believe; but in a strange way I am grateful for the experience of Kwinana because it gave me a perspective that the girls who had only known privilege did not have. Both of my aunties, Helen and Margaret, had also been educated at St Hilda's, and it was the first time I had a sense of belonging. Although I was an excellent student, I am not sure I would have done as well had I not completed my final year at that school. I hope June Jones felt rewarded in her choice when I got the top aggregate mark for the school that year. Shortly after I left the school she employed my father David as the school chaplain and, over the twenty years that followed, he became a greatly loved and respected member of the school community. Helen also returned to the school as a psychologist and careers advisor, and my brother Stephen even worked there for a time in the office. My reason for mentioning all this, is that June Jones later joined the UWA senate and became the chair of the UWA Centenary Trust for Women. She followed my career closely over the years and it was her invitation to give the Centenary Trust for Women keynote oration in 2007 that inspired me to document Monica's story more formally. It was really that event that made me 'put pen to paper', as they say.

As soon as my exams were done, I exploded out of the school gates with all the other girls. The relief was euphoric. At just sixteen, my whole future lay ahead of me. I was unconcerned that I had no idea what it might be. I did not have a care in the world, and the best thing was I was about to become a world traveller like Grandma.

We had such a wonderful time. I certainly have to agree that 'travel is the best education'. I saw so much, learned so much and met so many interesting people. Most importantly, the journey was a wonderful chance to really get to know Monica and to hear her amazing stories. That was when I knew that I had to follow her into medicine.

It was a white Christmas that year in England. The first thing I did when we arrived at our London hotel, the University Women's Club in Mayfair, was run down to play in the snow in Hyde Park. Monica was running not far behind. We celebrated my seventeenth birthday, just before Christmas, with Margaret's family in Shropshire, and that was the first day I saw the snow actually falling out of the sky. I met many of my English relatives for the first time, including Monica's sister Hope and her son Mike, who was also born in China. We were also there for Hope's second wedding, which was a Quaker ceremony. After a month in England we toured Scotland, and then Monica took me to see Holland, Germany, Italy, France and Switzerland. I know I scared Monica on a few occasions. In my naïve enthusiasm for exploring, I went out in Paris and Amsterdam at night. She was still talking about it twenty years later. Fortunately I was also born lucky and never came to any harm.

Never stop having fun

Monica survived Stanley by thirty years. Although she missed him, she found joy in every situation and I never heard her say a cross or negative word about anyone. She always said, 'If you can't enjoy life, then what is the point?'

For a short time, not long after Stanley died, Monica wrote and read some of the epilogues presented on ABC TV around midnight. Helen recalls vividly Monica reading them to her for practice, before going into the ABC studios to have them recorded. She also took every opportunity for community. She taught religious education at Hollywood High School, and continued her strong involvement in many of the cathedral activities. This group of friends grew particularly after Stanley died, when she would always go to morning tea in the Burt Hall on Sundays after the service.

In 1991, she was asked by Dr James Leavesley, a well-known author and radio personality at the time, to become patron of the Medical Museum. She accepted enthusiastically. In another strange coincidence, I happened to meet Leavesley's English nephew in Dubai around the same time, when our Malaysia Airlines flight was forced down with engine trouble. We were both stranded there for days, our passports taken by the authorities, but that is also another story.

Ten years later, in 2000, the editor of the museum's news-letter included the following report:

I asked Lady Prescott how she became involved with the Medical Museum and she wrote: 'On 1st November 1991, Dr James H. H. Leavesley, President of the Western Australian Health Care Museum invited me to become its Patron. I had met Dr Leavesley when he delivered some very interesting lectures in the South Perth Community Hospital and I was familiar with his good work as a general practitioner in South Perth. I had also thoroughly enjoyed reading some of his delightful books on famous people and their medical histories. At the same time I was keenly aware of the need to collect all the information possible about the early medical history of Western Australia. It was therefore with no hesitation that I accepted this invitation. Since being patron, I have been filled with admiration for the hard-working, enthusiastic people who have built up a museum of inestimable value to our State. It is well worth visiting.'

Lady Prescott lives in Perth, maintains a very active life, enjoys her children and grand-children, and is now mastering the computer. She worships regularly at St. George's Cathedral. Travel is one of her passions and she takes every opportunity to go overseas. She remains in touch with the Medical Museum and we appreciate her interest.[53]

This report was accompanied with a summary of Monica's fascinating life story, which of course you now know. As this note reminds us, Monica's greatest joys came from her family, her travel, her friends and her life at the cathedral. She travelled to England almost every year, until she was about ninety. She was still as physically fit as ever, but was starting to show early signs of losing her short-term memory. Her children were too worried to let her travel alone. Nigel and his wife Val often took their annual visit to London at the same time to keep an eye on her. On her final trip, her elder daughter, Helen, was her travelling companion. However, to prove her independence, Monica refused to sit with Helen on the plane, and once they arrived she chose to go off by herself to visit all of her favourite places. She always enjoyed returning to her 'clubs', the University Women's Club, where she had taken me on my very first visit to London, and later the Victory Services Club. She loved every minute she ever spent in London. So do I. She was always repeating the saying 'When you are tired of London you are tired of life'.

She never tired of visiting her favourite places, but as she got older, she gradually lost more and more of her friends, and her family became even more central to her life.

Many years after Stanley's death, Monica returned to Hong Kong with Helen. She loved that trip, exploring all of the places she still knew. There were so many memories of Stanley, and she missed him ever so much more. They had some of their happiest moments there: their reunion after many months of separation during the war, their wedding, their honeymoon. She loved visiting their church and had fun recalling the language and reading the signs. It was exciting to rediscover that she was still almost fluent in Chinese. Her heart was still very much with Stanley and with the Chinese.

Monica always loved to talk about her eight grandchildren. Each of her children gave her two grandchildren: Susan and Stephen (David's children), Elizabeth and Diana (Nigel's), Jasper and

Aaron (Helen's) and Douglas and Jessica (Margaret's). By the time she died she also had four great-grandchildren. She always seemed so proud of us all, and always knew what we were up to.

She had several godchildren as well. The only one I know of is Nicholas, a musician and the son of her lifelong friend Merle Davis. She showed me several CDs of his music. Monica also used to follow the careers of Merle's other children and collect newspaper clippings about their various successes. Two of Merle's other sons also studied medicine, a number of years ahead of me. When I first began my own research as a medical student in 1986, Monica presented me with a book by Merle's son Tim Davis on the key steps in undertaking good medical research. Merle Davis was as committed to her spiritual path as Monica. Even when Merle moved to England to enter a convent as Sister Michaela, they stayed strong friends and Monica saw her on most of her many trips back to England. Although it was a silent order, Merle (Sister Michaela) was apparently permitted to put aside her vows when Monica went to visit. I always thought Monica had such interesting friends!

Monica did have a few setbacks, but they were not enough to stop her for long. When she was about eighty-nine, she tripped over on an escalator and badly bruised her face and her pride. Shortly after that they discovered a melanoma on her face. She needed extensive surgery, but laughed this off as a facelift. Before long she was out and about again.

Monica never learned to drive. She never had any need to. If she wanted to go anywhere she would take public transport or just walk. If she had arthritis, I never saw any evidence of it. She was always very independent and nimble on her feet. I would sometimes bump into her on Rokeby Road, the main street

340

of Subiaco. I remember one time in particular. After a chance meeting, we had coffee while she told me about her new male friend, Hilary Greenwood, whom she had met through the Society of the Sacred Mission (SSM).

Nearly thirty years seemed a decent amount of time to wait after Stanley's death. I am not sure if the 'facelift' had anything to do with it, but she was amused that he was twenty-five years her junior. A toy boy. She insisted it was all quite innocent, and I believe her. Just a bit of fun, she said. He was a poet and a priest, and they had much in common. She enjoyed their theological debates. He used to write her poetry. She proudly showed me one of his poems:

Monica

She is no object of desire
Rousing within me lusty fire,
But adoration she incites
And shows me spiritual delights.

Lady I love you with the kind
Of love belonging to the blind

In fair exchange I ask of you
To love me as the angels do.

Hilary SSM

That was also the year she turned ninety, and she was very excited by the plans for her birthday. She wanted it to be 'just a family affair'. And Hilary. Her daughter Margaret came out from England specially. The day began with a special morning tea in her honour at St George's Cathedral. The chocolate-iced cake was big enough for the entire congregation to have a piece. She was thrilled with this. The cathedral community always remained a core to her life and her heart.

In the early evening her family all came together: children, grandchildren and even great-grandchildren. Everyone wanted her to know how much she was loved. Before the main dinner, all of her Australian grandchildren and their partners came to wish her well. There were drinks and toasts and sharing of many stories. Best of all, there was a special reading: a poem written by her daughters, in celebration of their most wonderful mother. Although this might seem more trite and light-hearted than the deeper sentiments of its authors, Monica absolutely loved it, and soon sent a copy to all of her friends, both locally and overseas.

Ode to our Mum

In the land of the long white cloud, far, far away,
Monica blonde and fair was born this February day.

With an adventurous Mum and Dad she was to travel early in
*   life.*
A love and passion to remain with her as a daughter, mother
*   and wife.*

In her teens in the north of England, for Medicine, to university
*   she went.*
A clever young lady was she with caring for others her bent.

For many long years she studied. Stanley spied her there one day.
A persistent and ardent lover, he stole her heart away.

Across the sea she sailed, into the face of war

To China a world so different to the man she had come to adore.

From there she escaped on a ship, facing perils and danger great
With young David a babe in arms to the shores of Australia her
*   fate.*

Young Stanley managed to follow fortunate for some of us here
Nigel was born, then Helen and Margaret, over the ensuing years.

To the west the family then travelled, over the treeless plain.
Perth, fairest city of all, a place they were to remain.

Behind every great man a woman, just the case with our Mum
*   and Dad*
For Dad in her had an ally, a loyal, loving, supportive fan.

Through their years of hard work and devotion, a true lady at
*   last she became*
When in shining armour, her knight was awarded with public
*   acclaim.*

Through good times and sad she's travelled with joy and faith in
*   her heart.*
Four children, eight grandchildren and great-grandchildren, well
*   James is the start.*

One day when St Peter she meets he will ask just what have
*   you done*
She will be able to say, with a spark in her eye, I have lived,
*   loved, been good and had fun.*

So charge your glasses all of you here. A toast this day we must
*   do*
To an adventurous lady of ninety years

Happy Birthday, God Bless, here's to you.

After the celebrations of the early evening, Monica wanted a more intimate dinner with just Hilary, her children and their partners: David and Jan, Nigel and Val, Helen and Paul, and Margaret. Paul had flown back from where he was working in Singapore to cook her favourite at her request: a poached salmon. It was a wonderful evening. Monica looked so happy. Hilary also gave her a special a birthday poem of his own, which she treasured just as much. She enjoyed his company immensely. They did not always agree on theological matters, but she told me their discussions were always lively, creative and gave them both much to think about.

> **To Monica from Hilary 4.2.03**
> *Lady you have to answer for a lot*
> *Of what we are and even what we're not*
> *So if at heaven's gate some angel Bumble*
> *Makes all our dismal apologies crumble*
> *We shall not hesitate to drop your name*
> *And say – if we are wrong she is to blame*
>
> *Dear one – the world looks different through your eyes*
> *And someday you will show us paradise*
>
> *A Happy Birthday*
> **Hilary SSM**

Then one day, in 2003, Hilary went to the United States on a theological conference, and did not return. He had a stroke while he was there and lapsed into a coma. He was dead in a week. It affected Monica deeply. He was a great friend. Another one lost.

After Hilary's death, Monica returned to Melbourne for

the scattering of his ashes. And it was Dunstan McKee, the monk who had followed and 'chaperoned' David and Jan home on the train from Melbourne in 1962, who spoke at Hilary's requiem, citing his writings on the Christian religion as a series of unresolvable paradoxes. She also had the chance to catch up with her old friend Father Lawrence Eyres.

I think a new loneliness set in around then. But she maintained her brave face. A great source of solace was her priest, Theresa Harvey. Monica was still a devout Anglican, and attended the cathedral regularly. It was such an important part of her daily life, she was a much loved and respected member of their community. She was full of admiration for Theresa Harvey, and often spoke of her to me. I met her only once, at Monica's funeral. Monica seemed to like Theresa's reserved nature, and the fact that she gave so little away about herself. Rather like Monica in many ways.

> She is so English, you never really know much about her. I rather like that sort of person. I am very fond of her indeed. She is a Canon now, and if they make women bishops, she should be one of the first.[54]

Monica started to plan her own funeral well ahead of time, but not because she was being morose or morbid. She just liked to be organised, and she took to it like she was planning one of her overseas trips. No longer able to travel to Europe, she channelled the same enthusiasm into arranging her departure from this world. It had to be at the cathedral, of course, and she thought it would be better if Theresa presided. She knew that it would be a strain on David and she did not want to put him through that.

Having said all of this, she was as lively as ever, and not showing any physical signs that she might be leaving us.

She had a few official engagements yet. In 2003, on its fiftieth anniversary, St Catherine's College honoured Monica's contribution in a special ceremony. Monica was celebrated along with other eminent people, including politician the Honourable. Dr Carmen Lawrence, who was the first woman to become Premier of a state of the Commonwealth of Australia. In her former career, Dr Lawrence had been my lecturer in behavioural science at UWA, and I had the chance to say hello again. This was a lovely occasion for Monica, and as old scholars of St Catherine's, Helen, Val and I were all invited as well. Monica gave a delightful speech of thanks and appreciation. At the end, she could not resist reminding her audience to always have fun, and let them in on her secret of skipping whenever possible. Although she was getting smaller with each passing year, she was getting ever more lively. Eight years later, in 2011, when I received a similar acknowledgement from St Catherine's College as an honorary fellow, I could not help thinking that Monica would be proud.

Another thing I am very glad about is that Monica lived to see me happily married in 2005. I did not marry until I was forty. It took me a while to find the right man, but I can tell you it was worth the wait. We are so very happy, and Monica adored Craig too. She said that 'he is just so easy to talk to', and I found she would tell him things she didn't tell the rest of the family. It was important to both of us that Monica should be there. And she was. I had the chance to acknowledge how important she was to me and how much I loved her in my wedding speech. My brother Stephen was married a few months later. It meant so much to all of us that she was with us.

Life in Perth, 2006–2007

Here is what Monica had to say of her life at the time we made the recording. As you will see, she was as excited about life as ever. She was still exploring. All of the other nursing home residents were content to stay inside, but not Monica. She loved running down the street. She was as girl-like as ever. In the beginning they tried to restrict her, but she would sneak out anyway, so in the end they just let her do her thing.

Fortunately I am very happy here, although I wish that I could be nearer to the cathedral. I don't get into the city any more much. Fortunately my priest Theresa Harvey comes to see me here.

I am physically very fit. I have always been active. I walk everywhere, and it helps a lot. They still let me out and I still go down to the shops every day. Unless you do that you are not going to meet other people.

I like to see babies and mothers and children. I don't want to be here looking at old ladies all day! I think that is the thing that keeps me young. The people that I meet at the coffee shop are usually glad to have someone to talk to. I usually say something and if they don't reply, I don't go on. But they nearly always do. Around here they are nearly always university graduates or professional people. I meet some very interesting people down there at the shops. But I don't know one other person from this institution here [the Sundowner Centre] who goes down the street [to Napoleon Street in Cottelsloe], not even on a bus. It's not far down there, but they just don't go out.

I believe in having a good time. I like the coffee shops. I have a piece of paper and I get a stamp for each cup of coffee I have, and when I have had my tenth I get one free! But no one here would know any of these things, because they never go out, apart from when one of their children come to take them out for a drive.

We are long-lived in our family. I am glad that I am active and fit for my age. I would rather die than be no good at all. Mother's people all lived to well in their eighties and that was quite old in those days. Dad's mother also lived until she was ninety. But so far I have won!

You can be assured that she told all of her story with perfect clarity of mind. Sometimes she would be confused about the present, but she had a better memory for the past than I will ever have. I am so glad that I took the time to record her thoughts and memories. I only wish I had more.

Her memory got worse in her final months. She still had many lucid moments, and she always knew who I was. She said the most frightening thing was waking up and not knowing where she was or even when. This was particularly a problem after an afternoon nap. But as soon as she got out for a walk and saw familiar sights, she was fine again: 'The worst thing is that I still know I have dementia'. Always a sense of humour.

At times she almost seemed frustrated that she was not showing any signs of getting nearer the next world. With the death of Muriel, her last surviving college friend in England, it was much harder to stay in the present.

Saying goodbye

It all began with another fall and a ride in an ambulance. At least that is what she thought it was. She was actually finding it harder to breathe. The melanoma she had several years before had spread to her chest and she had a large pleural effusion pressing on one of her lungs.

In May 2007, she was admitted to Bethesda Private Hospital. I think she knew how things might end, because she told me that 'the only way I will be getting out of here is in a box'. They tapped her effusion, removing over 1.5 litres of fluid. She was quite puzzled by how it got there, and I had to explain it several times. In the end she asked me to write it down so she didn't have to ask. When my relatives found the requested clinical description in her notebook, they thought me heartless, but I think I have been forgiven.

Her doctors eased her breathing and kept her comfortable; there was not much else to do. But she still knew who I was and she still seemed to have a clear idea of what was going on in my life. My husband Craig and I were building a house and she always remembered to ask about this and how we were going. Her spirits were buoyed when my brother Stephen told her that his wife Emma was pregnant again. She was thrilled to hope it would be a boy so the Prescott name would continue. And it was: James David Prescott was born six months later.

As the end grew closer, the family maintained a steady vigil at her bedside. It took a few weeks, but fortunately not too long. A story was repeating itself. I was reminded of how Monica described her own grandmother's last days.

She seemed to be only half there, but could somehow come back to say hello when I visited. On Thursday morning, 7 June, she was lucid and sitting out of bed but weak and struggling for breath. We had a good chat and it seemed like old times. It was only the next night that I saw her for the last time. By then she wasn't really there any more. The room was half in darkness. Craig and I stood on either side of her bed holding each of her hands. She was unconscious and suddenly so small. She was gone. Her body had withered overnight as her spirit started to leave it, so different from only the day before. I told her how much we loved her and how wonderful she was. I am sure she heard from somewhere, because I felt her grip tighten on mine.

It was very like Monica wrote of grandma Frances (my great-great-grandma) in 1941:

> Her mind by that time – or rather her spirit – was already in heaven...
> She used to lie quietly all day and only come back if someone came to
> talk to her.
>
> The last time I saw her was on Tuesday. She had gone by then. Her
> eyes had closed and she looked so calm and peaceful. We touched her
> and spoke to her but she just smiled in her sleep.[55]

350

I think her will to live had always been so positive and so strong that she found it hard to let go. We all told her it was all right to go now. Nigel and Helen were there too. David and Stephen had just been. In the heavy half-darkness I thought I could feel her old friends waiting to greet her. Especially Stanley. I can still imagine him waiting patiently on the other side of forever. He loved her so much.

She died the next morning, on 9 June 2007, when the family had all left the room. She was a very private person and we are quite convinced that she waited until she we had all gone out for a few moments to take her last breath. That was just how she was.

The funeral, on 13 June, was in St George's Cathedral, just as Monica wanted, with Theresa Harvey officiating. Quiet but lovely. It was an occasion to celebrate her life, and it did just that. In a way it was like any other family gathering we used to arrange around Grandma. Someone mused that at least this time we did not have to work out who was giving her a lift home. There was a sadness and yet a lightness at the same time. Dad had suggested that I say a few words, but I just couldn't. It was too soon for me, at that point. I don't think I could have spoken without crumbling. That was only for my own sense of loss. I was actually happy for Monica. I could feel both her satisfaction and her amusement at the proceedings.

I could also feel the echoes of the other occasions where we had all been there together. It was hard to believe it was almost thirty years since we had similarly gathered for Stanley's funeral. Only five years before that, when I was nine, I had walked down that same aisle in front of Grandpa Stanley. I was so proud and frightened that day as he escorted his daughter Margaret to

351

be married and I was her bridesmaid. After the wedding Monica had so proudly introduced me to all her friends. I loved being at her side.

I felt her there again as we gathered in Burt Hall next to the cathedral after the funeral. Many of the newer friends Monica had made at the cathedral were there and spoke of their fondness for her and of her faith and friendship. Tea and cake, and it felt just like the times Monica had taken me there after a Sunday service. It was nice to see some of our more distant relatives for the first time in many years.

My mother pointed out two blackbirds looking down from the rooftop as they drove Monica's coffin away. We let her go alone.

A public celebration

I was called to publicly reflect on Monica's life only a few weeks after her death. This started with the annual meeting of Centenary Trust for Women, and afterwards on the national ABC Radio program 'Life Matters' and several other events. As you now know, Monica had still been with us when I was first invited to speak to the trust, and we had all been looking forward to having her as a guest of honour. It was difficult to tell her story so soon after her death, but perhaps that made it especially poignant. It was a privilege to have such an opportunity to celebrate and commemorate her life.

As we gathered for lunch in Winthrop Hall, on 29 July 2007, I was touched to see so many people who had been part of her story. I saw the descendants of several of the foundation professors Stanley had appointed, especially friends and family of Professor Gordon King and Professor Neville Stanley. For me personally it meant a lot to see Neville's daughter, my friend and mentor Fiona Stanley gazing up at me as I delivered my address. There were also many people from the university and from St George's Cathedral who had known Monica and Stanley. I sat with the Governor-General Major General Michael Jeffery and his wife and with Sir James and Lady Cruthers, who also had enthralling stories to tell.

I told Monica's story from my heart and it moved many to tears. So many people there told me how inspired they were not only by her story, but by her attitudes to life.

There was much symmetry for me personally in the celebrations that day, as I reflected on how much of my grandparents' personal and public lives had touched mine. I attended the medical school that Stanley had founded; I had four wonderful years at St Catherine's College, eventually earning a place in the Prescott Wing; I took a year out of my medical studies to do research at Royal Perth Hospital and got my own taste of academic life; the little girl in the red shiny shoes became a great career mentor for me and I owe much to the encouragement of Fiona Stanley; I now have an academic career of my own and it was a Raine Foundation grant that helped me initiate my research career.

When I was promoted to full Professor in April 2007, I sat nervously under Stanley's portrait while I was waiting for my interview in the Prescott Room of the Vice-Chancellory. I know he was proud of me. I can still feel the warmth of his smile and see the mischievous twinkle in his eyes whenever I look at that painting.

I reflected on many of these things as I gave my address in Winthrop Hall. It was one of the important days of my life. Not for me, but because I was able to bring Monica and Stanley's story to life again. As I finished my storytelling a beam of sunlight passed through the stained-glass windows and I felt Winthrop Hall fill with light.

Last words

I have loved spending time with Monica and Stanley, together again through the pages of this book. This has brought me to know them in many ways that I did not while they were alive. I have treasured going back in time to when life was difficult, but somehow more simple, sharing something of day-to-day life in a century now past. I can only hope that the small fragments I have selected from their letters will give a true feeling of their hearts and minds. Now I am done, I can feel them with me, together always, reminding me and inspiring me anew to live the best life I can.

To honour her memory, and just as I did in the final words of my address in Winthrop Hall, I want to leave you with some of the important thoughts of which Monica was always reminding me. I also want to give her the last word!

Everyone can teach us something and we should look for that 'something' in everyone we meet, no matter who they are.

We should always look for the good in every situation, because it is always there!

We can do anything if we set our mind to it. (Monica was always repeating what has become a family motto) 'Where there is a will there is a way'.

Feel the success as though it has already happened.

We should never stop having fun. (Even in her nineties Monica would not be embarrassed to skip through the park and play on the swings.) Enjoy every breath you take. Why would you choose not to?

We never lose anything by giving. The energy of generosity creates more for everyone. (Monica was always selfless and generous.)

'Man man di'. We need to take time to enjoy life.

These thoughts may be simple and obvious, but they are unfortunately also too easily forgotten. If stories like Monica's can remind us of these simple principles then they are worth telling for that reason alone.

I want to able to say, as Monica did in her last days with us:

I love being alive.
But I have no fear of death.
Absolutely none.
I have had such a wonderful life.

Notes

NB: When consecutive quotes have been used from the same text, only the first instance is noted here.

FROM DISTANT LANDS: SHAPED BY THE STORIES OF OUR PAST

1   'The Late Rev. H. A. Job. One of the Empire's Finest and Most Brilliant Sons', 24 April 1947. Clippings kept by Monica from unknown London newspaper.
2   Unpublished autobiography 'Sursum Corda' by Eliza 'Amy' Gardiner (nee Watts b. 1856), sister to Frances Watts and Monica's great-aunt.
3   Same as above.
4   Unpublished autobiography of Frances Job (nee Watts b. 1851), Allen's mother and Monica's grandmother.
5   Unpublished autobiography 'Sursum Corda'.
6   Unpublished autobiography of Frances Job.
7   Unpublished autobiography 'Sursum Corda'.
8   http://en.wikipedia.org/wiki/Allen_Francis_Gardiner, accessed September 2009.
9   Recollections of the words of Allen Gardiner (II) from the unpublished autobiography 'Sursum Corda'.
10 Tom was a descendant of Reignold Jobe, born in Cornwall in 1646. Register of Descendants for Reignold JOBE, compiled by Warren Job (b. 1942).
11 Unpublished autobiography of Frances Job.
12 Unpublished autobiography 'Sursum Corda'.
13 Unpublished autobiography of Frances Job.
14 Transcript of taped interview with Monica Mary Prescott, recorded in her retirement home in Cottesloe, Western Australia, 11–12 November 2006.
15 'The Late Rev H. A. Job. One of the Empire's Finest and Most Brilliant Sons'.
16 Transcript of taped interview with Monica Mary Prescott.
17 Taken from Allen Job's letter to his mother, Frances Job, 138 Murdock Road, Handsworth, Birmingham, 29 September 1904.
18 Diary of Allen Job, 6 December 1906.
19 Diary of Allen Job, on board the SS *Mexican*, 9 December 1906.
20 Diary of Allen Job, on board the SS *Mexican*, 11 December 1906.

21   Transcript of taped interview with Monica Mary Prescott.

22   Diary of Allen Job, Peru, 1907.

23   Diary of Allen Job, Quitun, Peru, 4 June 1907.

24   Diary of Allen Job, St Domingo/Tambopata, Peru, 1907.

25   Diary of Allen Job, Curcero, Peru, Saturday 1 June 1907.

26   Diary of Allen Job, Peru, 1907.

27   Letter from Ethel Pulley (Monica's mother) to her parents, from Arequipa, Peru, 16–22 March 1908.

28   Letter from Ethel Pulley to her parents, from Tingo, Peru, 22 March 1908 (a footnote added to the letter dated 16 March 1908).

29   Transcript of taped interview with Monica Mary Prescott.

30   Diary of Allen Job, Indian Ocean, 8 August 1911.

31   Diary of Allen Job, Indian Ocean, 19 July 1911.

32   Transcript of taped interview with Monica Mary Prescott.

33   A. C. Bryer, *Chapel Next the Green: The Story of Twickenham Congregational Church*, B. L. Pearce, Twickenham, 1982.

34   Transcript of taped interview with Monica Mary Prescott.

35   G. C. Bolton, 'Prescott, Sir Stanley Lewis (1910–1978)', *Australian Dictionary of Biography*, Volume 16, Melbourne University Press, 2002, pp. 29–30.

36   Unpublished biography, 'John L. (Jack) Prescott 1873–1950', by Malcolm C. Prescott.

37   The terms of the Indenture of the Apprentice on 4th September 1888, as noted by Malcolm C. Prescott in the unpublished biography of his father, 'J. L. Prescott 1873–1950'.

38   Unpublished biography 'J. L. Prescott 1873–1950'.

39   Quotes taken by Malcolm Prescott from the obituary of John (Jack) Prescott published in an unspecified local newspaper, June 1950.

40   Unpublished biography, 'John L. (Jack) Prescott 1873–1950'.

41   Transcript of taped interview with Monica Mary Prescott.

CHINA: FORGING A NEW PATH

1   Transcript of taped interview with Monica Mary Prescott.

2   Letter from Stanley to his parents, on board the SS *Naldera*, October 1936.

3   Letter from Stanley to his parents, Shanghai, 14 November 1936.

4   Letter from Stanley to his parents, Tsinan, 24 November – 8 December 1936.

5   Christmas message from Monica and Stanley, December 1939.

6   Letters from Stanley to his parents, College of Language Studies, Peiping [Beijing], North China (via Siberia), 11–16 January 1937.

7   Letter from Stanley to his parents, Language School, Peiping, 20 February 1937.

8   Letters from Stanley to his parents, Language School, Peiping, 7 March 1937.

9   Letter from Stanley to his parents, College of Chinese Studies, Peking 25 April 1937.

10 Letter from Stanley to his parents, No. 5 Chin Sian Tsai, Peitaiho Beach, Hopei, 2 July 1937.

11 Same as above, 10 July 1937.

12 Same as above, 16 July 1937.

13 Same as above, 29 July 1937.

14 Same as above, 11 August 1937.

15 Same as above, 19 August 1937.

16 Letter from Monica to her parents, on board the SS *Corfu*, August 1937.

17 Professor Duncan Anderson, 'Nuclear Power: The End of the War Against Japan', www.bbc.co.uk/history/worldwars/wwtwo/nuclear_01.shtml.

18 http://en.wikipedia.org/wiki/Second_Sino-Japanese_War#cite_note-6.

19 *Daily Mirror.*

20 *City News*, 20 August 1937.

21 Transcript of taped interview with Monica Mary Prescott.

22 *Daily Mirror*, 23 September 1937.

23 *The Daily Sketch.*

24 Letter from Monica to her parents, Mission House, Kowloon, Hong Kong, 1–9 September 1937.

25 Letter from Stanley to his parents, 15 Ventris Road, Hong Kong, 2 September 1937.

26 Same as above, 9 September 1937.

27 Transcript of taped interview with Monica Prescott.

28 From a newspaper clipping in Monica's collections. Source unclear.

29 Letter from Stanley and Monica, The Towers Honeymoon Castle, 20 Broadwood Road, Hong Kong, 16 September 1937.

30 Letter from Stanley to his parents, 15 Ventris Road, Hong Kong, 23 September 1937.

31 Transcript of taped interview with Monica Mary Prescott.

32 Letter from Stanley to his parents, 15 Ventris Road, Hong Kong, 23 September 1937.

33 Letter from Stanley to his parents, 3 Conduit Rd, Hong Kong, 7 October 1937.

34 Same as above, 14 October 1937.

35 Transcript of taped interview with Monica Mary Prescott.

36 Letter from Stanley, 3 Conduit Road, Hong Kong, 17 November 1937.

37 Letter from Monica to her parents, 3 Conduit Rd, Hong Kong, 3 December 1937.

38 Letter from Stanley to his parents, 3 Conduit Rd, Hong Kong, 3 December 1937.

39 Same as above, 8 December 1937.

40 Letter from Monica to her parents, on board the SS *Huper*, 12 January 1938.

41 Letter from Stanley to his parents, 22 Seymore Road, Tsientin, 26 January 1938.

42   Letter from Stanley to his parents, c/o Methodist Mission, 33 Seymour Rd,
      Tsientin, 2 February 1938.
43   Letter from Stanley to his parents, College of Chinese Studies, Peking,
      11 March 1938.
44   Same as above.
45   Same as above, 29 April 1938.
46   Same as above, 7 May 1938.
47   Same as above, 20 May 1938.
48   Same as above, Peking, 3 June 1938.
49   Letter from Stanley to his parents, No. 5 Tung Po Lu, East Cliff, Peitaiho
      Beach, Hopei, N. China, June 1937.
50   Letter from Monica to her parents, No. 5 Tong Po Lu, East Cliff, Peitaiho
      Beach, Hopei, N. China, June 1937.
51   Letter from Stanley, Peitaiho Beach, August 1938.
52   Letter from Monica to her parents, Medical School, Cheeloo University,
      17 November 1938.
53   Letter from Stanley to his parents, Medical School, Cheeloo University,
      8 September 1938.
54   Letter from Monica to her parents, Medical School, Cheeloo University,
      8 September 1938.
55   Letter from Stanley to his parents, Cheeloo University, 8 September 1938.
56   Letter from Monica to her parents, Medical School, Cheeloo University,
      8 September 1938.
57   Same as above, 1 November 1938.
58   Transcript of taped interview with Monica Mary Prescott.
59   Letter from Monica, Wesley Bungalow, Cheeloo University, 17 November
      1938.
60   Letter from Stanley, Cheeloo University, 8 September 1937.
61   Letter from Monica, Cheeloo University, 12 September 1938.
62   Transcript of taped interview with Monica Mary Prescott.
63   Letter from Monica to her parents, Wesley Bungalow, Tsinan, 1938.
64   Transcript of taped interview with Monica Mary Prescott.
65   Letter from Monica, Tsinan, 22–26 September 1938.
66   From a letter Monica wrote in response to her father's queries about
      prostitutes, 4 January 1939.
67   Letter from Monica, Cheeloo University, 26 September 1938.
68   Letters from both Monica and Stanley, Tsinan, 27 September – 6 October
      1938.
69   Same as above, 13–20 October 1938.
70   Letter from Monica, Tsinan, 1 November 1938.
71   Same as above, 17 November 1937. As you can imagine, there are only
      sprawling city buildings visible from that spot now. But I was pleased to
      see that the rest of campus is still quite preserved, much as Monica had
      described it.

72   Letter from Monica, Cheeloo University, 2 December 1938.

73   Letters from Monica, Tsinan, 8–17 November 1938.

74   Notes from Stanley, Tsinan, 9–17 November 1938.

75   Letter from Monica, Cheeloo University, 15 December 1938.

76   Letter from Monica, Cheeloo University, 28 December 1938.

77   Letter from Monica, Tsinan, 4 January 1939.

78   Letters from Monica, 16–24 January 1939.

79   Letters from Monica, Cheeloo University, 4–20 January 1939.

80   Letter from acting president of the Cheeloo University, Dr Lair to the North China chairman, February 1939.

81   Letter from Monica to her parents, Shantung Christian University Hospital, 22 March 1939.

82   Letter from Stanley to his parents, Wesley House, Cheeloo University, 30 March 1939.

83   Letter from Monica to her parents, 10 May 1939.

84   Note from Stanley, 8 June 1939.

85   Transcript of taped interview with Monica Mary Prescott.

86   Letter from Monica to her parents, 1 June 1939.

87   Letter from Monica and Stanley to their parents, 10 September 1939.

88   Letter from Stanley to his parents, 16 September 1939.

89   Letter from Monica, 26 November 1939.

90   Same as above, 21 January 1940.

91   Same as above, 3 February 1940.

92   Same as above, 19 March 1940.

93   Same as above, 6–15 May 1940.

94   Same as above, 15 May 1940.

95   Same as above, 20 May 1940.

96   Same as above, 17 June 1940.

97   Letter from Stanley, 1 October 1940.

98   Same as above, 12 October 1940.

99   Letter from Monica, 28 October 1940.

100   Letter from Stanley, 20 November 1940.

101   Letters from Monica, 25–26 November 1940.

102   Transcript of taped interview with Monica Mary Prescott.

103   From note by David Lamplugh Prescott, 1980.

104   Transcript of taped interview with Monica Mary Prescott.

105   Letter from Stanley, 6 January 1941.

106   Same as above, 15 January 1941.

107   Australian Merchant Navy 'The Sea Supply Line', http://www.merchant-navy-ships.com/index.php?id=29,0,0,1,0,0, accessed 21 April 2008.

108   Transcript of taped interview with Monica Mary Prescott.

109   Letter from Monica to her parents, on board the *Neptuna* (near Manilla), Friday 24 January 1941.

110 Same as above, from Papua New Guinea, January 1941.
111 Australian Merchant Navy 'The Sea Supply Line'.
112 Same as above.

AUSTRALIA: WHERE DREAMS ARE MADE
1 Transcript of taped interview with Monica Mary Prescott.
2 Letter from Monica to her parents, 'Halcyon', Ward Street, Parkes, 27 February 1941.
3 Same as above, 5 March 1941.
4 Same as above, 25 March 1941.
5 Unpublished autobiography of Frances Job.
6 Letter from Monica, 25 March 1941.
7 Letter from Monica, 2 April 1941.
8 Letter from Monica, 16 April 1941.
9 Letter from Monica to her parents, 67 Bogan Street, Parkes, 21 April 1941.
10 Same as above, 1 May 1941.
11 Same as above, 18 May 1941.
12 Transcript of taped interview with Monica Mary Prescott.
13 Letter from Monica to her parents, Parkes, 28 May 1941.
14 Same as above, 20 June 1941.
15 Transcript of taped interview with Monica Mary Prescott.
16 Letter from Monica to her parents, Parkes, 23 July 1941
17 Letter from Monica to her parents, 3/108 Millswyn Street, South Yarra, Melbourne, 24 August 1941.
18 Same as above, 1 September 1941.
19 Same as above, 17 September 1941.
20 Letter from Monica to her parents, 27 Gordon Street, Hampton, Melbourne, 23 February 1942.
21 Same as above, January 1942.
22 Same as above, March 1942.
23 Same as above, January 1942.
24 'The Story of Thalidomide: A Lawyer's Account', an address by His Excellency Sir Zelman Cowen (AK, GCMG, GCVO KStJ, QC) Governor-General of the Commonwealth of Australia, on the occasion of the Annual Meeting of Royal Perth Hospital, in the ballroom of Government House, Perth, Western Australia, 3 October 1979.
25 Email from Jeremy Prescott, 2012.
26 Transcript of taped interview with Monica Mary Prescott.
27 Letter from Monica to her parents, St Vincent's Hospital, Melbourne, 16 May 1942.
28 Letter from Monica to her parents, Hampton, 28 August 1942.
29 Transcript of taped interview with Monica Mary Prescott.
30 The Chronicle, Ormond College, 1945.

31 From personal notes of David Lamplugh Prescott, 1980.

32 Newspaper clipping annotated by Monica with the words 'April 24th 1947'. The original source document was not recorded.

33 Transcript of taped interview with Monica Mary Prescott.

34 http://www.naa.gov.au/naaresources/publications/research_guides/guides/royalty/pages/chapter08/b.htm, accessed 5 June 2012.

35 Prime Minister Robert Menzies' press statement, dated 22 March 1954. NAA: A462, 825/14/48.

36 *Gazette of the University of Western Australia*, vol. 4, no. 1, May 1954.

37 Transcript of taped interview with Monica Mary Prescott.

38 G. C. Bolton, 'Prescott, Sir Stanley Lewis (1910–1978)', *Australian Dictionary of Biography*, published by the Australian National University, http://www.adb.online.anu.edu.au/biogs/A160034b.htm, accessed February 2008.

39 Comments of the Chancellor the Honourable Sir Lawrence Jackson in 1970, on the occasion of Stanley's retirement.

40 Reflection of Helen Silver, 2012.

41 Transcript of taped interview with Monica Mary Prescott.

42 *The West Australian*, 12 June 1965, p. 1.

43 Newspaper clipping (no date or details recorded), presumably from a local Peterborough paper.

44 *Daily News*, 1966 (date and page number missing).

45 G. C. Bolton, 'Prescott, Sir Stanley Lewis (1910–1978)'.

46 From the preface of Stanley's (unpublished) book: 'A graphic catalogue of the more common Chinese ideographs arranged phonetically, classified firstly according to final rhyming vowels, secondly according to initial consonants, and finally numerically, according to Soothill's (1911) phonetic list'.

47 G. C. Bolton, 'Prescott, Sir Stanley Lewis (1910–1978)'.

48 Transcript of taped interview with Monica Mary Prescott.

49 From eulogy by David L. Prescott in remembrance of his father, Stanley L. Prescott, July 1978.

50 The Royal Perth Hospital, *Servio News*, vol. 4, no. 11, 2, 20 July 1978.

51 *The Record*, Thursday 20 July 1978.

52 Transcript of taped interview with Monica Mary Prescott.

53 Western Australian Medical Museum, newsletter, April 2000.

54 Transcript of taped interview with Monica Mary Prescott.

55 Letter from Monica to her parents, Parkes, 18 May 1842.

Index

365

368